HOW TO AVOID THE LAKE OF FIRE!

A STUDY OF MANKIND'S OBLIGATIONS TO BELIEVE IN YESHUA HA MASHIACH (JESUS) AND TO KEEP THE WRITTEN TORAH OF YEHOVAH ELOHIM

Joy Collins Lyle

Martina Publishing, Inc.
South Carolina

 Correspondence and Ordering Information: Hardcopy editions, inquiries, or other information, please contact:

joylyle@yahoo.com or joycollinslyle@gmail.com
(put **BOOK ORDER** in subject line for books)

Most changes in parentheses, uppercase, underlining, bolding, and asterisks are done to add emphasis to the text. Most additions in brackets, except scripture references [KJV], are made by the author of this book and are solely the opinion of the author.

How To Avoid The Lake Of Fire!: A Study Of Mankind's Obligations To Believe In Yeshua Ha Mashiach (Jesus) And To Keep The Written Torah Of Yehovah Elohim /Joy Collins Lyle.

Martina Publishing, Inc.
www.ShielaMartina.com

Summary: This book will challenge Christians, Jews and others to think for themselves about what truth is and what it is not.

Library of Congress Control Number: 2016920890

ISBN-13: 978-0-9799344-3-8

[1. Hell —Lake of Fire. 2. Christianity—Jesus. 3. Written Torah—KJV. 4. Oral Torah—Judaism. 5. Church Hierarchy.] I. Title.

Printed in the United States of America

HERE IS THE PATIENCE OF THE SAINTS: HERE [ARE] THEY THAT KEEP THE COMMANDMENTS OF GOD, AND THE FAITH OF JESUS.

-Revelation 14:12[KJV]
Authorized King James
Version of THE HOLY BIBLE

CONTENTS

PREFACE

The overriding question each of us should ask ourselves is:

DO WE LOVE OUR FATHER OR NOT? ENOUGH TO WANT TO DO WHAT HE HAS TOLD US IN HIS WORD THAT PLEASES HIM– HIS WILL - THE THINGS HE DESIRES FOR HIS CHILDREN TO DO?

WHETHER WE HAVE TO OR NOT!!!

HOWEVER, SEE APPENDIX II RIGHT NOW FOR A LIST OF ABOMINATIONS AND OTHER SINS THAT WILL SEND YOU TO THE LAKE OF FIRE!!!

UNLESS YOU REPENT (TURN FROM THEM) AND RECEIVE FORGIVENESS IN YESHUA'S NAME!!!

INTRODUCTION

This book will challenge you to **"THINK FOR YOURSELF!"**

For Christians, there will be some things that I address that you may not agree with, at least at first, because they are completely different from what you have always believed or have been taught. I am not saying that I have it all right, and I am not asking that you believe all my commentary. But, **I AM ASKING YOU TO TRULY CAREFULLY CONSIDER THE SCRIPTURES QUOTED FOR YOURSELF!** Even a cursory review of church history will show you that all the "reformations" in the church were because people finally pushed to be able to get the scriptures in their own language, to read them for themselves and **<u>TO DECIDE TO OBEY ONLY THE BIBLE, NOT THE TRADITIONS OF MEN, EVEN IF THEY HAD TO LOSE THEIR LIFE TO DO SO</u>**! The Waldensians (or Waldenses) are a group that is a case in study, a Christian movement which started in Lyon, France, around the 1170's and spread to the Cottian Alps along the French and Italian border. They wanted to live only by the Bible, keeping Yehovah's laws, and because of this, were declared heretical by the Roman Catholic Church.

I need to explain that I have decided to use the Hebrew Names of Jesus, which is "Yeshua," and of God in their English pronunciation. Speaking God's name is not accepted practice among most Jews; instead they substitute the words "Lord", "Adonai", or "Ha Shem" for His actual Hebrew name of "Yehovah." "Elohim" is Hebrew for the title, "God," and in most scriptures in the Written Torah is right beside the name Yehovah, which is why I refer to Him as "Yehovah Elohim." The King James version of the Bible also usually translates the Hebrew name as "Lord" instead of "Yehovah." I would recommend a book by Keith E. Johnson, <u>His Hallowed Name Revealed Again, pg. 145,</u> to understand more on this subject. Mr. Johnson is a believer in Yeshua, but learned much of what he knows from Nehemiah Gordon, a Karaite Jewish man, who is not a believer in Yeshua. However, he is a Hebrew Bible scholar and a translator of the Dead Sea Scrolls. Also, consider the scripture from the Prophet Joel of the importance of being able to know and actually call on His Name – **YEHOVAH**:

[Joe 2:32 KJV] 32 And it shall come to pass, [that] **whosoever shall <u>CALL ON THE NAME</u> of the LORD shall be delivered**: for in mount Zion and in Jerusalem shall be deliverance, as the LORD hath said, and in the remnant whom the LORD shall call!!!

Now, to continue, the Waldensians were subjected to intense persecution and even burned in great numbers at the stake in 1215 A.D. I think the Roman Catholic Church missed Yeshua's Parable of the Wheat and the Tares in Matthew 13:24-30, 36-43. In this He said, even those who truly might be heretical were not to be rooted out and burned, but allowed to grow with the true believers until **YESHUA HIMSELF comes at the end of the age and sends His angels to gather them - (to be burned!)** The Waldensians were precursors to the Protestant Reformation that took place in the 1500's, and attempted to have more of Yehovah's laws re-established in the church during the reformation, such as the seventh day Sabbath. Although that did not happen, thankfully, the Protestant Reformation did reform much in the church. The man who is recognized as the leader of the Protestant Reformation, **MARTIN LUTHER, SAID, "A SIMPLE LAYMAN ARMED WITH SCRIPTURE IS GREATER THAN THE MIGHTIEST POPE WITHOUT IT."** This is a profound thought. Unfortunately, that first reformation just did not go quite far enough....

For Jews, I will present a Jewish Yeshua (Jesus), hopefully, you will come to believe is your Messiah, your Savior, the Son of God, the Son of Man, because He does not violate nor eradicate The Written Torah, as has been erroneously taught for millennia by Judaism and the church, but instead he practices and upholds it (Matthew 5:17-19.) But, He will require you to see that **ALL of the additions and subtractions from the Written Torah in Judaism** are **ALSO just traditions of men that Yehovah Elohim condemns (Deuteronomy 12:32/Isaiah 29:13-14/Matthew 15:1-20)**. More reformation is needed in Judaism too!

This book is a challenge for us to **CONTINUE THE REFORMATIONS** all the way back to the purity of Yehovah's Word, so we can avoid the Lake of Fire, and instead, be His True Saints and live in His presence forever!

[Revelation 14:12 KJV] HERE IS THE PATIENCE OF <u>THE SAINTS</u>: HERE [ARE] <u>THEY THAT KEEP THE COMMANDMENTS OF GOD</u>, AND <u>THE FAITH OF JESUS</u>.

<u>PARTIAL LIST OF IMPORTANT REFERENCE SCRIPTURES:</u>

Matthew 5:17-20/Matthew 7:21-23/Matthew 28:18-20 For All
Deuteronomy 12:32/Isaiah 29:13-14/Matthew 15:1-20 For Jews
Acts 15:1-29 For Gentiles
Acts 21:17-26 For Jews
Acts 13:42,44
Matthew 10:32-35
Acts 16:9-15
Revelation chapters 1-3, 7:9-17, 14:12, 12:17, 20:15, 3:1-6, 21:1-8, 21:24,27, 22:14-16, 22:19

THE END OF THE MATTER

Yehovah Elohim says in various places that He "**declares the end from the beginning.**"

So, I am going to try to do the same. If you continue reading this to the end, you will see repeated much of what I am writing here that I believe is the criteria that Yehovah Elohim, our Father, will use to determine **WHO WILL ULTIMATELY BE WITH HIM IN THE CITY OF THE NEW JERUSALEM THAT COMES DOWN OUT OF HEAVEN** to the New Earth after the 1000 year reign of the Messiah and **WHO WILL NOT!!!:**

[REV 21:1-4 KJV] 1 AND I SAW A NEW HEAVEN AND A NEW EARTH: FOR THE FIRST HEAVEN AND THE FIRST EARTH WERE PASSED AWAY; AND THERE WAS NO MORE SEA. 2 AND I JOHN SAW THE HOLY CITY, NEW JERUSALEM, COMING DOWN FROM GOD OUT OF HEAVEN, PREPARED AS A BRIDE ADORNED FOR HER HUSBAND. 3 AND I HEARD A GREAT VOICE OUT OF HEAVEN SAYING, BEHOLD, THE TABERNACLE OF GOD [IS] WITH MEN, AND HE WILL DWELL WITH THEM, AND THEY SHALL BE HIS PEOPLE, AND GOD HIMSELF SHALL BE WITH THEM, [AND BE] THEIR GOD. 4 AND GOD SHALL WIPE AWAY ALL TEARS FROM THEIR EYES; AND THERE SHALL BE NO MORE DEATH, NEITHER SORROW, NOR CRYING, NEITHER SHALL THERE BE ANY MORE PAIN: FOR THE FORMER THINGS ARE PASSED AWAY.

[Rev 21:5 KJV] - And HE THAT SAT UPON THE THRONE SAID, Behold, I make all things new. And he said unto me, WRITE: FOR THESE WORDS ARE TRUE AND FAITHFUL.

[Rev 21:6 KJV] - And he said unto me, It is done. I am Alpha and Omega, the beginning and the end. I will give unto him that is athirst of the fountain of the water of life freely.

[Rev 21:7 KJV] - He that OVERCOMETH shall INHERIT ALL THINGS; and I WILL BE HIS GOD, AND HE SHALL BE MY SON!!!

Rev 21:8 KJV – BUT, THE FEARFUL, and UNBELIEVING, and THE ABOMINABLE, and MURDERERS, and WHOREMONGERS, and SORCERERS, and IDOLATERS, and ALL LIARS, shall HAVE THEIR PART IN THE LAKE WHICH BURNETH WITH FIRE AND BRIMSTONE: WHICH IS THE SECOND DEATH.

<u>THIS IS THE FATHER HIMSELF SPEAKING!!!</u> <u>HE IS THE ONE SITTING ON THE THRONE</u>. He says <u>IF WE OVERCOME</u> we will be <u>His sons and daughters</u>!!!

<u>BUT, WHERE DO YOU FIND THE LAWS THAT ARE SPOKEN OF HERE?</u>

<u>IN THE WRITTEN TORAH!!! (The Written Torah is simply Genesis to Deuteronomy in Christian English Bibles, but, of course, it is originally written in Hebrew in the Hebrew Bible, and usually referred to as The Five Books of Moses).</u>

<u>THESE ARE EIGHT CATEGORIES OF COMMANDMENTS (WHICH ALSO INCLUDES BELIEF IN YESHUA) THAT MAY NOT BE BROKEN (WITHOUT REPENTANCE AND FORGIVENESS!) FOR PEOPLE TO BE ALLOWED IN YEHOVAH'S PRESENCE!</u>

<u>FOR EXAMPLE, THE WRITTEN TORAH IS THE ONLY PLACE THAT EXPLAINS WHAT THINGS ARE ABOMINABLE TO THE FATHER –</u> THERE ARE <u>MANY</u> OF THEM AND IT WOULD BE WELL WORTH YOUR TIME TO LOOK THEM UP!!! You can look up the words **ABOMINATION, ABOMINATIONS, and ABOMINABLE** in a Concordance, such as the Strong's Concordance, to find **<u>all the verses</u>** that will explain to you what is abominable to Yehovah. It also would be wise to see any ways you could be participating in idolatry, sorcery, or any of these other sins. **(SEE APPENDIX II AGAIN FOR A LIST OF ABOMINATIONS AND OTHER SINS THAT WILL SEND YOU TO THE LAKE OF FIRE!)**The Father **<u>does not differentiate in this verse</u>** between unbelievers or Jewish believers in Yeshua, believers from The House of Israel, gentile believers that are joined to Israel by the Mosaic Covenant (proselytes/devout men and women), or completely gentile believers in Yeshua!

CONCERNING <u>THE NEW JERUSALEM</u> (OR, I BELIEVE, <u>HEAVEN</u>, AS WE CALL IT NOW), <u>THESE LAWS ARE FOR EVERYONE</u> IT SEEMS!

The Apostle John is shown the New Jerusalem, how wonderful it is, in the next verses, 9-27. But, he **<u>ALSO</u>** says **THOSE WHO PRACTICE THESE CERTAIN SINS WILL NOT BE THERE!:**

[Rev 21:24-27 KJV] 24 **AND <u>THE NATIONS OF THEM WHICH ARE SAVED SHALL</u>**

WALK IN THE LIGHT OF IT and **THE KINGS OF THE EARTH** do bring their glory and honour into it. 25 And the gates of it shall not be shut at all by day: for there shall be no night there. 26 And **THEY** shall bring the glory and honour of the nations into it. 27 **And there shall IN NO WISE enter into it ANYTHING THAT DEFILETH, NEITHER [WHATSOEVER] WORKETH ABOMINATION, OR [MAKETH] A LIE: BUT THEY WHICH ARE WRITTEN IN THE LAMB'S BOOK OF LIFE.**

Maybe to be **SURE** we understand this, it is reiterated again in the very last chapter of the Book of Revelation, in speaking of the New Jerusalem.

[Rev 22:15-16 KJV] 15 For WITHOUT [are] DOGS, AND SORCERERS, AND WHOREMONGERS, AND MURDERERS, AND IDOLATERS, AND WHOSOEVER LOVETH AND MAKETH A LIE. 16 I Jesus have sent mine angel to testify unto you these things IN THE CHURCHES. I am the root and the offspring of David, [and] the bright and morning star.

According to Revelation 21:8, the word WITHOUT here has to be the Lake of Fire!!! Notice that this is WRITTEN TO THE CHURCHES, SO I THINK HE IS MAKING THE POINT FOR YOU NOT TO THINK THAT YOU WILL BE EXEMPT BECAUSE OF YOUR BELIEF IN YESHUA! In fact, belief in Yeshua is part of these commandments! (See Appendix II).

If you put all three of these scriptures together, it seems that the word "DOGS" in the above verse Revelation 22:15 combine many of the sins listed in Revelation 21:8 (fearful, unbelieving and abominable) that will cause one to be thrown into the Lake of Fire. In the same way, the word "DEFILED" in Revelation 21:27 combines others (fearful, unbelieving, murderers, whoremongers, sorcerers, idolaters). So, I believe it behooves us to quote it again!:

Rev 21:8 KJV - BUT, THE FEARFUL, and UNBELIEVING, and THE ABOMINABLE, and MURDERERS, and WHOREMONGERS, and SORCERERS, and IDOLATERS, and ALL LIARS, shall HAVE THEIR PART IN THE LAKE WHICH BURNETH WITH FIRE AND BRIMSTONE: WHICH IS THE SECOND DEATH.

I BELIEVE UNDERSTANDING THIS IS OF UTMOST IMPORTANCE!

In addition, **I BELIEVE YEHOVAH, OUR FATHER, DESIRES FOR ALL OF HIS WRITTEN TORAH TO BE KEPT**. Yeshua said that those who **DO YEHOVAH'S COMMANDMENTS** as given in **the Written Torah, even the least of them**, and **teach them to others**, will be called **GREAT in the Kingdom of Heaven** and those who **do not keep even the least of the commandments** and **do not teach them to others** will be called **LEAST in the Kingdom of Heaven**. Remember that this is Yeshua himself speaking:

[MAT 5:19 KJV] 19 WHOSOEVER THEREFORE SHALL BREAK ONE OF THESE LEAST COMMANDMENTS, AND SHALL TEACH MEN SO, HE SHALL BE CALLED THE LEAST IN THE KINGDOM OF HEAVEN: BUT WHOSOEVER SHALL DO AND TEACH [THEM], THE SAME SHALL BE CALLED GREAT IN THE KINGDOM OF HEAVEN.

NOTE THAT HE DOES NOT SAY THAT THEY WILL NOT BE IN THE KINGDOM OF HEAVEN – JUST THE LEAST!

HOWEVER, THIS NEGATES OUR IDEA THAT THERE ARE NO BIG SINS OR LITTLE SINS. YESHUA JUST SPOKE OF LEAST COMMANDMENTS!
OBVIOUSLY, THE ONES THAT WILL HAVE YOU THROWN IN THE LAKE OF FIRE MUST BE THE BIGGEST SINS!!!

I don't presume to know everything about the Kingdom of Heaven, which starts with the 1000 year reign of the King of Kings, Yeshua ha Mashiach, when he returns to this earth. Nor do I know all about the New Heavens and the New Earth, right afterwards, when The Father, Yehovah Elohim **HIMSELF** comes down to reign forever in the heavenly New Jerusalem that has come to earth.

BUT, ONE THING I KNOW FOR SURE BASED ON THESE SCRIPTURES - HE STILL DEMANDS THAT AT LEAST THESE EIGHT CATEGORIES OF COMMANDMENTS BE KEPT, EVEN IN THE NEW JERUSALEM!!!

[Rev 22:14 KJV] 14 BLESSED [are] they that DO HIS COMMANDMENTS, that they may have RIGHT TO THE TREE OF LIFE, and MAY ENTER IN THROUGH THE GATES INTO THE CITY.

WILL IT BE WORTH IT? ABSOLUTELY!

But, keep reading. There is MUCH MORE to understand all the way to the end!!!

SO, NOW, FOR THE REST OF THE MATTER!:

I believe that **its possible** that whether we are **OBLIGATED** to keep **ALL OF**

<u>THE WRITTEN TORAH</u>, even from the beginning of our walk as believers in Yeshua, is according to which group of believers we belong to. However, regardless of which one we are in, **ALL MANKIND HAS TO COME INTO THE NEW COVENANT WITH THE FATHER <u>THROUGH THE DOOR, YESHUA HA MASHIACH</u>!!! WE HAVE TO BELIEVE IN HIM!**

From my research, I think there are **<u>FOUR GROUPS OF PEOPLE THAT HAVE (OR WILL) COME INTO FAITH IN YESHUA that EVENTUALLY WILL BE MADE INTO ONE GROUP</u>!** We will review each one in the next few chapters...

CHAPTER 1

Believers in Yeshua from the House of Judah

(HOUSE OF JUDAH) JEWS - According to II Chronicles 11:1-17, the House of Judah was the tribe of Judah, the tribe of Benjamin, the Levites from all Israel, and those from the other tribes that wanted to continue to seek Yehovah Elohim after The Father took the Kingdom from King Solomon, King David's son. Yehovah, because of Solomon's fall into idolatry, stripped the Kingdom from his son, Rehoboam, and gave it to a man named Jeroboam, making him King of the House of Israel. Yehovah left him one tribe – Judah- for King David's sake, however. All the kings of Judah to come were described as to whether they followed Yehovah the way their Father David did, keeping His commandments, statutes, and judgments – or not.

[1Ki 11:11-13 KJV] 11 Wherefore the LORD said unto Solomon, Forasmuch as this is done of thee, and **THOU HAST NOT KEPT MY COVENANT AND MY STATUTES, WHICH I HAVE COMMANDED THEE**, I will surely rend the kingdom from thee, and will give it to thy servant. 12 Notwithstanding in thy days I will not do it for David thy father's sake: [but] I will rend it out of the hand of thy son. 13 Howbeit I will not rend away all the kingdom; [but] will give one tribe to thy son for David my servant's sake, and for Jerusalem's sake which I have chosen.

As I stated earlier, the servant to whom Yehovah gave the kingdom was named Jeroboam. King Jeroboam, who became ruler over the House of Israel, unfortunately was not faithful to keep Yehovah's Written Torah either!

[2Ch 11:1-17 KJV] 1 And when Rehoboam was come to Jerusalem, he gathered of the house of Judah and Benjamin an hundred and fourscore thousand chosen [men], which were warriors, to fight against Israel, that he might bring the kingdom again to Rehoboam. 2 But the word of the LORD came to Shemaiah the man of God, saying, 3 Speak unto Rehoboam the son of Solomon, king of Judah, and to all Israel in Judah and Benjamin, saying, 4 Thus saith the LORD, Ye shall not go up, nor fight against your brethren: return every man to his house: for this thing is done of me. And they obeyed the words of the LORD, and returned from going against Jeroboam. 5 And Rehoboam dwelt in Jerusalem, and built cities for defence in Judah. 6 He built even Bethlehem, and Etam, and Tekoa, 7 And Bethzur, and Shoco, and Adullam, 8 And Gath, and Mareshah, and Ziph, 9 And Adoraim, and Lachish, and Azekah, 10 And Zorah, and Aijalon, and Hebron, which [are] in Judah and in Benjamin fenced cities. 11 And he fortified the strong holds, and put captains in them, and store of victual, and of oil and wine. 12 And in every several city [he put] shields and spears, and made them exceeding strong, having **JUDAH** and **BENJAMIN** on his side. 13 **AND THE PRIESTS AND THE LEVITES THAT [WERE] IN ALL ISRAEL RESORTED TO HIM OUT OF ALL THEIR COASTS. 14 FOR THE LEVITES LEFT THEIR SUBURBS AND THEIR POSSESSION, AND CAME TO JUDAH AND JERUSALEM: FOR JEROBOAM AND HIS SONS HAD CAST THEM OFF FROM EXECUTING THE PRIEST'S OFFICE UNTO THE LORD**: 15 And he ordained him priests for the high places, and for the devils, and for the calves which he had made. **16 AND AFTER THEM OUT OF ALL THE TRIBES OF ISRAEL SUCH AS SET THEIR HEARTS TO SEEK THE LORD GOD OF ISRAEL CAME TO JERUSALEM, TO SACRIFICE UNTO THE LORD GOD OF THEIR FATHERS.** 17 So they strengthened the kingdom of Judah, and made Rehoboam the son of Solomon strong, three years: **FOR THREE YEARS THEY WALKED IN THE WAY OF DAVID AND SOLOMON.**

Because later, as I will discuss below, the Kingdom of Israel (or House of Israel) was divorced from Yehovah, the Kingdom of Judah (or House of Judah) was all that was left of the nation of Israel by the time Yeshua was born and so they were called Jews. **- THE JEWS WERE ISRAEL and THEY WERE STILL UNDER THE 1ST COVENANT! THEREFORE, JEWISH BELIEVERS IN YESHUA ARE ABSOLUTELY TO CONTINUE KEEPING THE WRITTEN TORAH (LAW) OF MOSES ACCORDING TO MATTHEW 5:17-19 AND ACTS 21:18-25.** These Jewish believers in Yeshua who did still keep the Torah were called Nazarenes (Notzrim in Hebrew transliteration), or the Nazarene sect of Jews, in the first few centuries.

Interestingly, there are also many believers in Yeshua today that are finding that they have Jewish heritage that was hidden to them in the past! Consequently, they definitely should also learn and keep all of the Written Torah.

CHAPTER 2

Believers in Yeshua from the House of Israel (Ephraim)

HOUSE OF ISRAEL (EPHRAIM) –The House of Israel are those from the rest of the tribes of Israel that The Father put under the rule of Jeroboam when he took the Kingdom of Israel from Solomon. In scripture, The Father refers to them as "Ephraim" much of the time because the tribe of Ephraim was their head tribe. King Jeroboam was commanded by Yehovah to keep all the Written Torah. But, he made the people two golden calves to worship in Bethel and Dan instead of letting them go to Jerusalem to worship the True God (Yehovah) as they were commanded. He also changed the times of the feasts that Yehovah had set up. He did all this because he was afraid of losing the people back to the King of Judah if they went to Jerusalem to worship as Yehovah had commanded in the Written Torah. The Father was not pleased at all. He told Jeroboam, because he had not kept his commandments, that his seed would not continue to be the kings of Israel. All the later kings of Israel that The Father did allow would even be described as to whether they followed the sins of Jeroboam or not. Most did and many even went further into idolatry by leading the people into Baal worship. Years later, the House of Israel was completely divorced by Yehovah for continuing to break his laws, even though he sent many prophets to warn them to repent and turn back to the Written Torah. They were overtaken by the Kingdom of Assyria, as the prophets prophesied to them would happen if they did not repent. Then, they were scattered to all the countries of the world, intermarrying with gentiles. The story is told in the book of Hosea. You should read at least the first three chapters, but the whole book tells about the divorce and the future redemption of the House of Israel. However, a synopsis is here in Hosea chapter 1:

[Hos 1:1-11 KJV] 1 The word of the LORD that came unto Hosea, the son of Beeri,
in the days of Uzziah, Jotham, Ahaz, [and] Hezekiah, kings of Judah, and in the days
of Jeroboam the son of Joash, king of Israel. 2 The beginning of the word of the
LORD by Hosea. And the LORD said to Hosea, Go, take unto thee a wife of
whoredoms and children of whoredoms: for the land hath committed great
whoredom, [departing] from the LORD. 3 So he went and took Gomer the
daughter of Diblaim; which conceived, and bare him a son. 4 And the LORD said

unto him, Call his name Jezreel; for yet a little [while], and I will avenge the blood of Jezreel upon the house of Jehu, and **WILL CAUSE TO CEASE THE KINGDOM OF THE HOUSE OF ISRAEL.** 5 And it shall come to pass at that day, that I will break the bow of Israel in the valley of Jezreel. 6 And she conceived again, and bare a daughter. And [God] said unto him, Call her name Loruhamah: **FOR I WILL NO MORE HAVE MERCY UPON THE HOUSE OF ISRAEL; BUT I WILL UTTERLY TAKE THEM AWAY.** 7 But I will have mercy upon the house of Judah, and will save them by the LORD their God, and will not save them by bow, nor by sword, nor by battle, by horses, nor by horsemen. 8 Now when she had weaned Loruhamah, she conceived, and bare a son. 9 **THEN SAID [GOD], CALL HIS NAME LOAMMI: FOR YE [ARE] NOT MY PEOPLE, AND I WILL NOT BE YOUR [GOD]. 10 YET THE NUMBER OF THE CHILDREN OF ISRAEL SHALL BE AS THE SAND OF THE SEA, WHICH CANNOT BE MEASURED NOR NUMBERED; AND IT SHALL COME TO PASS, [THAT] IN THE PLACE WHERE IT WAS SAID UNTO THEM, YE [ARE] NOT MY PEOPLE, [THERE] IT SHALL BE SAID UNTO THEM, [YE ARE] THE SONS OF THE LIVING GOD. 11 <u>THEN SHALL THE CHILDREN OF JUDAH AND THE CHILDREN OF ISRAEL BE GATHERED TOGETHER, AND APPOINT THEMSELVES ONE HEAD,</u> AND THEY SHALL COME UP OUT OF THE LAND: FOR GREAT [SHALL BE] THE DAY OF JEZREEL.**

SO THE HOUSE OF ISRAEL WAS NO LONGER IN THE 1ST COVENANT – THEY WERE DIVORCED! There may have been some groups that knew they had come from these tribes, but most just lost their identity altogether and, for all practical purposes, were gentiles:

[Hos 8:8 KJV] 8 Israel is swallowed up: now shall they be among the Gentiles as a vessel wherein [is] no pleasure. [Hos 7:8-9 KJV] 8 Ephraim, he hath mixed himself among the people; Ephraim is a cake not turned. 9 Strangers have devoured his strength, and he knoweth [it] not: yea, gray hairs are here and there upon him, yet he knoweth not.

I believe it's possible that many of the gentile believers in Yeshua, even through the ages, are actually from these lost tribes. The New Covenant is the plan that The Father made to bring them (and everyone, as we will see later) back into covenant with Himself, according to Jeremiah 31:31-34 and many other prophecies::

[Jer 31:31-33 KJV] 31 **BEHOLD, THE DAYS COME, SAITH THE LORD, THAT I WILL MAKE A NEW COVENANT WITH THE HOUSE OF ISRAEL, AND WITH THE HOUSE OF JUDAH**: 32 Not according to the covenant that I made with their fathers in the day [that] I took them by the hand to bring them out of the land of Egypt; which **MY COVENANT THEY BRAKE, ALTHOUGH I WAS AN HUSBAND UNTO THEM**, saith the LORD: 33 But this [shall be] the covenant that I will make with the house of Israel; After those days, saith the LORD, **I WILL PUT MY LAW IN THEIR INWARD PARTS**, and write it in their hearts; and will be their God, and they shall be my people. Read **Ezekiel 37:15-28** to see that **<u>The Father will reunite all 12 tribes of Israel:</u>**

[Eze 37:15-28 KJV] 15 The word of the LORD came again unto me, saying, 16 Moreover, thou son of man, take thee one stick, and write upon it, For Judah, and for the children of Israel his companions: then take another stick, and write upon it, For Joseph, the stick of Ephraim, and [for] all the house of Israel his companions: 17 And join them one to another into one stick; and they shall become one in thine hand. 18 And when the children of thy people shall speak unto thee, saying, Wilt thou not shew us what thou [meanest] by these? 19 Say unto them, <u>THUS SAITH THE LORD GOD; BEHOLD, I WILL TAKE THE STICK OF JOSEPH, WHICH [IS] IN THE HAND OF EPHRAIM, AND THE TRIBES OF ISRAEL HIS FELLOWS, AND WILL PUT THEM WITH HIM, [EVEN] WITH THE STICK OF JUDAH, AND MAKE THEM ONE STICK, AND THEY SHALL BE ONE IN MINE HAND</u>. 20 And the sticks whereon thou writest shall be in thine hand before their eyes. 21 And say unto them, Thus saith the Lord GOD; Behold, I will take the children of Israel from among the heathen, whither they be gone, and will gather them on every side, and bring them into their own land: 22 And I will make them one nation in the land upon the mountains of Israel; and one king shall be king to them all: and they shall be no more two nations, neither shall they be divided into two kingdoms any more at all: 23 Neither shall they defile themselves any more with their idols, nor with their detestable things, nor with any of their transgressions: but I will save them out of all their dwellingplaces, wherein they have sinned, and will cleanse them: so shall they be my people, and I will be their God. 24 And David my servant [shall be] king over them; and they all shall have one shepherd: <u>THEY SHALL ALSO WALK IN MY JUDGMENTS, AND OBSERVE MY STATUTES, AND DO THEM</u>. 25 And they shall dwell in the land that I have given unto Jacob my servant, wherein your fathers have dwelt; and they shall dwell therein, [even] they, and their children, and their children's children for ever: and my servant David [shall be] their prince for ever. 26 Moreover I will make a covenant of peace with them; it shall be an everlasting covenant with them: and I will place them, and multiply them, and will set my sanctuary in the midst of them for evermore. 27 My tabernacle also shall be with them: yea, I will be their God, and they shall be

my people. 28 And the heathen shall know that I the LORD do sanctify Israel, when my sanctuary shall be in the midst of them for evermore.
(See these scriptures also: Genesis 48:19, 5:3, 8:8, Amos 9:9, Jeremiah 31:18-19, Zechariah 10:7, Romans 9:24-26, 11:25-26, Ephesians 2:11-22)

So, if you KNOW that you are from one of the lost tribes of Israel, by DNA testing or any other way that the Father allows you to know, then Ezekiel 37:24 above makes it clear that it is The Father's will for you to keep all of the Written Torah.

There are many in the Hebrew Roots Movement of Christianity that submit the theory that all of the believers in Yeshua that are not Jewish and have been in the gentile Christian churches are totally from these lost tribes. I believe that many, maybe the majority, are as well, but not all.

CHAPTER 3

Believers in Yeshua from Gentiles Joined to Israel by the Mosaic Covenant (Proselytes/Devout)

<u>GENTILES JOINED TO ISRAEL BY THE MOSAIC COVENANT (PROSELYTES/DEVOUT)</u> – Many of us did not truly understand that the Father Yehovah Elohim ALWAYS had allowed gentiles that wanted to worship Him to join Israel, even before Yeshua came! There were exceptions – the seven Canaanite nations that Yehovah replaced with the nation of Israel in the Promised Land were not allowed to join Israel. He obviously truly hated their **ABOMINABLE CUSTOMS**, which he explains in the entire chapter of Leviticus 18 as to why they were displaced and eliminated – men, women, and children. (Remember practicing "abominations" will keep you out of the New Jerusalem that comes down out of heaven!!!) There were other stipulations with some of the other nations. But, most other "strangers," as the King James version of the Bible calls gentiles, were <u>welcomed</u> to "sojourn" with biological or natural Israelites. **They had to obey the Written Torah just like Israel did, though! But, then they were to be treated as part of the family! Yehovah has always been so merciful!**

[Num 15:15-16 KJV] 15 **ONE ORDINANCE [SHALL BE BOTH] FOR YOU OF THE CONGREGATION, AND ALSO FOR THE STRANGER THAT SOJOURNETH [WITH YOU], <u>AN ORDINANCE FOR EVER IN YOUR GENERATIONS</u>: <u>AS YE [ARE], SO SHALL THE STRANGER BE BEFORE THE LORD</u>.** 16 **ONE LAW AND ONE MANNER SHALL BE FOR YOU, AND FOR THE STRANGER THAT SOJOURNETH WITH YOU.**

[Lev 19:33-34 KJV] 33 And if a stranger sojourn with thee in your land, ye shall not vex him. 34 **<u>[BUT] THE STRANGER THAT DWELLETH WITH YOU SHALL BE UNTO YOU AS ONE BORN AMONG YOU, AND THOU SHALT LOVE HIM AS THYSELF</u>**; for ye were strangers in the land of Egypt: I [am] the LORD your God.

The Moabite woman, Ruth, would have been one of these strangers! (See the Book of Ruth.) After her husband died, she said to her Jewish mother in law, Naomi: [Rth 1:16 KJV] 16 And Ruth said, Intreat me not to leave thee, [or] to return from following after thee: for whither thou goest, I will go; and where thou lodgest, I will lodge: **thy people [shall be] my people, and thy God my God.**

EVEN AS A MOABITE WOMAN, SHE MARRIED INTO ISRAEL AND BECAME A GENTILE PROSELYTE, TRULY FROM HER HEART, RUTH BECAME AN INTEGRAL PART OF THE NATION OF ISRAEL AS THE GREAT-GRANDMOTHER OF KING DAVID AND, AS SUCH, EVEN IN THE LINEAGE OF YESHUA HA MASHIACH!

So these gentiles joined to Israel would submit to the entire Mosaic Covenant, even circumcision . They were commonly called Proselytes or Devout Men/Women or God Fearers in the New Testatment and should **ABSOLUTELY** continue to keep the Written Torah, even after coming to faith in Yeshua. They are part of Israel.

Many of us have missed the presence of these Devout Gentiles joined to Israel as we have read the New Covenant. A possible one that obviously became a believer in Yeshua is the Ananias that Yeshua instructed to go lay hands on Saul (Paul) so that he could regain his sight. **PAUL SAYS THAT ANANIAS KEPT THE TORAH, EVEN AS A BELIEVER, AND BECAUSE OF THIS, HAD A GOOD REPUTATION AMONG THE JEWISH PEOPLE IN DAMASCUS!**

[Act 22:12-13 KJV] 12 And **ONE ANANIAS, A DEVOUT MAN ACCORDING TO THE LAW, HAVING A GOOD REPORT OF ALL THE JEWS WHICH DWELT [THERE]**,
13 Came unto me, and stood, and said unto me, Brother Saul, receive thy sight. And the same hour I looked up upon him.

It's possible that Ananias was a Jewish believer; however, the fact that it was pointed out that he was "devout", a term usually used to describe Gentile Proselytes, makes this a possibility.

Take for example, Cornelius, a Roman Centurion, a Gentile who definitively was termed "devout":

[Act 10:1-6 KJV] 1 There was a certain man in Caesarea called Cornelius, a
centurion of the band called the Italian [band], 2 **[A] DEVOUT [MAN], AND ONE THAT FEARED GOD WITH ALL HIS HOUSE, WHICH GAVE MUCH ALMS TO THE PEOPLE, AND PRAYED TO GOD ALWAY**. 3 He saw in a vision evidently about the
ninth hour of the day an angel of God coming in to him, and saying unto him,
Cornelius. 4 And when he looked on him, he was afraid, and said, What is it, Lord?
And he said unto him, Thy prayers and thine alms are come up for a memorial

before God. 5 And now send men to Joppa, and call for [one] Simon, whose surname is Peter: 6 He lodgeth with one Simon a tanner, whose house is by the sea side: he shall tell thee what thou oughtest to do.

It's **possible** that Peter had to be instructed by Yehovah that it was all right for him to go into Cornelius's house because he was already supposed to be being treated as part of Israel, but may not have been because of the Oral Torah (which we will discuss later)... there is certainly nothing in the Written Torah to prevent it.

Personally, I believe these are the best scriptures, Numbers 15:15-16 and Leviticus 19:33-34, along with Ruth's and Ananias's example, to give us a clue of how Yehovah Elohim WOULD EXPECT ANY GENTILES, who later came into Israel through the New Covenant by belief in Yeshua, to live. They were to keep the Written Torah and be treated like natural Israel. Israel was to be ONE nation – not divided!

CHAPTER 4

Believers in Yeshua from the Completely Gentiles

Completely gentiles would be those believers in Yeshua who had never entered into covenant with Yehovah Elohim, nor were they part of any of the tribes of Israel, but Yehovah chose them and put His name upon them, allowing them to come into the New Covenant by faith in Yeshua ha Mashiach! The two scriptures below state this clearly.

[Isa 49:5-6 KJV] 5 **And now, saith the LORD that <u>formed me from the womb [to be] his servant</u>, to bring Jacob again to him, <u>THOUGH ISRAEL BE NOT GATHERED</u>**, yet shall I be glorious in the eyes of the LORD, and my God shall be my strength. 6 **<u>AND HE SAID, IT IS A LIGHT THING THAT THOU SHOULDEST BE MY SERVANT TO RAISE UP THE TRIBES OF JACOB, AND TO RESTORE THE PRESERVED OF ISRAEL: I WILL ALSO GIVE THEE FOR A LIGHT TO THE GENTILES, THAT THOU MAYEST BE MY SALVATION UNTO THE END OF THE EARTH!</u>**

<u>[Amo 9:11-12 KJV] 11 In that day will I raise up the tabernacle of David that is fallen, and close up the breaches thereof; and I will raise up his ruins, and I will build it as in the days of old: 12 That they may possess the remnant of Edom, and OF ALL THE HEATHEN, WHICH ARE CALLED BY MY NAME, saith the lord that doeth this.</u>

Also, the "sons of the stranger" (the gentiles) are prophesied to be gathered to the natural nation of Israel when Yehovah sends Yeshua, whose name actually is translated as "salvation"!:

[Isa 56:1-8 KJV] 1 Thus saith the LORD, Keep ye judgment, and do justice: for <u>MY SALVATION [IS] NEAR TO COME</u>, and my righteousness to be revealed. 2 Blessed [is] the man [that] doeth this, and the son of man [that] layeth hold on it; that keepeth the sabbath from polluting it, and keepeth his hand from doing any evil. 3 <u>NEITHER LET THE SON OF THE STRANGER, THAT HATH JOINED HIMSELF TO THE LORD, SPEAK, SAYING, THE LORD HATH UTTERLY SEPARATED ME FROM HIS PEOPLE</u>: neither let the eunuch say, Behold, I [am] a dry tree. 4 For thus saith the LORD unto the eunuchs that keep my

sabbaths, and choose [the things] that please me, and take hold of my covenant; 5 Even unto them will I give in mine house and within my walls a place and a name better than of sons and of daughters: I will give them an everlasting name, that shall not be cut off. 6 ALSO THE SONS OF THE STRANGER, THAT JOIN THEMSELVES TO THE LORD, TO SERVE HIM, AND TO LOVE THE NAME OF THE LORD, TO BE HIS SERVANTS, EVERY ONE THAT KEEPETH THE SABBATH FROM POLLUTING IT, AND TAKETH HOLD OF MY COVENANT; 7 EVEN THEM WILL I BRING TO MY HOLY MOUNTAIN, AND MAKE THEM JOYFUL IN MY HOUSE OF PRAYER: THEIR BURNT OFFERINGS AND THEIR SACRIFICES [SHALL BE] ACCEPTED UPON MINE ALTAR; FOR MINE HOUSE SHALL BE CALLED AN HOUSE OF PRAYER FOR ALL PEOPLE. 8 The Lord GOD which gathereth the outcasts of Israel saith, <u>Yet will I gather [others] to him, BESIDE THOSE that are gathered unto him.</u>

(Although we will be discussing this later, notice that these gentile believers <u>WILL BE</u> making burnt offerings and sacrifices, keeping the Sabbath, and actually keeping all of the Covenant (the Written Torah) at this time, which I believe is the Millennial Kingdom of the Mashiach. If the gentile believers will be keeping the Written Torah then, why would they not now, as they await Yeshua ha Mashiach's return?)

Maybe this is why **YESHUA** said **<u>AFTER HIS RESURRECTION</u>**:

[Luk 24:46-47 KJV] 46 And said unto them, Thus it is written, and thus it behoved Christ to suffer, and to rise from the dead the third day: 47 And that repentance and remission of sins should be preached in his name **<u>AMONG ALL NATIONS</u>**, beginning at Jerusalem.

The operative word here is **ALL – NOT JUST THE NATION OF THE JEWS OR THE NATIONS WHERE THE LOST TRIBES OF ISRAEL HAD BEEN SCATTERED! Paul also said when relating what Yeshua said to him when he was blinded on the way to Damascus:**

[Act 26:15-18 KJV] 15 And I said, Who art thou, Lord? And he said, I am Jesus whom thou persecutest. 16 But rise, and stand upon thy feet: for I have appeared unto thee for this purpose, to make thee a minister and a witness both of these things which thou hast seen, and of those things in the which I will appear unto thee; 17 Delivering thee from the people, and [from] <u>THE GENTILES, UNTO WHOM NOW I SEND THEE</u>, 18 <u>TO OPEN THEIR EYES, [AND] TURN [THEM TO] FROM DARKNESS TO LIGHT, AND [FROM] THE POWER OF SATAN UNTO GOD</u>, THAT THEY MAY RECEIVE FORGIVENESS OF SINS, AND

INHERITANCE AMONG THEM WHICH ARE SANCTIFIED BY FAITH THAT IS IN ME.

Also, the Book of the Revelation of Yeshua ha Mashiach written by the Apostle John says:

[Rev 7:9-10 KJV] 9 After this I beheld, and, lo, <u>A GREAT MULTITUDE, WHICH NO MAN COULD NUMBER, OF ALL NATIONS, AND KINDREDS, AND PEOPLE, AND TONGUES</u>, stood before the throne, and before the Lamb, clothed with white robes, and palms in their hands; 10 And cried with a loud voice, saying, Salvation to our God which sitteth upon the throne, and unto the Lamb.

Other confirming scriptures are Acts 1:7-8 and Revelation 14:6-7.

Most Christians today, of course, believe that complete gentiles could become believers in Yeshua, because most of us are! But, it wasn't always this way**! THE ENTIRE CONGREGATION OF BELIEVERS IN YESHUA WERE INITIALLY ONLY JEWISH! THEY WERE MESSIANIC JEWS (NAZARENES)!** As stated before, even today, there are some in the Hebrew Roots Movement that think everyone who becomes a believer in Yeshua can only come from one of the twelve tribes of Israel. **BUT, OUR FATHER IS SO GLORIOUS AND MERCIFUL THAT HE HAS ALLOWED EVEN COMPLETELY GENTILES TO COME INTO THE CONGREGATION OF ISRAEL THROUGH THE NEW COVENANT!**

BUT, ALSO, AS A THOUGHT TO CONSIDER – IF 3 OUT OF THESE 4 GROUPS OF BELIEVERS IN YESHUA ARE TO KEEP THE WRITTEN TORAH, WOULD IT NOT BE REASONABLE TO THINK THAT EVEN THE 4TH GROUP SHOULD TOO, SINCE YESHUA SAID THERE WOULD ONLY BE ONE FOLD AND ONE SHEPHERD?

[Jhn 10:16 KJV] 16 **And OTHER SHEEP I HAVE, WHICH ARE NOT OF THIS FOLD: them also I must bring, and they shall hear my voice; and there shall be ONE FOLD, [and] ONE SHEPHERD.**

We do need to note that <u>all the nations, even completely gentiles, knew some things that were sinful from the beginning of time. Some of these are, as Genesis relates</u>: Murder - Genesis 9:5-6, Adultery – Genesis 20:3, Homosexuality – Genesis 19:1-28 (Yehovah would not have punished Sodom and Gomorrah if they had not known better), Incest – Genesis 19: 29-38 (the daughters had to make their father drunk or he would not have had sexual relations with them). There are different ideas about how they knew these things, generally referred to as the Noahide laws by the Jewish people.

HOWEVER, ALL FOUR GROUPS SIMPLY HAVE TO BELIEVE THAT YESHUA OF NAZARETH IS THE SON OF GOD IN ORDER TO COME INTO THE NEW COVENANT THAT WILL GIVE THEM ETERNAL LIFE – THE RESURRECTION! THIS TRULY IS AN AGE OF GRACE!!

CHAPTER 5

Simply Believe in Yeshua to Come into the New Covenant – Even Jews!

It **seems too simple** to some people that the only thing people have to do is believe that Yeshua is the Son of God **to come** into the New Covenant that offers eternal life. **But, Yeshua tells us it is very similar to what Yehovah did for Israel when they had murmured and complained against him and Moses, and he brought fatally poisonous snakes to punish them. But, because of his great mercy, he gave them an INCREDIBLY SIMPLE SALVATION. If they would simply look at a brass serpent that Moses was instructed to put on a stake, they would be totally healed. Here is the story:**

[Num 21:4-9 KJV] 4 And they journeyed from mount Hor by the way of the Red sea, to compass the land of Edom: and the soul of the people was much discouraged because of the way. 5 And the people spake against God, and against Moses, Wherefore have ye brought us up out of Egypt to die in the wilderness? for [there is] no bread, neither [is there any] water; and our soul loatheth this light bread. 6 And the LORD sent fiery serpents among the people, and they bit the people; and much people of Israel died. 7 Therefore the people came to Moses, and said, We have sinned, for we have spoken against the LORD, and against thee; pray unto the LORD, that he take away the serpents from us. And Moses prayed for the people. 8 **AND THE LORD SAID UNTO MOSES, MAKE THEE A FIERY SERPENT, AND SET IT UPON A POLE: AND IT SHALL COME TO PASS, THAT EVERY ONE THAT IS BITTEN, WHEN HE LOOKETH UPON IT, SHALL LIVE. 9 AND MOSES MADE A SERPENT OF BRASS, AND PUT IT UPON A POLE, AND IT CAME TO PASS, THAT IF A SERPENT HAD BITTEN ANY MAN, WHEN HE BEHELD THE SERPENT OF BRASS, HE LIVED.**

YESHUA SAYS THAT HE IS LIKE THIS BRASS SERPENT! He states in the Book of John:

[JHN 3:14-18 KJV] 14 AND AS MOSES LIFTED UP THE SERPENT IN THE WILDERNESS, EVEN SO MUST THE SON OF MAN BE LIFTED UP: 15 THAT WHOSOEVER BELIEVETH IN HIM SHOULD NOT PERISH, BUT HAVE ETERNAL LIFE. 16 For God so loved the world, that he gave his only begotten Son, that whosoever believeth in him should not perish, but have everlasting life. 17 For God sent not his Son into the world to condemn the world; but that the world through him might be saved. 18 He that believeth on him is not condemned: but he that believeth not is condemned already, because he hath not believed in the name of the only begotten Son of God.

SO, DO NOT MAKE THE MISTAKE OF THINKING THAT THE JEWISH PEOPLE DO NOT HAVE TO COME TO FAITH IN YESHUA TO HAVE ETERNAL LIFE. Speaking to the Jews of his day He said, in [Jhn 8:24 KJV], " I said therefore unto you, that ye shall die in your sins: **FOR IF YE BELIEVE NOT THAT I AM [HE], YE SHALL DIE IN YOUR SINS.**"

YEHOVAH ELOHIM has made it necessary for there to be a blood sacrifice to atone for the sins of the Israelites:

[Lev 17:11 KJV] 11 FOR THE LIFE OF THE FLESH [IS] IN THE BLOOD: AND I HAVE GIVEN IT TO YOU UPON THE ALTAR TO MAKE AN ATONEMENT FOR YOUR SOULS: FOR IT [IS] THE BLOOD [THAT] MAKETH AN ATONEMENT FOR THE SOUL.

******Isaiah 52:13 through all of Isaiah 53 describes Yehovah Elohim's merciful provision for a man , the Messiah himself, to be the "Suffering Servant" that SHEDS HIS BLOOD for the Israelite people TO COMPLETELY ATONE FOR THEIR SINS. When he returns, (See Daniel 7:13-14) everyone will be astonished at him, as he will be highly exalted at that point as Messiah the King!!!******

[Isa 52:13-15 KJV] 13 Behold, MY SERVANT shall deal prudently, HE SHALL BE EXALTED AND EXTOLLED, AND BE VERY HIGH.

14 AS MANY WERE ASTONIED AT THEE; HIS VISAGE WAS SO MARRED MORE THAN ANY MAN, AND HIS FORM MORE THAN THE SONS OF MEN:

15 SO SHALL HE SPRINKLE MANY NATIONS; THE KINGS SHALL SHUT THEIR MOUTHS AT HIM: FOR [THAT] WHICH HAD NOT BEEN TOLD THEM SHALL THEY SEE; AND [THAT] WHICH THEY HAD NOT HEARD SHALL THEY CONSIDER.

Isa 53:1 KJV - WHO HATH BELIEVED OUR REPORT? and to whom is THE ARM OF THE LORD revealed?

Isa 53:2 KJV - For he shall grow up before him as a tender plant, and as a root out of a dry ground: he hath no form nor comeliness; and when we shall see him, [there is] no beauty that we should desire him.

Isa 53:3 KJV - HE IS DESPISED AND REJECTED OF MEN; A MAN OF SORROWS, AND ACQUAINTED WITH GRIEF: AND WE HID AS IT WERE [OUR] FACES FROM HIM; HE WAS DESPISED, AND WE ESTEEMED HIM NOT.

Isa 53:4 KJV - Surely he hath borne our griefs, and carried our sorrows: yet we did esteem him stricken, smitten of God, and afflicted.

Isa 53:5 KJV - BUT HE [WAS] WOUNDED FOR OUR TRANSGRESSIONS, [HE WAS] BRUISED FOR OUR INIQUITIES: THE CHASTISEMENT OF OUR PEACE [WAS] UPON HIM; AND WITH HIS STRIPES WE ARE HEALED.

Isa 53:6 KJV - All we like sheep have gone astray; we have turned every one to his own way; AND THE LORD HATH LAID ON HIM THE INIQUITY OF US ALL.

Isa 53:7 KJV - He was oppressed, and he was afflicted, yet he opened not his mouth: he is brought as a lamb to the slaughter, and as a sheep before her shearers is dumb, so he openeth not his mouth.

Isa 53:8 KJV - He was taken from prison and from judgment: and who shall declare his generation? for he was cut off out of the land of the living: FOR THE TRANSGRESSION OF MY PEOPLE WAS HE STRICKEN.

Isa 53:9 KJV - And he made his grave with the wicked, and with the rich in his death; because he had done no violence, neither [was any] deceit in his mouth.

****Isa 53:10 KJV - Yet it pleased the LORD to bruise him; he hath put [him] to grief: WHEN THOU SHALT MAKE HIS SOUL AN OFFERING FOR SIN, he shall see [his] seed, he shall prolong [his] days, and the pleasure of the LORD shall prosper in his hand.

Isa 53:11 KJV - HE SHALL SEE OF THE TRAVAIL OF HIS SOUL, [AND] SHALL BE SATISFIED: BY HIS KNOWLEDGE SHALL MY RIGHTEOUS SERVANT JUSTIFY MANY; FOR HE SHALL BEAR THEIR INIQUITIES.

Isa 53:12 KJV - Therefore will I divide him [a portion] with the great, and he shall divide the spoil with the strong; BECAUSE HE HATH POURED OUT HIS

SOUL UNTO DEATH: and he was numbered with the transgressors; and HE BARE THE SIN OF MANY, AND MADE INTERCESSION FOR THE TRANSGRESSORS.

Wow! How incredibly merciful!!!

Eternal life requires us to have our names written in the Book of Life. The Book of Daniel speaks of this Book of life too:

[Dan 12:1-3 KJV] 1 And at that time shall Michael stand up, the great prince which standeth for the children of thy people: and there shall be a time of trouble, such as never was since there was a nation [even] to that same time: and at that time thy people shall be delivered, **EVERY ONE THAT SHALL BE FOUND WRITTEN IN THE BOOK**. 2 **And many of them that sleep in the dust of the earth shall awake, some to everlasting life, and some to shame [and] everlasting contempt.** 3 And they that be wise shall shine as the brightness of the firmament; and they that turn many to righteousness as the stars for ever and ever.

This Book of life is that which The Father Yehovah Elohim calls **The Lamb's** Book of Life in the Book of Revelation – its Yeshua's, the Lamb's, Book of Life! In speaking of the New Jerusalem that will come down out of heaven to the New Earth, The Father says:

Rev 21:27 KJV - And there shall in no wise enter into it anything that defileth, neither [whatsoever] worketh abomination, or [maketh] a lie: but **they which are written in THE LAMB'S Book of Life.**

The Jews from the House of Judah, the lost tribes of the House of Israel, and even the gentile proselytes joined to Israel by the Mosaic Covenant, **ALL** have to believe in Yeshua. They have to be "born again" as Yeshua terms it (or "born anew" as I have heard is already a Jewish concept). This is proven by many scriptures in the Psalms and the Prophets, but I will list a few below:

Isa 28:16 KJV - Therefore thus saith the Lord GOD, Behold, I lay in Zion for a foundation a stone, a tried stone, a precious corner [stone], a sure foundation: he that BELIEVETH shall not make haste.

Isa 8:13 KJV - **Sanctify the LORD of hosts himself**; and [let] him [be] your fear, and [let] him [be] your dread.

Isa 8:14 KJV - **And he shall be for a sanctuary; but for a stone of stumbling and for a rock of offence to both the houses of Israel**, for a gin and for a snare to the inhabitants of Jerusalem.

Isa 8:15 KJV - And many among them shall stumble, and fall, and be broken, and be snared, and be taken.

<u>YESHUA SAYS HE IS THIS STONE:</u>

Psa 118:22 KJV - The stone [which] the builders refused is become the head [stone] of the corner.

Psa 118:23 KJV - This is the LORD'S doing; it [is] marvellous in our eyes.

Mat 21:42 KJV - Jesus saith unto them, Did ye never read in the scriptures, The stone which the builders rejected, the same is become the head of the corner: this is the Lord's doing, and it is marvellous in our eyes?

<u>YESHUA COMES "IN THE NAME OF YEHOVAH," SO MANY OF THE PROPHECIES CONCERNING WHAT YEHOVAH ELOHIM WILL DO ARE ACTUALLY FULFILLED BY YESHUA (IN HIS FIRST COMING AND IN HIS SECOND COMING!):</u>

The Book of Psalms confirms that Yehovah will give this power of attorney to operate in His name to the Messiah:

<u>[PSA 118:26 KJV] 26 BLESSED [BE] HE THAT COMETH IN THE NAME OF THE LORD: WE HAVE BLESSED YOU OUT OF THE HOUSE OF THE LORD.</u>

Remember Yeshua also said to Jews:

MAT 23:39 KJV - FOR I SAY UNTO YOU, <u>YE SHALL NOT SEE ME HENCEFORTH, TILL YE SHALL SAY, BLESSED [IS] HE THAT COMETH IN THE NAME OF THE LORD.</u>

<u>THE NAME OF THE LORD IS YEHOVAH!</u>

Also, concerning the House of Israel, specifically, Hosea, the prophet, wrote:

Hsa 1:10 KJV - **Yet <u>the number of the children of Israel</u> shall be as the sand of the sea, which cannot be measured nor numbered; and it shall come to pass, [that] <u>in the place where it was said unto them, Ye [are] not my people, [there] it shall be said unto them, [Ye are] the sons of the living God.</u>**

Hsa 1:11 KJV - **THEN shall <u>the children of Judah and the children of Israel be gathered together</u>, and <u>appoint themselves ONE HEAD</u>**, and they shall come up out of the land: for great [shall be] the day of Jezreel.

I BELIEVE THAT ONE HEAD IS THE MASCHIAH (MESSIAH) OF ALL ISRAEL, YESHUA OF NAZARETH!

IT IS IMPORTANT FOR EVERYONE TO REMEMBER, HOWEVER, THAT THE FATHER HAS PROPHESIED THAT AT THE END OF THE AGE, WHEN YESHUA RETURNS ON THE DAY OF YEHOVAH, THAT THERE WILL BE (SOME) JEWISH PEOPLE WHO WILL BE GIVEN THE SPIRIT OF GRACE TO BELIEVE IN YESHUA <u>AS THEY SEE HIM RETURN</u> TO DEFEND JERUSALEM AND JUDAH, ALBEIT WITH MOURNING. SO, <u>ALTHOUGH THEY ARE NOT BELIEVERS IN YESHUA NOW, WE MUST REMEMBER THAT THE FATHER IS NOT THROUGH WITH THE JEWISH PEOPLE! WE ARE TO BE RESPECTFUL OF THEIR HONORABLE POSITION AS THE SONS OF ABRAHAM, ISAAC, AND JACOB, THE CHILDREN OF ISRAEL, AND HAVE PRESERVED THE WRITTEN TORAH THROUGH THOUSANDS OF YEARS SO THAT WE CAN EVEN KNOW THE ONE TRUE GOD! WE ARE TO BLESS THEM!! THEY MAY BE PART OF THE REMNANT WHO WILL BE GIVEN FAITH TO BELIEVE IN YESHUA AT THE VERY END! THEY ARE STILL IN THE 1ST COVENANT WITH YEHOVAH!</u> AGAIN, THERE ARE SO MANY PROPHECIES, BUT JUST ONE TO VERIFY THIS IS ZECHARIAH 12:

[Zec 12:1-14 KJV] 1 The burden of the word of the LORD for Israel, saith the LORD,
which stretcheth forth the heavens, and layeth the foundation of the earth, and
formeth the spirit of man within him. 2 Behold, I will make Jerusalem a cup of
trembling unto all the people round about, when they shall be in the siege both
against Judah [and] against Jerusalem. 3 And in that day will I make Jerusalem a
burdensome stone for all people: all that burden themselves with it shall be cut in
pieces, though all the people of the earth be gathered together against it. 4 In that
day, saith the LORD, I will smite every horse with astonishment, and his rider with
madness: and I will open mine eyes upon the house of Judah, and will smite every
horse of the people with blindness. 5 And the governors of Judah shall say in their
heart, The inhabitants of Jerusalem [shall be] my strength in the LORD of hosts
their God. 6 In that day will I make the governors of Judah like an hearth of fire
among the wood, and like a torch of fire in a sheaf; and they shall devour all the
people round about, on the right hand and on the left: and Jerusalem shall be
inhabited again in her own place, [even] in Jerusalem. 7 **THE LORD ALSO SHALL
SAVE <u>THE TENTS OF JUDAH</u> FIRST**, that the glory of the house of David and the
glory of the inhabitants of Jerusalem do not magnify [themselves] against Judah. 8
**IN THAT DAY SHALL THE LORD DEFEND THE INHABITANTS OF JERUSALEM;
AND HE THAT IS FEEBLE AMONG THEM AT THAT DAY SHALL BE AS DAVID;
AND THE HOUSE OF DAVID [SHALL BE] AS GOD, AS THE ANGEL OF THE LORD**

BEFORE THEM. 9 And it shall come to pass in that day, [that] I will seek to destroy all the nations that come against Jerusalem. 10 **AND I WILL POUR UPON <u>THE HOUSE OF DAVID</u>, AND UPON <u>THE INHABITANTS OF JERUSALEM</u>, THE SPIRIT OF GRACE AND OF SUPPLICATIONS: AND <u>THEY SHALL LOOK UPON ME WHOM THEY HAVE PIERCED, AND THEY SHALL MOURN FOR HIM, AS ONE MOURNETH FOR [HIS] ONLY [SON], AND SHALL BE IN BITTERNESS FOR HIM, AS ONE THAT IS IN BITTERNESS FOR [HIS] FIRSTBORN.</u>** 11 In that day shall there be a great mourning in Jerusalem, as the mourning of Hadadrimmon in the valley of Megiddon. 12 And the land shall mourn, every family apart; the family of the house of David apart, and their wives apart; the family of the house of Nathan apart, and their wives apart; 13 The family of the house of Levi apart, and their wives apart; the family of Shimei apart, and their wives apart; 14 All the families that remain, every family apart, and their wives apart.

[Zec 13:1 KJV] 1 In that day there shall be a fountain opened to <u>the house of David</u> and to <u>the inhabitants of Jerusalem</u> for sin and for uncleanness.

But, the reason I said **ONLY SOME** of the Jewish people will believe and be saved when Yeshua ha Mashiach returns is because of the next chapter:

[Zec 13:8-9 KJV] 8 And it shall come to pass, [that] IN ALL THE LAND, saith the LORD, TWO PARTS THEREIN SHALL BE CUT OFF [AND] DIE; BUT THE THIRD SHALL BE LEFT THEREIN. 9 And <u>I will bring the third part through the fire, and will refine them as silver is refined, and will try them as gold is tried: they shall call on my name, and I will hear them: I will say, It [is] my people: and they shall say, The LORD [is] my God.</u>

THAT MEANS THAT THE SIMPLE GOSPEL MESSAGE THAT YESHUA, THE ONE LIFTED UP ON A STAKE LIKE THE BRASS SERPENT, IS THE SON OF GOD, NEEDS TO BE GIVEN EVEN TO THE JEWISH PEOPLE NOW – LATER MAY BE TOO LATE!

In fact, **YESHUA** said to start the preaching of the gospel in **Jerusalem, then Judea and Samaria, and then to the uttermost parts of the earth!** In other words, the message of salvation through belief in Yeshua is first to Israel and then to the gentiles. In fact, he also said the job in Israel (to the Jews) would not be finished before he came back!

[Act 1:8 KJV] 8 But ye shall receive power, after that the Holy Ghost is come upon you: and **YE SHALL BE WITNESSES UNTO ME BOTH IN JERUSALEM, AND IN ALL JUDAEA, AND IN SAMARIA, AND UNTO THE UTTERMOST PART OF THE EARTH.**

[Mat 10:23 KJV] 23 But when they persecute you in this city, flee ye into another: **FOR VERILY I SAY UNTO YOU, YE SHALL NOT HAVE GONE OVER THE CITIES OF ISRAEL, TILL THE SON OF MAN BE COME.**

Since belief in Yeshua as the Mashiach is of greatest importance, we need to try to get rid of every stumbling block that would hinder anyone, especially Jews, from that belief.

Yeshua is not only THE SON OF GOD, but also THE SON OF MAN. His human genealogy has to be from the royal line of King David in order for him to be the Mashiach:

> The genealogy of Yeshua through his **only earthly parent Miriam** is detailed in Matthew's account of the origin of the 'king of heaven.' The Messiah *must* be from the lineage of King David (Jeremiah 23:5). Though translations derived from the Greek text of Matthew confuse the genealogy, the Ancient Hebrew text of Matthew's Gospel, from which the Aramaic and later, the Greek were translated, clearly details Miriam's lineage through her ***father*** Yoseph ben Yaakov through the kingly line of David through Solomon. Luke's Gospel, on the other hand, details the lineage of Miriam's ***husband*** Yoseph ben Eli through David's son Nathan...It is clear that the *Yoseph ben Yaakov* mentioned in Matthew 1:16 and the *Yoseph ben Eli* cited in Luke 3:23 (which is the Yoseph who is Miriam's husband in Matthew 1:19) are two different men with two distinct genealogical lines back to David – yet they both bear a very common Israelite name. A woman marrying a man with the same first name as her father is very common in every culture – this led a careless translator into profound error .... When Yoseph ben Yaakov is accurately identified as Miriam's **father** in Matthew 1:16, it puts Miriam in the thirteenth generation from the Babylonian captivity. This puts her son Yeshua in the fourteenth generation. The Greek text *reports* that Yeshua is the fourteenth generation, but it did not correctly identify Yoseph ben Yaakov as the *father* (as opposed to the husband) of Miriam. Even a novice can see that the Greek genealogy of Yeshua (and all subsequent translations) are in obvious error because they do not add up to fourteen generations....There is only one ancient Biblical source that maintains the correct lineage of Yeshua, through his mother, to King David – and that is the ancient Hebrew Matthew that has been preserved in Jewish archives. As of Yom Kippur, 2012, twenty-eight separate manuscripts of ancient *original language* Hebrew Matthew have been discovered, fourteen of

> them by Karaite scholar Nehemiah Gordon....In two of the oldest manuscripts of the Ancient Hebrew Matthew copied into the appendix of Shem Tov Ibn Shaprut's "Even Bochan" we have the accurate lineage of Yeshua that shows his direct ancestral path to the throne of David – "Yoseph ***avi*** Miriam" – Yoseph the father of Miriam of whom was born Yeshua. (Rood 44-45)

You can also see The Chronological Gospels: The Life and Seventy Week Ministry of the Messiah, pages 44-48, a resource listed in the Recommended Reading and Research page, for further information and pictorial documentation of one of the Hebrew Matthew Manuscripts.

When reading the Gospels, notice carefully that Yeshua refers to himself as "The Son of Man" most of the time during his ministry. I think this is because the Jews had the prophecy from Daniel that the Mashiach is called the Son of Man (which most Gentile Believers have missed completely!):

[Dan 7:13-14 KJV] 13 I saw in the night visions, and, behold, [one] like THE SON OF MAN CAME WITH THE CLOUDS OF HEAVEN, and CAME TO THE ANCIENT OF DAYS, and they brought him near before him. 14 And there was given him dominion, and glory, and a kingdom, that all people, nations, and languages, should serve him: his dominion [is] an everlasting dominion, which shall not pass away, and HIS KINGDOM [THAT] WHICH SHALL NOT BE DESTROYED.

However, they also were told in this verse that the Son of Man, the Mashiach, will be coming in the clouds of heaven. Yeshua was on earth. But, this was his first coming to fulfill the prophecies as the sacrifice for Israel's sins (as discussed above – Isaiah 53, etc.) He says definitively that He is returning, at his second coming, with the clouds of heaven!

[Mat 24:27-31 KJV] 27 FOR AS THE LIGHTNING COMETH OUT OF THE EAST, AND SHINETH EVEN UNTO THE WEST; SO SHALL ALSO THE COMING OF THE SON OF MAN BE. 28 For wheresoever the carcase is, there will the eagles be gathered together. 29 Immediately after the tribulation of those days shall the sun be darkened, and the moon shall not give her light, and the stars shall fall from heaven, and the powers of the heavens shall be shaken: 30 And then shall appear the sign of the Son of man in heaven: and then shall all the tribes of the earth mourn, and THEY SHALL SEE THE SON OF MAN COMING IN THE CLOUDS OF HEAVEN WITH POWER AND GREAT GLORY. 31 And he shall send his angels with a great sound of a trumpet, and they shall

gather together his elect from the four winds, from one end of heaven to the other.

(I believe vs. 28 is referencing "the marriage supper of the lamb" where the fowls of heaven will be feasting on the carnage that takes place when Yeshua returns to fight for Jerusalem and Judah!)

THE PROPHECY FROM DANIEL 7:13-14 SHOULD MAKE IT ABUNDANTLY CLEAR THAT THE MASHIACH WILL NOT BE A REGULAR JEWISH MAN THAT IS LIVING ON EARTH. HE IS COMING FROM HEAVEN!!!

Yeshua, the Son of Man, who is also the Son of God as prophesied in the scriptures above, is coming to rule the whole earth by the authority given him by the Ancient of Days, HIS FATHER YEHOVAH!

MANY SCRIPTURES ARE AVAILABLE FOR YOU TO REVIEW AND SEE THAT YESHUA FULFILLED PROPHECIES WRITTEN ABOUT HIMSELF AS THE MESSIAH. BELOW ARE A FEW HE HAS FULFILLED AND OTHERS THAT HE WILL FULFILL!:

Psalm 16:8-11 Yeshua, as David's son, will be resurrected
Psalm 110 Yeshua is David's Sovereign and is also David's Son and will be resurrected (receiving the dew of his youth) and the High Priest after order of Melek Zadik
Psalm 69 Prophecies that Yeshua fulfilled
*****Isaiah52:13- Isaiah 53 Yeshua became the sacrifice for Israel's sins (Isaiah 53:4,5,8,10) AND Yehovah says that He will be the Exalted King (Isaiah 52:13-15)**
*****Psalm 22 Prophecies that Yeshua fulfilled**
Psalm 2 Yeshua is the Son of Elohim
Proverbs 30:4 What is the Creator's name and what is His Son's name?
Psalm 118:22 Yeshua claims to be this stone the builders rejected
Psalm 118:26 Yeshua comes in the Name of Yehovah
Deuteronomy 18:18-19 Yeshua is the Prophet that is like Moses that was promised
Psalm 49:15 – Resurrection promised
Joel 2:28-29 Ruach ha Kodesh will be poured upon Yehovah's servants
Isaiah 55:3-5 Yeshua was given the sure mercies of David
Isaiah 49:5-6 Yehovah extends this salvation even to all people (foreigners)- not just the twelve tribes of Israel-through His Servant, Yeshua
Isaiah 56:1-8 Yehovah extends this salvation even to all people (foreigners) who

enter into covenant with Him and keep his Sabbaths
Psalm 17:13-15 - Resurrection promised
Isaiah 62:11 Yeshua is coming!

SO, NOW, WHAT ABOUT THE WRITTEN TORAH THAT YEHOVAH GAVE TO ISRAEL AT MOUNT SINAI – THE COVENANT HE GAVE TO MOSES , IN THE FORM OF COMMANDMENTS, STATUTES, AND JUDGMENTS, FOR HIS PEOPLE TO OBEY? IS THIS WRITTEN TORAH STILL VALID TODAY FOR BELIEVERS IN YESHUA OR HAS IT BEEN NULLIFIED BY YESHUA'S SACRIFICIAL DEATH?

DID YESHUA TELL ANYONE TO STOP KEEPING THE WRITTEN TORAH?

ABSOLUTELY NOT!

(Neither did he remove the BLESSINGS OF KEEPING THE WRITTEN TORAH! See Deuteronomy 28:1-14)

CHAPTER 6

The Obligation to Keep the Written Torah – Believers from the House of Judah, the House of Israel, and the Devout Gentiles

AS I ALREADY STATED, CONCERNING THE FIRST GROUP OF BELIEVERS IN YESHUA—THE MESSIANIC JEWS—THERE SHOULD BE NO DISPUTE THAT THEY SHOULD ABSOLUTELY CONTINUE TO KEEP THE WRITTEN TORAH, EVEN ACCORDING TO THE NEW TESTAMENT!

I BELIEVE INCLUDED WITH THEM WOULD BE THOSE FROM THE HOUSE OF ISRAEL AND THE GENTILES WHO HAD JOINED THEMSELVES TO THE JEWS (ISRAEL) THROUGH THE MOSAIC COVENANT - THE PROSELYTES /DEVOUT MEN AND WOMEN AS THEY ARE CALLED IN THE NEW TESTAMENT.
(I will speak in the first person during most of this section, as I have reason to believe that I may have Jewish ancestry, although raised as a complete gentile believer in Yeshua. My having Jewish lineage is not definitive, however, and I am just grateful to be a believer in Yeshua that tries to keep the Written Torah!)

The number one reason I have come to believe that Messianic Jews are to keep the Written Torah is that **YESHUA WAS TALKING TO HIS JEWISH FOLLOWERS, DISCIPLES**, when he stated Matthew 5:17-20.

MATTHEW 5:19 IS THE PIVOTAL VERSE THAT CONVINCED ME OF THE CONTINUING VALIDITY OF THE WRITTEN TORAH ABOUT 13 YEARS AGO, SO I WILL REITERATE IT OFTEN IN THIS BOOK:

[MAT 5:17-20 KJV] 17 THINK NOT THAT I AM COME TO DESTROY THE LAW, OR THE PROPHETS: I am not come to destroy, but to fulfil. 18 For verily I say unto you, Till heaven and earth pass, one jot or one tittle shall in no wise pass from the law, till all be fulfilled.

19 WHOSOEVER THEREFORE SHALL BREAK ONE OF THESE LEAST COMMANDMENTS, AND SHALL TEACH MEN SO, HE

SHALL BE CALLED THE LEAST IN THE KINGDOM OF HEAVEN: BUT WHOSOEVER SHALL DO AND TEACH [THEM], THE SAME SHALL BE CALLED GREAT IN THE KINGDOM OF HEAVEN. 20 For I say unto you, That **EXCEPT YOUR RIGHTEOUSNESS SHALL EXCEED [THE RIGHTEOUSNESS] OF THE SCRIBES AND PHARISEES, YE SHALL IN NO CASE ENTER INTO THE KINGDOM OF HEAVEN.**

CLEARLY, YESHUA TOLD HIS JEWISH FOLLOWERS TO KEEP THE WRITTEN TORAH!!!

(BUT HE ALSO SAID THE "RIGHTEOUSNESS" OF THE SCRIBES AND PHARISEES, WHICH WAS BASED ON MAN-MADE LAWS, WOULD NOT EVEN GET THEM INTO THE KINGDOM OF GOD!)

ACTS 21: 17-26 ALSO VERIFIES THIS WAS THE BELIEF OF THE APOSTLES. These verses refer back to the Council of Jerusalem in the first century that is described in Acts 15. (SEE APPENDIX I – AUTHORITY IN THE CHURCH – FOR A FULL STUDY ON THIS AND OTHER COUNCILS!!!) REMEMBER THAT THE ENTIRE CHURCH WAS MESSIANIC JEWISH TO START WITH SO THERE WAS NO QUESTION THAT THEY WERE TO CONTINUE KEEPING THE COVENANT. It was only when (complete) gentiles became believers in Yeshua by the grace of Yehovah that there even was a question about anyone not keeping the Torah. REMEMBER THAT YESHUA HIMSELF IS A MESSIANIC JEW – HE DECLARED THAT HE IS THE MESSIAH, THE SON OF GOD, AND HE IS A JEW! HE CERTAINLY KEPT THE WRITTEN TORAH –HE EVEN KEPT IT PERFECTLY!!

Act 21:17 KJV - And when we were come to Jerusalem, the brethren received us gladly.

Act 21:18 KJV - And the [day] following **Paul went in with us unto James; and all the elders were present**. [This was a meeting in front of at least some of the apostles and other leaders in Jerusalem]

Act 21:19 KJV - And when he had saluted them, he declared particularly what things God had wrought among the Gentiles by his ministry.

******Act 21:20 KJV - And when they heard [it], they glorified the Lord, and said unto him, THOU SEEST, BROTHER, HOW MANY THOUSANDS OF JEWS THERE ARE WHICH BELIEVE; AND THEY ARE ALL ZEALOUS OF THE LAW:**

******ACT 21:21 KJV - AND THEY ARE INFORMED OF THEE, THAT THOU TEACHEST ALL THE JEWS WHICH ARE AMONG THE GENTILES TO FORSAKE MOSES, SAYING THAT THEY OUGHT NOT TO CIRCUMCISE [THEIR] CHILDREN, NEITHER TO WALK AFTER THE CUSTOMS.**

Act 21:22 KJV - What is it therefore? the multitude must needs come together: for they will hear that thou art come.

Act 21:23 KJV - Do therefore this that we say to thee: We have four men which have a vow on them;

******Act 21:24 KJV - Them take, and purify thyself with them, and be at charges with them, that they may shave [their] heads: and all may know that those things, whereof they were informed concerning thee, are nothing; BUT [THAT] THOU THYSELF ALSO WALKEST ORDERLY, AND KEEPEST THE LAW.******

Act 21:25 KJV - As touching the Gentiles which believe, **WE have written [and] concluded** that they observe no such thing, save only that they keep themselves from [things] offered to idols, and from blood, and from strangled, and from fornication.

Act 21:26 KJV - **Then Paul took the men, and the next day purifying himself with them entered into the temple, to signify the accomplishment of the days of purification, until that an offering should be offered for every one of them.**

******SO, PAUL A MESSIANIC JEW, STILL KEPT THE TORAH!!! ******

This shows that even at the very beginning of the church, the congregation of believers in Yeshua, there was a problem with understanding if the Torah was to still be observed and if so, who was to observe it. IT ALSO LETS US KNOW THAT PAUL, AS WONDERFUL AS HE WAS IN SPREADING THE GOSPEL OF YESHUA, (AND HE WORKED EXTREMELY HARD – TRAVELING AND MINISTERING CONTINUALLY), WAS INSTRUMENTAL IN THIS MISUNDERSTANDING, EVEN AMONG THE JEWISH BELIEVERS.

HOWEVER, HE WAS WILLING TO DO WHAT THE APOSTLES ASKED HIM TO DO TO CONVINCE THE JEWISH BELIEVERS THAT HE DID NOT MEAN FOR THEM TO STOP KEEPING THE TORAH!

ACTUALLY, PAUL'S LETTERS (EPISTLES) ARE THE ONLY SCRIPTURES I HAVE FOUND THAT WOULD EVEN INTIMATE THAT THE WRITTEN TORAH WAS NOT STILL VALID.

ALL OF THE GOSPELS, AS WELL AS THE LETTERS OF THE APOSTLE PETER AND THE APOSTLE JOHN, EVEN THE BOOK OF JUDE, ABSOLUTELY TELL THE PEOPLE NOT TO SIN, DEFINING SIN AS THE TRANSGRESSION OF THE TORAH!

Just a few verses that show this are below, but even a cursory reading of **1ST, 2ND, AND 3RD JOHN AND 1ST AND 2ND PETER** will show these are not isolated verses. Everyone needs to read these books carefully to see for themselves.

[1Pe 1:13-17 KJV] 13 Wherefore gird up the loins of your mind, be sober, and hope to the end for the grace that is to be brought unto you at the revelation of Jesus Christ; 14 **AS OBEDIENT CHILDREN**, not fashioning yourselves according to the former lusts in your ignorance: 15 But **AS HE WHICH HATH CALLED YOU IS HOLY, SO BE YE HOLY IN ALL MANNER OF CONVERSATION; 16 BECAUSE IT IS WRITTEN, BE YE HOLY; FOR I AM HOLY.** 17 And if ye call on the Father, who without respect of persons **judgeth according to every man's work, pass the time of your sojourning [here] in fear:**

The word "conversation" would be translated today as "behavior."

1Jo 2:1 KJV - My little children, **THESE THINGS , WRITE I UNTO YOU, THAT YE SIN NOT**. And if any man sin, we have an advocate with the Father, Jesus Christ the righteous:

1Jo 2:2 KJV - And he is the propitiation for our sins: and not for ours only, but also for [the sins of] the whole world.

1Jo 3:4 KJV - **WHOSOEVER COMMITTETH SIN TRANSGRESSETH ALSO THE LAW: FOR SIN IS THE TRANSGRESSION OF THE LAW.**

SO, THE WRITTEN TORAH COULD NOT HAVE BEEN "NAILED TO THE CROSS" IF IT WAS TO STILL BE KEPT BY THE BELIEVING JEWS, PAUL HIMSELF STILL KEEPING IT!!

IN FACT, WE SHOULD NOTE THAT THE NEXT VERSES SHOW THAT PAUL'S ARREST AND SUBSEQUENT DELIVERY TO ROME WAS BECAUSE OF HIS

ATTEMPT TO PROVE TO THE BELIEVING JEWS THAT HE STILL KEPT THE TORAH HIMSELF, AND THAT EVERYTHING THAT THEY HAD HEARD ABOUT HIM NEGATING THE KEEPING OF THE TORAH WAS NOT TRUE!!:

Act 21:26 KJV - Then Paul took the men, and the next day purifying himself with them entered into the temple, to signify the accomplishment of the days of purification, until that an offering should be offered for every one of them.

Act 21:27 KJV - And when the seven days were almost ended, the Jews which were of Asia, when they saw him in the temple, stirred up all the people, and laid hands on him,

Act 21:28 KJV - Crying out, Men of Israel, help: This is the man, that teacheth all [men] every where against the people, and THE LAW, and this place: and further brought Greeks also into the temple, and hath polluted this holy place.

Act 21:29 KJV - (For they had seen before with him in the city Trophimus an Ephesian, whom they supposed that Paul had brought into the temple.)

Act 21:30 KJV - And all the city was moved, and the people ran together: and they took Paul, and drew him out of the temple: and forthwith the doors were shut.

Act 21:31 KJV - And as they went about to kill him, tidings came unto the chief captain of the band, that all Jerusalem was in an uproar.

Act 21:32 KJV - Who immediately took soldiers and centurions, and ran down unto them: and when they saw the chief captain and the soldiers, they left beating of Paul.

Act 21:33 KJV - Then the chief captain came near, and took him, and commanded [him] to be bound with two chains; and demanded who he was, and what he had done.

Act 21:34 KJV - And some cried one thing, some another, among the multitude: and when he could not know the certainty for the tumult, he commanded him to be carried into the castle.

THIS IS WORTH REITERATING!!

ANYTHING IN PAUL'S LETTERS that would lead Jewish believers to not keep the Torah, **EVEN TO NOT CIRCUMCISE THEIR MALE CHILDREN**, he proved was **NOT**

HIS INTENT by his going to the temple and purifying himself with the four men who had a vow (probably a Nazirite vow) on them and being arrested while he was there, spending the rest of his life as a prisoner. **He even testified, every time he was questioned, that he had done nothing against the laws of the Jews! That seems to be debatable based on some of the wording in his epistles (letters), but he definitely was saying THAT IT WAS NOT HIS INTENT!**

I know the issue of circumcision is controversial – however, this is a place we need to stop **and hear what Yeshua has to say above all others.** He said that circumcision, although it is in the Written Torah, the Law, really is of "The Fathers" (**the COVENANTS WITH ABRAHAM, ISAAC AND JACOB**); in other words, it was before the Written Torah of the Mosaic Covenant. So, I believe biological Jews or anyone from the other 11 tribes, if DNA ever proves they are descendants of Abraham, Isaac, and Jacob, , should absolutely continue to circumcise their children, even once they become believers in Yeshua. Read: [Jhn 7:21-24 KJV] 21 Jesus answered and said unto them, I have done one work, and ye all marvel. **22 Moses therefore gave unto you circumcision; (NOT BECAUSE IT IS OF MOSES, BUT OF THE FATHERS;)** and ye on the Sabbath day circumcise a man. 23 If a man on the Sabbath day receive circumcision, that the law of Moses should not be broken; are ye angry at me, because I have made a man every whit whole on the Sabbath day? 24 Judge not according to the appearance, but judge righteous judgment. Obviously, the point Yeshua is making here is about judging righteously what is acceptable to do on the Sabbath. However, in doing so, Y**eshua himself still clarifies the circumcision question as being BEFORE the Law (Just like Tithing is before the Law, as the Christian Church always points out!!!)** Also, read Ezekiel 44:1-9, which many Bible teachers believe, as I do, describes the coming temple service during the Millennial Reign of Yeshua ha Mashiach. It describes The Father's thoughts on circumcision [even for strangers (gentiles)!]

[Eze 44:1-9 KJV] 1 Then he brought me back the way of the gate of the outward sanctuary which looketh toward the east; and it [was] shut. 2 Then said the LORD unto me; This gate shall be shut, it shall not be opened, and no man shall enter in by it; because the LORD, the God of Israel, hath entered in by it, therefore it shall be shut. 3 [It is] for the prince; the prince, he shall sit in it to eat bread before the LORD; he shall enter by the way of the porch of [that] gate, and shall go out by the way of the same. 4 Then brought he me the way of the north gate before the house: and I looked, and, behold, the glory of the LORD filled the house of the LORD: and I fell upon my face. 5 And the LORD said unto me, Son of man, mark well, and behold with thine eyes, and hear with thine ears all that I say unto thee concerning all the ordinances of the house of the LORD, and all the laws thereof; and mark well the entering in of the house, with every going forth of the sanctuary. 6 And thou shalt say to the rebellious, [even] to the house of Israel, **Thus saith the Lord GOD; O ye house of Israel, let it suffice you of all your abominations, 7 In that ye have brought [into my sanctuary] strangers, uncircumcised in heart, and uncircumcised in flesh, to be in my sanctuary, to pollute it, [even] my house, when ye offer my bread, the fat and the blood, and they have broken my covenant because of all your abominations. 8 And ye have not kept the charge of mine holy things: but ye have set keepers of my charge in my sanctuary for yourselves. 9 Thus saith the Lord GOD; NO STRANGER, UNCIRCUMCISED IN HEART, NOR UNCIRCUMCISED IN FLESH, shall enter into my sanctuary, OF ANY STRANGER THAT [IS] AMONG THE CHILDREN OF ISRAEL.**

NOTE: THIS IS YEHOVAH ELOHIM, HIMSELF, GIVING HIS INSTRUCTIONS ON THE NECESSITY FOR CIRCUMCISION, EVEN FOR GENTILES, IN ORDER TO COME INTO HIS TEMPLE – MOST PROBABLY THE MILLENIAL KINGDOM TEMPLE WHEN YESHUA REIGNS ON EARTH IN JERUSALEM!!!

IT SOUNDS LIKE THE CHRISTIAN CHURCH HAS POSSIBLY HAD IT WRONG ALL THESE YEARS...

Continuing on, a very important point that needs to be brought out is that we only can keep parts of the Written Torah today. Obviously, the temple was still standing at the point Acts was written and all the apostles and Paul continued to go to the temple very often, and also made sacrifices there. They continued making sacrifices, I believe, because there were many different types of offerings and sacrifices, that were commanded to be made to Yehovah Elohim. I personally do not believe they made (or would have had to make) sacrifices for sin, even though Jews that did not believe in Yeshua would have.

I BELIEVE THAT YESHUA HAS PAID THE SACRIFICE FOR SIN TOTALLY!

ISAIAH 52-53 PERFECTLY DESCRIBES THE FATHER'S PLAN TO LAY ON YESHUA HA MASHIACH ALL OF MAN'S INIQUITY (AND THEN, AT HIS SECOND COMING,TO BECOME EXTOLLED!)

[Isa 52:13-15 KJV] 13 Behold, MY SERVANT shall deal prudently, HE SHALL BE EXALTED AND EXTOLLED, AND BE VERY HIGH.

14 AS MANY WERE ASTONIED AT THEE; HIS VISAGE WAS SO MARRED MORE

THAN ANY MAN, AND HIS FORM MORE THAN THE SONS OF MEN:

15 SO SHALL HE SPRINKLE MANY NATIONS; THE KINGS SHALL SHUT THEIR MOUTHS AT HIM: FOR [THAT] WHICH HAD NOT BEEN TOLD THEM SHALL THEY SEE; AND [THAT] WHICH THEY HAD NOT HEARD SHALL THEY CONSIDER.

Isa 53:1 KJV - WHO HATH BELIEVED OUR REPORT? and to whom is THE ARM OF THE LORD revealed?

Isa 53:2 KJV - For he shall grow up before him as a tender plant, and as a root out of a dry ground: he hath no form nor comeliness; and when we shall see him, [there is] no beauty that we should desire him.

Isa 53:3 KJV - HE IS DESPISED AND REJECTED OF MEN; A MAN OF SORROWS, AND ACQUAINTED WITH GRIEF: AND WE HID AS IT WERE [OUR] FACES FROM HIM; HE WAS DESPISED, AND WE ESTEEMED HIM NOT.

Isa 53:4 KJV - Surely he hath borne our griefs, and carried our sorrows: yet we did esteem him stricken, smitten of God, and afflicted.

Isa 53:5 KJV - BUT HE [WAS] WOUNDED FOR OUR TRANSGRESSIONS, [HE WAS] BRUISED FOR OUR INIQUITIES: THE CHASTISEMENT OF OUR PEACE [WAS] UPON HIM; AND WITH HIS STRIPES WE ARE HEALED.

Isa 53:6 KJV - All we like sheep have gone astray; we have turned every one to his own way; AND THE LORD HATH LAID ON HIM THE INIQUITY OF US ALL.

Isa 53:7 KJV - He was oppressed, and he was afflicted, yet he opened not his mouth: he is brought as a lamb to the slaughter, and as a sheep before her shearers is dumb, so he openeth not his mouth.

Isa 53:8 KJV - He was taken from prison and from judgment: and who shall declare his generation? for he was cut off out of the land of the living: FOR THE TRANSGRESSION OF MY PEOPLE WAS HE STRICKEN.

Isa 53:9 KJV - And he made his grave with the wicked, and with the rich in his death; because he had done no violence, neither [was any] deceit in his mouth.

******Isa 53:10 KJV - Yet it pleased the LORD to bruise him; he hath put [him] to grief: WHEN THOU SHALT MAKE HIS SOUL AN OFFERING FOR SIN, he shall**

see [his] seed, he shall prolong [his] days, and the pleasure of the LORD shall prosper in his hand.

Isa 53:11 KJV - HE SHALL SEE OF THE TRAVAIL OF HIS SOUL, [AND] SHALL BE SATISFIED: BY HIS KNOWLEDGE SHALL MY RIGHTEOUS SERVANT JUSTIFY MANY; FOR HE SHALL BEAR THEIR INIQUITIES.

Isa 53:12 KJV - Therefore will I divide him [a portion] with the great, and he shall divide the spoil with the strong; BECAUSE HE HATH POURED OUT HIS SOUL UNTO DEATH: and he was numbered with the transgressors; and HE BARE THE SIN OF MANY, AND MADE INTERCESSION FOR THE TRANSGRESSORS.

I PERSONALLY BELIEVE THIS IS COMPLETELY DEFINITIVE ABOUT YESHUA, THE COMING KING MESSIAH, BEING THE COMPLETE SACRIFICE FOR SIN - THE LAMB OF GOD WHO CAME AND TOOK AWAY THE SIN OF THE WORLD!!!

I believe that when a believer in Yeshua sins, he is to ask, humbly, The Father Yehovah to have mercy on him and forgive him, pleading the blood of Yeshua's sacrifice as payment for his sin. I believe that the Father will. I also believe that person should repent, "teshuvah" in Hebrew, which means to completely turn around and not continue in that sin, asking The Father for help to not do it again. If the person does commit, even the same thing, again, he should repeat this. The Father knows each person's heart - he is not mocked. He knows if it is true repentance or not. But, since Yeshua tells us to forgive seventy times seven the person that asks forgiveness from us, are we better than God? Obviously, then, the Father can forgive the same sin again!

HOWEVER, THERE ARE OTHER SACRIFICES BESIDES THOSE FOR SIN! I have studied these different sacrifices and offerings through the last 10 years, but still don't feel qualified to expound on them, as they are not something that is practiced right now with no temple. However, reading through Leviticus will show that there were daily morning and evening sacrifices, Sabbath offerings, New Moon offerings, peace offerings, thanksgiving offerings, and many more, that had nothing to do with sin. Here, we see Paul, as a Messianic Jew, with these four other Messianic Jewish men, ending their Nazarite vow, planning to make offerings at the temple :

<u>Acts 21:26 KJV - Then Paul took the men, and the next day purifying himself with them entered into the temple, to signify the accomplishment of the days of purification, UNTIL THAT AN OFFERING SHOULD BE OFFERED FOR EVERY ONE OF THEM.</u>

We also see through the Book of Acts where Paul would go to Jerusalem for the Feasts of Pesach (Passover) and Shavuot (Pentecost), where the prescribed sacrifices were presumably being made. As The Father has not seen fit for the Temple to be rebuilt yet, we can only honor the Feasts (Yehovah's Appointed Times) today, at their proper time according to the Written Torah (not the mathematically derived Rabbinic Jewish calendar which has gotten off through the centuries.) **HOWEVER, NO SACRIFICES ARE MADE NOW, SINCE NO SACRIFICES ARE EVER TO BE MADE OUTSIDE OF JERUSALEM AND ALSO ONLY ON YEHOVAH'S BIBLICALLY DEDICATED ALTAR!** So, this is an example of where we keep the part of the Written Torah that we can, but not all of it. In addition, there were laws that were just for the priests, some that were just for the Levites, some just for men, some just for women, etc. **So, we should keep the parts of the Torah <u>WE</u> are supposed to keep and can keep!**

Now, continuing our discussion of Paul, Peter wrote also, **<u>that there were people who misinterpreted Paul's letters because there were some things in them that were hard to understand. But that it was to their destruction!!</u>** Peter goes on to say for the believers in Yeshua not to fall from their own steadfastness to the error of the wicked:

2Pe 3:14 KJV - Wherefore, beloved, seeing that ye look for such things, be diligent that ye may be found of him in peace, **<u>without spot, and blameless.</u>**

2Pe 3:15 KJV - And account [that] the longsuffering of our Lord [is] salvation; even as **<u>our beloved brother Paul also according to the wisdom given unto him hath written unto you;</u>**

<u>2Pe 3:16 KJV - As also in all [his] epistles, speaking in them of these things; IN WHICH ARE SOME THINGS HARD TO BE UNDERSTOOD, WHICH THEY THAT ARE UNLEARNED AND UNSTABLE WREST, AS [THEY DO] ALSO THE OTHER SCRIPTURES, UNTO THEIR OWN DESTRUCTION.</u>

2Pe 3:17 KJV - Ye therefore, beloved, seeing ye know [these things] before, **<u>BEWARE LEST YE ALSO, BEING LED AWAY WITH THE ERROR OF THE WICKED, FALL FROM YOUR OWN STEDFASTNESS.</u>**

Here Peter called Paul a beloved brother, so obviously he was convinced that Paul was not purposely leading the believers to turn from keeping the Torah, but that unlearned men were interpreting his letters so. **I believe that we have inherited this misunderstanding.**

For example, one of the main premises of those who believe we are not to try to keep the Torah is that most of Paul's letters say that we are saved by grace and not by "works." But, in his letter to Titus, he makes it clear that, after we are saved by grace, that good works, righteous and Godly living should follow. We know how to do that by learning the Written Torah:

[Tit 2:11-14 KJV] 11 For the grace of God that bringeth salvation hath appeared to all men, 12 Teaching us that, denying ungodliness and worldly lusts, we should live soberly, righteously, and godly, in this present world;
13 Looking for that blessed hope, and the glorious appearing of the great God and our Saviour Jesus Christ; 14 Who gave himself for us, that he might redeem us from all iniquity, and purify unto himself a peculiar people, zealous of **good works**.

CHAPTER 7

The Fallacy of the Oral Torah and the Validity of the Written Torah

I BELIEVE THAT, POSSIBLY, THE REASON PAUL SEEMED IN HIS LETTERS TO BE COMING AGAINST KEEPING THE TORAH, IS THAT HE HAD BEEN BURNT BY THE ADDITIONS TO THE WRITTEN TORAH HIMSELF! THESE ADDITIONS EVENTUALLY BECAME KNOWN AS THE ORAL TORAH. REMEMBER THAT HE CALLED HIMSELF A "PHARISEE OF PHARISEES." HE SAID HE WAS "RAISED AT THE FEET OF GAMALIEL," ONE OF THE REVERED SAGES EVEN TODAY IN JUDAISM. PAUL KNEW THE DIFFICULTY AND THE FUTILITY OF TRYING TO OBSERVE ALL OF THOSE EXTRA LAWS.

According to Rabbinic Judaism, the "Oral Torah" or "Oral Law" (Hebrew: תורה שבעל פה, *Torah she-be-`al peh*, lit "Torah that is spoken") represents those laws, statutes, and legal interpretations that **WERE NOT RECORDED** in the *Five Books of Moses*, the "Written Torah" (Hebrew: תורה שבכתב, *Torah she-bi-khtav*, lit. "Torah that is written"), **BUT NONETHELESS ARE REGARDED BY JEWS AS PRESCRIPTIVE AND CO-GIVEN.** This holistic Jewish code of conduct encompass a wide swath of ritual, worship, God-man and interpersonal relationships, from dietary laws to Sabbath and festival observance to marital relations, agricultural practices, and civil claims and damages.

According to Jewish tradition, the Oral Torah was passed down orally in an unbroken chain from generation to generation until its contents were finally committed to writing following the destruction of the Second Temple in 70 CE, when Jewish civilization was faced with an existential threat.

The major repositories of the Oral Torah are the *Mishnah*, compiled between 200–220 CE by Rabbi Yehudah haNasi, and the *Gemara*, a series of running commentaries and debates concerning the Mishnah, which together comprise the *Talmud*, the preeminent text of Rabbinic Judaism. In fact, two "versions" of the Talmud exist: one produced in Jerusalem c. 300-350 CE (the Jerusalem Talmud), and second, more extensive Talmud compiled in Babylonia and published c. 450-500 CE (the Babylonian Talmud).

BELIEF THAT THE ORAL TORAH WAS TRANSMITTED ORALLY FROM GOD TO MOSES ON MOUNT SINAI DURING THE EXODUS FROM EGYPT IS A FUNDAMENTAL TENET OF FAITH OF ORTHODOX AND HAREDI JUDAISM, AND WAS RECOGNIZED AS ONE OF THE THIRTEEN PRINCIPLES OF FAITH BY MAIMONIDES. However, not all branches of Rabbinic Judaism accept the divine provenance of the Oral Torah, such that Conservative and (to a greater extent) Reform Jews give deference to the Talmudic sages while empowering themselves to formulate and adopt their own rulings and interpretations.

THERE HAVE ALSO BEEN HISTORICAL DISSENTERS TO THE ORAL TORAH IN ITS ENTIRETY, INCLUDING ADHERENTS TO KARAITE JUDAISM, WHO ATTEMPT TO DERIVE THEIR RELIGIOUS PRACTICE STRICTLY FROM THE WRITTEN TORAH, USING SCRIPTURE'S MOST NATURAL MEANING TO FORM THEIR BASIS OF JEWISH LAW. (Wikipedia contributors, "Oral Torah")

(See also the Appendix IV - Oral Torah for more information).

BECAUSE OF THE TRANSLATIONS FROM GREEK TO ENGLISH OF THE NEW TESTAMENT THROUGH THE PAST 2000 YEARS, IT IS POSSIBLE THAT PAUL'S REFERENCES TO THE LAW WERE REALLY ABOUT THESE ADDITIONS TO THE WRITTEN TORAH THAT YESHUA HIMSELF CAME AGAINST VEHEMENTLY. THAT IS THE ONLY WAY I CAN JUSTIFY THAT PAUL ACTUALLY SAID IN HIS LETTER TO THE CORINTHIANS: [1CO 6:12 KJV] 12 ALL THINGS ARE LAWFUL UNTO ME, BUT ALL THINGS ARE NOT EXPEDIENT: ALL THINGS ARE LAWFUL FOR ME, BUT I WILL NOT BE BROUGHT UNDER THE POWER OF ANY." AS A JEWISH BELIEVER, HE SHOULD HAVE KNOWN THAT HE ABSOLUTELY WAS TO CONTINUE TO KEEP THE LAW (WRITTEN TORAH) BUT COULD HAVE MEANT THAT HE WAS NOT UNDER THE ORAL TORAH. THE OTHER POSSIBILITY IS THAT THIS LETTER WAS WRITTEN PRIOR TO HIS BEING CALLED TO ACCOUNT AND PROVE THAT HE DID KEEP THE TORAH IN ACTS 21:17-26. (SINCE YESHUA MADE CLEAR THAT HE WAS ONLY COMING AGAINST THE ORAL TORAH, THE "TRADITIONS OF THE ELDERS," AND THAT HE FULLY UPHELD THE WRITTEN TORAH, IT WOULD HAVE MADE IT EASIER IF PAUL'S LETTERS HAD MADE THAT SAME DISTINCTION!!!)

Particularly, today, I absolutely believe there are Christian pastors (usually gentile, but sometimes even Messianic Jewish!) who preach an extreme grace message that leaves out any responsibility on our part to live right, which is to learn and start keeping the commandments, statutes, and judgments (the Written Torah) after our confession of belief in Yeshua. **I BELIEVE THIS IS BECAUSE OF**

THEIR OWN MISUNDERSTANDING ABOUT WHAT IS SIN AND WHAT IS NOT. They have been raised in or have been part of very judgmental churches that called everything even remotely fun or pleasurable to be sin, and were constantly coming under UNDUE CONDEMNATION by others and even their own consciences. Finally, out of frustration and rebellion to this "FALSE LEGALISM", they decided that they would not subject themselves to it anymore. But, so that their conscience could not condemn them anymore, they adopted the belief that we are not "under the law" (which is good and true legalism – the Written Torah). I have actually heard ministers' testimonies that support my observation. Sin is not smoking cigarettes, watching movies, drinking alcohol moderately, women cutting their hair nor wearing make-up, jewelry, or pretty clothes. It is also not sin to do pleasurable things on the Sabbath that are not work. **Many different Christian denominations have condemned all of these things in an attempt to define sin, basically making man-made laws. IF THESE MINISTERS HAD JUST BEEN TAUGHT, INSTEAD, THAT SIN IS DEFINED IN THE BIBLE AS THE TRANSGRESSION OF THE (WRITTEN) TORAH, THEY MOST LIKELY WOULD NOT HAVE FELT THE NEED TO REBEL AGAINST ANYTHING EVEN SMELLING OF "THE LAW"!!**

THIS MISUNDERSTANDING OF SIN HAS TRULY HINDERED THE CHURCH FOR 2000 YEARS!

I want to share a story that brings out the problem with this **extreme grace message** that has gotten so prevalent in the last few years (**grace with no law** – no actual understanding of what constitutes sinning against Yehovah Elohim).

Around March of 2016, I was watching a "Praise the Lord" program on Trinity Broadcasting Network (TBN), which is a Christian television network that I listen to a lot. It has truly been a blessing throughout the last 26 years that I have been striving to serve Yehovah Elohim. However, this night, the guest preacher that was being interviewed (I truly have no idea what his name is), surprised me when **he pulled up his shirt sleeve and showed a tattoo with the words, "Leviticus 19:28" imprinted on his forearm. He said, "Do you know what this is? This is the verse that says not to put tattoos on your body!" I was totally stunned! He went on to say that he did that to show that we are under grace and not under law! Talk about REBELLION directly in Yehovah's Face!** He continued talking throughout the program about the Holy Spirit leading him…The host just smiled – I think he didn't really know how to respond. Well, I was responding - sitting in my living room shouting at the TV! **I wanted for the host to ask him, "Well, are you going to go out and murder to prove that you are not 'under the law'? How about committing adultery?" Seriously!!**

[Lev 19:28 KJV] 28 Ye <u>shall not</u> make any cuttings in your flesh for the dead, **nor print any marks upon you**: **I [am] the LORD.**

The Apostle John strives to make this clear:

1John 3:4 KJV - **WHOSOEVER COMMITTETH SIN TRANSGRESSETH ALSO THE LAW: <u>FOR SIN IS THE TRANSGRESSION OF THE LAW</u>**.

CHAPTER 8

Yeshua's Words Have Supremacy over Paul's Words

Going back to our discussion of Paul, there is another point I think that needs to be made. **IN THE CHRISTIAN CHURCH, I THINK WE HAVE LIFTED PAUL TO A PLACE THAT WE SHOULD NOT HAVE.** He was a wonderful ambassador of Yeshua! However, he is not Yeshua! **THE FATHER MADE IT CLEAR THAT NO ONE'S WORDS WERE MORE IMPORTANT THAN YESHUA'S - NOT MOSES'S, NOT ELIJAH'S - AND NOT PAUL'S!!! In other words, not even the Written Torah as Yehovah gave to Moses in the 1st Covenant or Elijah's words representing all the prophets AND NOT EVEN PAUL'S WORDS are greater than Yeshua's words!**

WE ARE COMMANDED TO FOLLOW YESHUA (WHO DID KEEP THE WRITTEN TORAH, BY THE WAY); WE ARE NOT COMMANDED TO FOLLOW PAUL.

Also, Paul was an apostle, but he was NOT one of the Twelve Apostles. This has been a point of confusion in Christianity. **BUT, PAUL HIMSELF SAYS SO IN I CORINTHIANS 15!:**

[1Co 15:1-8 KJV] 1 Moreover, brethren, I declare unto you the gospel which I preached unto you, which also ye have received, and wherein ye stand; 2 By which also ye are saved, if ye keep in memory what I preached unto you, unless ye have believed in vain. 3 For I delivered unto you first of all that which I also received, how that Christ died for our sins according to the scriptures; 4 And that he was buried, and that he rose again the third day according to the scriptures: 5 And that he was seen of Cephas, **THEN OF THE TWELVE**: 6 After that, he was seen of above five hundred brethren at once; of whom the greater part remain unto this present, but some are fallen asleep. 7 After that, he was seen of James; **THEN OF ALL THE APOSTLES**. 8 And **LAST OF ALL HE WAS SEEN OF ME** also, as of one born out of due time.

Remember that Acts 1 records that Judas Iscariot's position as one of the twelve disciples/apostles was replaced with a disciple named Matthias that had been following Yeshua from the beginning. Peter led them in prayer to Yehovah:

[Act 1:21-26 KJV] 21 **WHEREFORE OF THESE MEN WHICH HAVE COMPANIED**

WITH US ALL THE TIME THAT THE LORD JESUS WENT IN AND OUT AMONG US, 22 BEGINNING FROM THE BAPTISM OF JOHN, UNTO THAT SAME DAY THAT HE WAS TAKEN UP FROM US, MUST ONE BE ORDAINED TO BE A WITNESS WITH US OF HIS RESURRECTION. 23 And they appointed two, Joseph called Barsabas, who was surnamed Justus, and Matthias. 24 And they prayed, and said, Thou, Lord, which knowest the hearts of all [men], shew whether of these two **THOU HAST CHOSEN**, 25 That he may take part of this ministry and apostleship, from which Judas by transgression fell, that he might go to his own place. 26 And they gave forth their lots; and the lot fell upon **MATTHIAS; AND HE WAS NUMBERED WITH THE ELEVEN APOSTLES**.

IS THIS IMPORTANT? YES!!

Yeshua told the TWELVE apostles this:

[Luk 22:28-30 KJV] 28 **YE ARE THEY WHICH HAVE CONTINUED WITH ME IN MY TEMPTATIONS.** 29 And I appoint unto you a kingdom, as my Father hath appointed unto me; 30 That ye may eat and drink at my table in my kingdom, and **SIT ON THRONES JUDGING THE <u>TWELVE</u> TRIBES OF ISRAEL.**

So, Yeshua said the criteria to be one of the Twelve Apostles was that they had been **WITH HIM** in his temptations on earth.

The Twelve Apostles are honored even more by The Father, because the **NEW JERUSALEM IN HEAVEN** (that will be coming to earth!) actually is built on **TWELVE FOUNDATIONS that have the names of these TWELVE APOSTLES! That means that THE TWELFTH APOSTLE'S NAME THERE WILL BE <u>MATTHIAS</u> AS THE REPLACEMENT OF JUDAS!**

[Rev 21:14 KJV] 14 And the wall of the city had twelve foundations, and in them **THE NAMES OF THE TWELVE APOSTLES OF THE LAMB.**

So, the Twelve Apostles are distinguished from <u>others who were called out as apostles, which translated means "sent ones</u>." Paul and Barnabas (not just Paul-by the way; do we generally call Barnabas, the Apostle Barnabas?) were called and <u>sent out by the Holy Spirit</u>:

[Act 13:1-3 KJV] 1 Now there were in the church that was at Antioch certain prophets and teachers; as Barnabas, and Simeon that was called Niger, and Lucius of Cyrene, and Manaen, which had been brought up with Herod the tetrarch, and Saul. 2 As they ministered to the Lord, and fasted, **THE HOLY GHOST SAID, SEPARATE ME BARNABAS AND SAUL FOR THE WORK WHEREUNTO I HAVE**

CALLED THEM. 3 And when they had fasted and prayed, and laid [their] hands on them, they **SENT [THEM]** away.

So, in our study of scripture we should not put Paul's words (which we have already been told by Peter could be hard to understand) above the words of Yeshua. We also may need to pay more special attention to the gospels and the epistles written by **those we know to be of the Twelve Apostles, the future Judges of Israel – Matthew, Peter and John.** I am very grateful for Paul's diligence in spreading the gospel of Yeshua ha Mashiach. But, Paul's letters, epistles, were sent to particular congregations and we don't always know all the circumstances he may have been addressing or the culture. **In any event, if there is EVER a discrepancy in our understanding of scriptures, <u>WE DEFINITELY NEED TO GIVE YESHUA'S WORDS PREEMINENCE</u> – found in <u>Matthew, Mark, Luke, John, Acts, and The Revelation!</u>**

<u>Hear what The Father says about "hearing Yeshua"</u>:

Mar 9:2 KJV - And after six days Jesus taketh [with him] Peter, and James, and John, and leadeth them up into an high mountain apart by themselves: and he was transfigured before them.

Mar 9:3 KJV - And his raiment became shining, exceeding white as snow; so as no fuller on earth can white them.

Mar 9:4 KJV - And there appeared unto them Elias with Moses: and they were talking with Jesus.

Mar 9:5 KJV - And Peter answered and said to Jesus, Master, it is good for us to be here: and let us make three tabernacles; one for thee, and one for Moses, and one for Elias.

Mar 9:6 KJV - For he wist not what to say; for they were sore afraid.

Mar 9:7 KJV - And **<u>there was a cloud that overshadowed them: and a voice came out of the cloud, saying, THIS is my beloved Son: HEAR HIM.</u>**

<u>Although this controversy over Yeshua's words having preeminence over Paul's words may seem foreign to some Christians, this is an issue that has been debated throughout the centuries</u>! It seems that there were some Christians during the Protestant Reformation who thought that the Book of James , because it proclaims that "faith without works is dead," contradicted Paul's teachings that only faith is necessary. Many people have not heard of Carlstadt but he was called in 1505 to the new University of Wittenberg, and he put the school on the map by being the first of its teachers to issue a publication. Though it has now been determined that he was three years younger than Martin Luther, he was his senior on the faculty and actually presided at the ceremony in which Luther was granted his doctoral degree. There was a move to take the Book of James out of the Bible, which Carlstadt didn't agree with. Consider one man's research in the following:

> In 1517, Andreas Bodenstein von Carlstadt (or Karlstadt) (1486-1541) and Luther began the Reformation together. (See bio by Beitenholz; see also "Carlstadt," *Wikipedia*.)
>
> "In fact, Carlstadt was as much or more of the Reformation's founder than Luther. This fact is obscured because of a later falling out between Carlstadt and Luther over their differences on issues like Paul.
>
> One of the key issues that divided these two men was Carlstadt's clear position in 1520 which held that ***JESUS'S WORDS HOLD SUPREMACY OVER THOSE OF PAUL'S***, and hence James's epistle is not to be dismissed as canon merely upon the fact it contradicts Paul.
>
> ...Carlstadt wrote:
>
> Oportet enim servos dominis obsequi, atque sicut Spiritus Apostoli in came non fuit par vel major Domino, ita quoque pectus ***Paulinum sub literis non habet autoritatus tantundem, quantum habet Christus***.
>
> In translation, Carlstadt said:
>
> **It is necessary in fact to preserve obedience to the Lord, and as the Spirit of the Apostles is not a guide equal or greater than the Lord, thus also the heart of *PAUL WITHIN HIS LETTERS DOES NOT HAVE AS MUCH AUTHORITY AS HAS CHRIST.*** ("Carlstadt: Elevating Jesus Over Paul," *Jesus' Words Only*)

There are those who say that Paul's words were mistranslated. That may or may not be true. But, there are so many instances in his letters that concern the Law that are "hard to understand", as Peter says, that I am not convinced that they are mistranslated.

So, this is a good place, then, to remember Yeshua's words concerning the Written Torah as written in Matthew 5:17-19. **HE** said **NOT** to think He was coming to get rid of the Law and if you will keep it and teach it to others, you will be great in the Kingdom of God (my paraphrase)!

I know that discussing this is hard, but we need to want to follow the truth , not just our traditional understanding. It is okay to change as long as we are changing to follow the truth! Let us examine this important example of one difference between what Paul preached and what Yeshua preached. Paul preached:

[1Co 8:1-12 KJV] 1 **NOW AS TOUCHING THINGS OFFERED UNTO IDOLS**, we know that we all have knowledge. Knowledge puffeth up, but charity edifieth. 2 And if any man think that he knoweth any thing, he knoweth nothing yet as he ought to know. 3 But if any man love God, the same is known of him**. 4 AS CONCERNING THEREFORE THE EATING OF THOSE THINGS THAT ARE OFFERED IN SACRIFICE UNTO IDOLS, WE KNOW THAT AN IDOL [IS] NOTHING IN THE WORLD, AND THAT [THERE IS] NONE OTHER GOD BUT ONE.** 5 For though there be that are called gods, whether in heaven or in earth, (as there be gods many, and lords many,) 6 But to us [there is but] one God, the Father, of whom [are] all things, and we in him; and one Lord Jesus Christ, by whom [are] all things, and we by him. **7 HOWBEIT [THERE IS] NOT IN EVERY MAN THAT KNOWLEDGE: FOR SOME WITH CONSCIENCE OF THE IDOL UNTO THIS HOUR EAT [IT] AS A THING OFFERED UNTO AN IDOL; AND THEIR CONSCIENCE BEING WEAK IS DEFILED. 8 BUT MEAT COMMENDETH US NOT TO GOD: FOR NEITHER, IF WE EAT, ARE WE THE BETTER; NEITHER, IF WE EAT NOT, ARE WE THE WORSE.** 9 But take heed lest by any means this liberty of yours become a stumblingblock to them that are weak. 10 For if any man see thee which hast knowledge **SIT AT MEAT IN THE IDOL'S TEMPLE,** shall not the conscience of him which is weak be emboldened to eat those things which are offered to idols; 11 And through thy knowledge shall the weak brother perish, for whom Christ died? 12 But when ye sin so against the brethren, and wound their weak conscience, ye sin against Christ.

So, Paul basically is saying it is ok to eat meat sacrificed to idols, because idols are not really gods. (By the way, why would any believer even be going to an idol's temple??? I have heard that it was the meat market that is being referred to, but note that the verbiage says "sit at meat in the idol's temple". This sounds like actually eating there.)

HOWEVER, YESHUA SAID SOMETHING VERY DIFFERENT IN THE BOOK OF THE REVELATION THAT HE GAVE TO THE APOSTLE JOHN TO TELL THE CHURCHES:

[Rev 2:14, 16 KJV] 14 But **I HAVE A FEW THINGS AGAINST THEE**, because thou hast there them that hold the doctrine of Balaam, who taught Balac to cast a stumblingblock before the children of Israel, **TO EAT THINGS SACRIFICED UNTO IDOLS**, and to commit fornication. ... 16 **REPENT; OR ELSE I WILL COME UNTO THEE QUICKLY, AND WILL FIGHT AGAINST THEM WITH THE SWORD OF MY MOUTH.**

[Rev 2:20 KJV] 20 Notwithstanding **I HAVE A FEW THINGS AGAINST THEE,**

because thou sufferest that woman Jezebel, which calleth herself a prophetess, **TO TEACH AND TO SEDUCE MY SERVANTS TO COMMIT FORNICATION, AND TO EAT THINGS SACRIFICED UNTO IDOLS.**
SO, YESHUA CLEARLY DOES NOT WANT HIS PEOPLE TO EAT MEATS SACRIFICED TO IDOLS! Paul was telling the believers it was ok.... Who are we to believe?

YESHUA!!!

In fact, Yeshua uses the word "REPENT" quite a bit in what he wants spoken to the churches in the first three chapters of The Revelation. Everyone should read those three chapters! I feel like He is setting things straight that had already gotten off track, even in the early churches.

THIS BOOK ENDS WITH AN ADMONITION THAT NO ONE IS TO TAKE AWAY ONE WORD FROM IT OR HE WILL LOSE HIS SALVATION (REVELATION 22:19) SO IT WOULD BEHOOVE US TO LISTEN TO IT CAREFULLY!!!:

[Rev 22:19 KJV] 19 And if any man shall take away from the words of the book of this prophecy, **GOD SHALL TAKE AWAY HIS PART OUT OF THE BOOK OF LIFE, AND OUT OF THE HOLY CITY**, and [from] the things which are written in this book.

So, what does this all mean? **AS I STATED BEFORE, I THINK THAT IF THERE IS EVER ANY CONFUSION BETWEEN THE WORDS THAT WE READ OF PAUL'S (OR ANY ONE ELSE'S) AND THE WORDS THAT WE READ OF YESHUA'S, THE SAFEST DECISION IS TO UNQUESTIONABLY FOLLOW YESHUA'S WORDS!!**

Paul was a wonderful "apostle" sent out and was extremely faithful to preach the gospel of Yeshua Ha Mashiach. But, it is possible, even probable, just like other preachers of the Gospel of Yeshua through the ages that have not gotten every single doctrine correct, that he did not have the correct understanding on this particular issue of keeping the Written Torah. Again, think of the many wonderful preachers that we listen to even today, but maybe don't agree with them on every point, based on our understanding of the scripture...

If you do read Paul's epistles, be careful to remember that YESHUA said to keep the Written Torah, even the least of it, so anything that seems to be to the contrary should be ignored. I personally think it would be best to read the four Gospels, the Epistles(letters) written by the Twelve Apostles, the Revelation of Yeshua ha Mashiach , as well as the Written Torah to get a very good understanding of this first. Then, when you read Acts 15 and Paul's letters, you will be able to discern truth from error. If ANYONE'S words contradict Yeshua's words, we are to listen to YESHUA!!!

Chapter 9

The Obligation to Keep the Written Torah – Completely Gentile Believers – According to Yeshua

NOW, IT IS CLEAR THAT THE BELIEVING JEWS, BELIEVERS FROM THE HOUSE OF ISRAEL (IF THEY KNOW FOR SURE THAT THEY ARE) , AND THE BELIEVING GENTILE PROSELYTES WHO ARE JOINED TO ISRAEL ARE OBLIGATED TO KEEP THE WRITTEN TORAH. WHAT ABOUT THE COMPLETE GENTILES THAT ARE BELIEVERS IN YESHUA?

ARE COMPLETE GENTILES OBLIGATED TO KEEP THE WRITTEN TORAH???

AGAIN, NOTE THAT THIS IS THE ONLY ONE OF THE FOUR GROUPS OF BELIEVERS FOR WHICH THERE SHOULD EVEN BE A QUESTION...

FIRST, LET'S SEE WHAT YESHUA SAYS AGAIN IN WHAT WAS MY PIVOTAL VERSE, MATTHEW 5:19:

[Mat 5:19 KJV] 19 **WHOSOEVER** therefore shall break one of these least commandments, and shall teach men so, he shall be called the least in the kingdom of heaven: but **WHOSOEVER** shall do and teach [them], the same shall be called great in the kingdom of heaven.

BUT, you say, he was talking only to Jews! That is true. **AT THAT TIME!**

However, after his resurrection , he told those same Jewish disciples to go into all the world and teach the gentiles about him and to teach them to OBSERVE EVERYTHING THAT HE HAD TOLD THEM TO DO!:

Mat 28:18 KJV - And Jesus came and spake unto them, saying, All power is given unto me in heaven and in earth.

Mat 28:19 KJV - GO YE THEREFORE, and TEACH ALL NATIONS, baptizing them in the name of the Father, and of the Son, and of the Holy Ghost:

Mat 28:20 KJV - <u>Teaching THEM to OBSERVE ALL THINGS WHATSOEVER I HAVE COMMANDED YOU</u>: and, lo, I am with you alway, [even] unto the end of the world. Amen.

THIS IS AN EXTREMELY IMPORTANT POINT WORTH REITERATING! YESHUA TOLD HIS TWELVE APOSTLES TO TEACH ALL THE GENTILES (ALL NATIONS) ABOUT HIM AND FOR THEM TO DO AND OBSERVE EVERYTHING HE HAD TOLD THE APOSTLES TO DO!!! YESHUA MADE NO DIFFERENCE, IT SEEMS, BETWEEN JEW AND GENTILE BELIEVERS!

Remember in <u>Matthew 5:19</u>, Yeshua had said to his disciples, "**WHOSOEVER**" would keep the commandments and teach them to others would be great in the Kingdom! **If we can believe that the "WHOSOEVER" in JOHN 3:16 CONCERNING SALVATION IS FOR US GENTILES, when he was talking to Jews, we should believe that "WHOSOEVER" in Matthew 5:19 applies to us gentiles as well!!!**

Jhn 3:16 KJV - For God so loved the world, that he gave his only begotten Son, that **<u>WHOSOEVER</u>** believeth in him should not perish, but have everlasting life.

BASED ON THESE STATEMENTS OF YESHUA'S, I BELIEVE THAT <u>HE TEACHES</u> THAT COMPLETE GENTILES <u>ARE</u> TO LEARN <u>THE WRITTEN TORAH</u>, EVEN THE LEAST OF THE COMMANDMENTS, JUST LIKE THE JEWISH BELIEVERS! HOWEVER, EVEN IF YOU, AS A COMPLETELY GENTILE BELIEVER , ARE NOT "<u>OBLIGATED</u>" TO KEEP ALL OF THE WRITTEN TORAH (<u>AT LEAST AT THE BEGINNING OF YOUR JOURNEY UNTIL YOU HAVE LEARNED IT</u>), <u>IF YOU WANT YOUR FATHER TO SEE YOU AS GREAT IN THE KINGDOM OF GOD</u>, <u>YOU WILL</u>! <u>IT'S YOUR CHOICE</u>!

NEXT, WE CAN LOOK AT WHAT OTHERS HAVE TO SAY ON THIS SUBJECT. (HOWEVER, REMEMBER THAT YESHUA'S WORDS SHOULD ALWAYS TRUMP ANYONE ELSE'S!!)

CHAPTER 10

The Obligation to Keep the Written Torah – Completely Gentile Believers – According to the Jerusalem Council; Emperor Constantine's and Other Church Councils' Perversion of Christianity

According to Acts 15 (specifically Acts 15:29) , this question was ADDRESSED AND DECIDED by THE APOSTLES AND ELDERS at THE COUNCIL OF JERUSALEM IN THE FIRST CENTURY:

(PLEASE SEE APPENDIX I ENTITLED "AUTHORITY IN THE CHURCH" THAT I HAVE WRITTEN, QUESTIONING WHETHER THIS COUNCIL AND SUBSEQUENT CHURCH COUNCILS HAD TRUE YEHOVAH-GIVEN AUTHORITY OVER THE BELIEVERS IN YESHUA OR NOT!)

The setting for this starts in Antioch where Paul and Barnabas were preaching and many gentiles were coming to faith in Yeshua.

Act 15:1 KJV - And certain men which came down from Judaea taught the brethren, [and said], Except ye be circumcised after the manner of Moses, ye cannot be saved.

Act 15:2 KJV - When therefore Paul and Barnabas had no small dissension and disputation with them, they determined that **Paul and Barnabas, and certain other of them, should go up to Jerusalem unto the apostles and elders about this question.**

Act 15:3 KJV - And being brought on their way by the church, they passed through Phenice and Samaria, declaring the conversion of the Gentiles: and they caused great joy unto all the brethren.

Act 15:4 KJV - And when they were come to Jerusalem, they were received of the church, and [of] the apostles and elders, and they declared all things that God had done with them.

Act 15:5 KJV - But **there rose up certain of the sect of the Pharisees which believed, saying, That it was needful to circumcise them, and to command [them] to keep the law of Moses.**

Act 15:6 KJV - And the apostles and elders came together for to consider of this matter.

Act 15:7 KJV - And when there had been much disputing, Peter rose up, and said unto them, Men [and] brethren, ye know how that a good while ago God made choice among us, that the Gentiles by my mouth should hear the word of the gospel, and believe.

Act 15:8 KJV - And God, which knoweth the hearts, bare them witness, giving them the Holy Ghost, even as [he did] unto us;

Act 15:9 KJV - And put no difference between us and them, **purifying their hearts by faith**.

Act 15:10 KJV - Now therefore why tempt ye God, to put a yoke upon the neck of the disciples, which neither our fathers nor we were able to bear?

(Remember that before Yeshua's perfect sacrifice of Himself for sin, there was forgiveness in the Written Torah for most sins by offerings, but there was no forgiveness for some sins – there was a death penalty or, in some cases, the penalty of being cut off from Israel! This may be what Peter was referring to. As I mentioned before concerning Paul's teachings, it is also possible that Peter was referring to the burdensome Oral Torah additions which were too much for them or their fathers to bear. **REGARDLESS, THE FATHER CERTAINLY NEVER SAID THAT THE WRITTEN TORAH WAS TOO HARD TO BEAR, OR HE WOULDN'T HAVE EXPECTED THEM TO KEEP IT!** [Deu 30:10-16 KJV] 10 If thou shalt hearken unto the voice of the LORD thy God, **TO KEEP HIS COMMANDMENTS AND HIS STATUTES WHICH ARE WRITTEN IN THIS BOOK OF THE LAW**, [and] if thou turn unto the LORD thy God with all thine heart, and with all thy soul. 11 **FOR THIS COMMANDMENT WHICH I COMMAND THEE THIS DAY, IT [IS] NOT HIDDEN FROM THEE, NEITHER [IS] IT FAR OFF. 12 IT [IS] NOT IN HEAVEN, THAT THOU SHOULDEST SAY, WHO SHALL GO UP FOR US TO HEAVEN, AND BRING IT UNTO US, THAT WE MAY HEAR IT, AND DO IT? 13 NEITHER [IS] IT BEYOND THE SEA, THAT THOU SHOULDEST SAY, WHO SHALL GO OVER THE SEA FOR US, AND BRING IT UNTO US, THAT WE MAY HEAR IT, AND DO IT? 14**

BUT THE WORD [IS] VERY NIGH UNTO THEE, IN THY MOUTH, AND IN THY HEART, THAT THOU MAYEST DO IT. 15 See, I have set before thee this day life and good, and death and evil; **16 IN THAT I COMMAND THEE THIS DAY TO LOVE THE LORD THY GOD, TO WALK IN HIS WAYS, AND TO KEEP HIS COMMANDMENTS AND HIS STATUTES AND HIS JUDGMENTS,** that thou mayest live and multiply: and the LORD thy God shall bless thee in the land whither thou goest to possess it.)

Peter continues:

Act 15:11 KJV - **But we believe that through the grace of the Lord Jesus Christ we shall be saved, even as they.** (Later, the Jewish believers **were determined** by James and these same elders to still be **OBLIGATED** to continue to keep the Written Torah in Acts 21[Acts 21:24]. Of course, if they did sin but repented, forgiveness by the blood of Yeshua was still available to them, too.)

Act 15:12 KJV - Then all the multitude kept silence, and gave audience to Barnabas and Paul, declaring what miracles and wonders God had wrought among the Gentiles by them.

Act 15:13 KJV - And after they had held their peace, James answered, saying, Men [and] brethren, hearken unto me:

Act 15:14 KJV - **Simeon hath declared how God at the first did visit the Gentiles, to take out of them a people for his name.**

Act 15:15 KJV - And to this agree the words of the prophets; **as it is written, (See Amos 9: 11-12)**

Act 15:16 KJV - After this I will return, and will build again the tabernacle of David, which is fallen down; and I will build again the ruins thereof, and I will set it up:

Act 15:17 KJV - That the residue of men might seek after the Lord**, and all the Gentiles, upon whom my name is called, saith the Lord, who doeth all these things.**

Act 15:18 KJV - Known unto God are all his works from the beginning of the world.

Act 15:19 KJV - **Wherefore MY SENTENCE IS, that we trouble not them, which from among the Gentiles are turned to God:**

Act 15:20 KJV - BUT THAT WE WRITE UNTO THEM, THAT THEY ABSTAIN FROM POLLUTIONS OF IDOLS, AND [FROM] FORNICATION, AND [FROM]

THINGS STRANGLED, AND [FROM] BLOOD.

These are some laws from the Written Torah in Exodus and Leviticus. Leviticus 17:10-17 said for Israel and the strangers [gentiles] that sojourned among them not to eat blood and things strangled would have had the blood kept inside. Also, LEVITICUS 18 [READ WHOLE CHAPTER] SPECIFIES ALL TYPES OF SEXUAL SIN (ALL THE INCEST, ADULTERY, FORNICATION, SEXUAL RELATIONS DURING A WOMAN'S MENSTRUAL PERIOD, HOMOSEXUALITY, AND BESTIALITY) THAT ISRAEL AND THE STRANGERS (GENTILES) THAT SOJOURNED AMONG THEM WERE NOT TO COMMIT .

YEHOVAH HATED ALL OF THESE.

HOMOSEXUALITY IS EVEN CALLED AN ABOMINATION – LEVITICUS 18:22 KJV: THOU SHALT NOT LIE WITH MANKIND, AS WITH WOMANKIND: IT [IS] ABOMINATION.) LEVITICUS 20:13 PUTS THE DEATH PENALTY ON IT.

THE FATHER ALSO MADE SURE HIS PEOPLE DID NOT EVEN GET CLOSE TO HOMOSEXUALITY BY THIS COMMANDMENT:

[Deu 22:5 KJV] 5 THE WOMAN SHALL NOT WEAR THAT WHICH PERTAINETH UNTO A MAN, NEITHER SHALL A MAN PUT ON A WOMAN'S GARMENT: for ALL THAT DO SO [ARE] ABOMINATION UNTO THE LORD THY GOD. (Sort of rules out Yehovah's approval of transgenderism, too....it is ABOMINATION, which will keep you out of the New Jerusalem at the very least – unless you repent!)

THE COMMITTING OF ALL THOSE SEXUAL SINS WAS ONE OF THE MAIN REASONS THAT HE CAST OUT THE SIX NATIONS OF THOSE CANAANITE GENTILES (ALL DESCENDANTS OF CANAAN THAT WERE CURSED BY YEHOVAH according to [Gen 9:25 KJV] 25 And he said, Cursed [be] Canaan; a servant of servants shall he be unto his brethren.) YEHOVAH CAST THEM OUT OF THE LAND OF CANAAN FOR THESE INIQUITOUS PRACTICES AND BROUGHT THE CHILDREN OF ISRAEL IN TO TAKE THEIR PLACE, RENAMING IT THE LAND OF ISRAEL!

[LEV 18:24-30 KJV] 24 DEFILE NOT YE YOURSELVES IN ANY OF THESE THINGS: FOR IN ALL THESE THE NATIONS ARE DEFILED WHICH I CAST OUT BEFORE YOU: 25 AND THE LAND IS DEFILED: THEREFORE I DO VISIT THE INIQUITY THEREOF UPON IT, AND THE LAND ITSELF VOMITETH OUT HER INHABITANTS. 26 YE SHALL THEREFORE KEEP MY STATUTES AND MY

JUDGMENTS, AND SHALL NOT COMMIT [ANY] OF THESE ABOMINATIONS; [NEITHER] ANY OF YOUR OWN NATION, NOR ANY STRANGER THAT SOJOURNETH AMONG YOU: **27 (FOR ALL THESE ABOMINATIONS HAVE THE MEN OF THE LAND DONE, WHICH [WERE] BEFORE YOU, AND THE LAND IS DEFILED;) 28 THAT THE LAND SPUE NOT YOU OUT ALSO, WHEN YE DEFILE IT, AS IT SPUED OUT THE NATIONS THAT [WERE] BEFORE YOU. 29 FOR WHOSOEVER SHALL COMMIT ANY OF THESE ABOMINATIONS, EVEN THE SOULS THAT COMMIT [THEM] SHALL BE CUT OFF FROM AMONG THEIR PEOPLE. 30 THEREFORE SHALL YE KEEP MINE ORDINANCE, THAT [YE] COMMIT NOT [ANY ONE] OF THESE ABOMINABLE CUSTOMS, WHICH WERE COMMITTED BEFORE YOU, AND THAT YE DEFILE NOT YOURSELVES THEREIN: I [AM] THE LORD YOUR GOD.**

(Yehovah's dealing with Sodom and Gomorrah, both Canaanite cities, [Genesis 10:19] also lets us know that he takes sexual sin very seriously. Read Genesis 13:12 forward.)

Next, idolatry was forbidden in the first two commandments in Exodus 20:1-6. ANYTHING TO DO WITH IDOLATRY ANGERS YEHOVAH. He is a jealous God! So, Israel, and then later the gentile believers in Yeshua as well, were not to eat foods sacrificed to idols , of course!

Then James says something very interesting!!:

*********Act 15:21 KJV - FOR MOSES OF OLD TIME HATH IN EVERY CITY THEM THAT PREACH HIM, BEING READ IN THE SYNAGOGUES EVERY SABBATH DAY. ********

Act 15:22 KJV - Then pleased it the apostles and elders, with the whole church, to send chosen men of their own company to Antioch with Paul and Barnabas; [namely], Judas surnamed Barsabas, and Silas, chief men among the brethren:

Act 15:23 KJV - And they wrote [letters] by them after this manner; The apostles and elders and brethren [send] greeting unto the brethren which are of the Gentiles in Antioch and Syria and Cilicia:

Act 15:24 KJV - Forasmuch as we have heard, that certain which went out from us have troubled you with words, subverting your souls, saying, [Ye must] be circumcised, and keep the law: to whom **WE gave no [such] commandment**:

Act 15:25 KJV - It seemed good unto us, being assembled with one accord, to send chosen men unto you with our beloved Barnabas and Paul,

Act 15:26 KJV - Men that have hazarded their lives for the name of our Lord Jesus Christ.

Act 15:27 KJV - We have sent therefore Judas and Silas, who shall also tell [you] the same things by mouth.

Act 15:28 KJV - **For it seemed good to the Holy Ghost, and to us, to lay upon you no greater burden than these necessary things;**

Act 15:29 KJV - That ye abstain from meats offered to idols, and from blood, and from things strangled, and from fornication: from which if ye keep yourselves, ye shall do well. Fare ye well.

Act 15:30 KJV - So when they were dismissed, they came to Antioch: and when they had gathered the multitude together, they delivered the epistle:

Act 15:31 KJV - [Which] when they had read, they **REJOICED** for the consolation.

We should note a few things here. First, after having decided to obey the Written Torah even as a gentile believer in Yeshua, I have come to wonder at **these gentiles REJOICING at not being held responsible to do so. IT SEEMS TO ME THAT REJOICING MIGHT NOT HAVE BEEN THE BEST RESPONSE!!!**

WHY? BECAUSE THE FATHER HAS SAID OVER AND OVER THROUGHOUT THE TORAH AND THE PSALMS AND THE PROPHETS THAT HIS COMMANDMENTS, STATUTES, AND JUDGMENTS ARE HIS DESIRES, HIS WILL, AND ARE GOOD!!!

[Psa 19:8 KJV] 8 The statutes of the LORD [are] right, REJOICING THE HEART: the commandment of the LORD [is] pure, enlightening the eyes.

PSALM 119, THE LONGEST CHAPTER IN THE BIBLE, IS JUST ONE OF HUNDREDS OF SCRIPTURES THAT STATE THIS. JUST ONE SECTION STATES:

[Psa 119:9-16 KJV] 9 BETH. Wherewithal shall a young man cleanse his way? by taking heed [thereto] according to thy word. 10 With my whole heart have I sought thee: O LET ME NOT WANDER FROM THY COMMANDMENTS. 11 THY WORD HAVE I HID IN MINE HEART, THAT I MIGHT NOT SIN AGAINST THEE. 12 Blessed [art] thou, O LORD: teach me thy statutes. 13 With my lips have I declared all the judgments of thy mouth. 14 I have rejoiced in the way of thy testimonies, as [much as] in all riches. 15 I will meditate in thy precepts, and have respect unto thy ways. 16 I will delight myself in thy statutes: I will not forget thy word.

Second, **ALTHOUGH THESE GENTILES WERE NOT "COMMANDED " TO KEEP ALL OF THE TORAH, THEY DID HAVE COMMANDMENTS.** Read Acts 15:20 above again. **THESE WERE NOT SUGGESTIONS, but COMMANDMENTS FROM THE TORAH TO THE GENTILE BELIEVERS! It's possible that these commandments were designed by the elders to be those adhered to in order for the lawless but believing gentiles to even be considered part of the congregation of Believing Torah Observant Israel! But, then they were to go to the synagogue on the Sabbath and start learning the Written Torah and keeping it little by little, growing in holiness as I believe Acts 15:21 directed.**

Sadly, the modern church has almost completely disregarded the fornication laws. They also regularly eat rare meat that very well may still have the blood inside. Most American Christians haven't been exposed to meat sacrificed to idols yet, thankfully, at least not knowingly. But, that could easily change and may have already. I have been told that meats marked "halal" in the grocery stores are meats that are permissible to eat under Islamic Shariah Law and **MAY have been dedicated to the god Allah (which is NOT the same as Yehovah Elohim!!)**

I DON'T WANT TO GLOSS OVER THE FORNICATION ISSUE! Probably a majority of believers have actually accepted fornication, heterosexual and more recently, homosexual, as normal in the modern church. (I even just heard this week, July 2016, that the current Pope Francis of the Catholic Church, says that Christians owe an apology to homosexuals – a practice Yehovah calls abominable!) Now, even openly living together without marriage, and even worse, having children, not just one child, but a whole family, without marriage, is becoming normal in the modern church. We have become more and more lawless rather than more and more holy. In Matthew 15:18-19, Yeshua says fornication is one of the sins that causes defilement!

Continuing on, note that although nothing was mentioned in Acts 15: 20 about completely gentile believers committing no murder, no stealing, no taking the name of Yehovah in vain, no bowing down to graven images, no disrespecting your father and mother, etc., traditionally we have believed they were also not to do these. Why? Most gentile believers in Yeshua, even today, would say that they believe they should keep the 10 commandments. But, why?? The 10 commandments are the foundation of "The Law" – The Written Torah! The Law that gentiles are not supposed to have to keep??? I have heard different pastors say that the 10 commandments are the "moral law" and that is why they are still to be kept. I'm sorry, but the only distinctions that Yehovah makes in speaking of The Written Torah, that I have found, are that there are <u>commandments, statutes, and judgements</u>,

three divisions. I believe they are all moral! See what Psalm 19 says and you judge if they are all moral:

[Psa 19:7-11 KJV] 7 THE LAW OF THE LORD [IS] PERFECT, converting the soul: the testimony of the LORD [is] sure, making wise the simple. 8 THE STATUTES OF THE LORD [ARE] RIGHT, REJOICING THE HEART: the COMMANDMENT OF THE LORD [IS] PURE, enlightening the eyes. 9 The fear of the LORD [is] CLEAN, enduring for ever: THE JUDGMENTS OF THE LORD [ARE] TRUE [AND] RIGHTEOUS ALTOGETHER. 10 MORE TO BE DESIRED [ARE THEY] THAN GOLD, yea, than much fine gold: sweeter also than honey and the honeycomb. 11 Moreover by them is thy servant warned: [and] in keeping of them [there is] great reward.

The slippery slope of completely gentile believers in Yeshua claiming that they are not bound to keep "The Law" is resulting in our world falling into more and more sin – **more and more blatantly pagan practices – breaking even more and more of even the 10 commandments!**

ONE OF THE MOST DANGEROUS OF THESE IS BREAKING THE SECOND COMMANDMENT TO NOT BOW DOWN TO GRAVEN IMAGES!!!

Daniel chapters 7 through 12 and Revelation 13 prophesy that one day there is going to be an extremely powerful world government which will be the last of the 4 kingdoms on earth (before Yeshua destroys and sets up the Kingdom of God on earth - Revelation 19 and 20). Ezekiel 38 and 39 list at least some of the countries who will be part of that kingdom. I believe they may be present day Russia and may be some of the countries adjoining it. Russia may be the land of Magog, Meshek and Tubal, Persia is probably Iran, Togarmah may be Turkey, Gomer may be Germany, the countries of Libya and Ethiopa are probably the same as today or could be larger areas. The scripture says there will be other countries with these and they all will come against Israel in the last days. Gog of Magog (Ezekiel 38: 2-3), may be the actual name of the ruler of this kingdom, termed the King of the North (Daniel 11:40) and the first beast (Revelation 13:1), who is actually going to have a statue (idol – image) of himself and IT WILL BE REQUIRED THAT EVERYONE BOW DOWN TO IT IN WORSHIP! People will actually worship satan (the dragon) that empowers this openly satanic king and will worship him because he is so powerful (Daniel 11:36-37 and Revelation 13:4). He will be involved in dark sorcery and witchcraft (Daniel 8:23-25). He eventually defiles the Temple in Jerusalem with the "abomination that makes desolate" (possibly that image of himself) and magnifies himself

above every god and blasphemes the true God, expecting worship of himself. He builds his palace on the Temple Mount (Daniel 11:41-45)! Then there will be a second beast, termed the "false prophet," which may be another king that works satanic, occultic miracles (Revelation 13:11-18). We are not given any clues as to what nations he has control over, but it says he has two horns like a lamb but speaks like a dragon, exercising all the authority of the first beast. He is the one that causes the image of the first beast to be made and, through his satanic power, miraculously makes the image of the first beast to be able to speak! That false prophet beast requires that if you don't worship the first beast and his image (BOWING DOWN TO A GRAVEN IMAGE), and don't take his "mark" in your hand or your forehead, and his number, you will not be able to buy or sell and will be killed! (The technology for this is, of course, already here in the form of a scannable chip that can be inserted under the skin.) BUT, IF YOU DO WORSHIP THE FIRST BEAST, AND BOW DOWN TO HIS IMAGE, AND TAKE HIS MARK, CALLED THE "MARK OF THE BEAST," OR THE NUMBER OF HIS NAME, YOU WILL LOSE YOUR SALVATION – YOUR NAME WILL BE TAKEN OUT OF THE LAMB'S BOOK OF LIFE!!!!

[Revelation 13:1-18 KJV] 1 And I stood upon the sand of the sea, and saw a beast
rise up out of the sea, having seven heads and ten horns, and upon his horns ten
crowns, and upon his heads the name of blasphemy. 2 And the beast which I saw
was like unto a leopard, and his feet were as [the feet] of a bear, and his mouth as
the mouth of a lion: and **THE DRAGON GAVE HIM HIS POWER, AND HIS SEAT,
AND GREAT AUTHORITY.** 3 And I saw one of his heads as it were wounded to
death; and his deadly wound was healed: and **ALL THE WORLD WONDERED
AFTER THE BEAST. 4 AND THEY WORSHIPPED THE DRAGON WHICH GAVE
POWER UNTO THE BEAST: AND THEY WORSHIPPED THE BEAST, SAYING,
WHO [IS] LIKE UNTO THE BEAST? WHO IS ABLE TO MAKE WAR WITH HIM?** 5
And there was given unto him a mouth speaking great things and blasphemies;
and power was given unto him to continue forty [and] two months. 6 And he
opened his mouth in blasphemy against God, to blaspheme his name, and his
tabernacle, and them that dwell in heaven. 7 And **IT WAS GIVEN UNTO HIM TO
MAKE WAR WITH THE SAINTS, AND TO OVERCOME THEM**: and power was
given him over all kindreds, and tongues, and nations. 8 and **ALL THAT DWELL
UPON THE EARTH SHALL WORSHIP HIM, WHOSE NAMES ARE NOT WRITTEN
IN THE BOOK OF LIFE OF THE LAMB SLAIN FROM THE FOUNDATION OF THE
WORLD. 9 IF ANY MAN HAVE AN EAR, LET HIM HEAR.** 10 He that leadeth into
captivity shall go into captivity: he that killeth with the sword must be killed with
the sword. Here is the patience and the faith of the saints. 11 And I beheld another

beast coming up out of the earth; and he had two horns like a lamb, and he spake as a dragon. 12 And he exerciseth all the power of the first beast before him, and causeth the earth and them which dwell therein to worship the first beast, whose deadly wound was healed. 13 And he doeth great wonders, so that he maketh fire come down from heaven on the earth in the sight of men, 14 And deceiveth them that dwell on the earth by [the means of] those miracles which he had power to do in the sight of the beast; saying to them that dwell on the earth, that they should make an image to the beast, which had the wound by a sword, and did live. 15 **AND HE HAD POWER TO GIVE LIFE UNTO THE IMAGE OF THE BEAST, THAT THE IMAGE OF THE BEAST SHOULD BOTH SPEAK, AND CAUSE THAT AS MANY AS WOULD NOT WORSHIP THE IMAGE OF THE BEAST SHOULD BE KILLED. 16 AND HE CAUSETH ALL, BOTH SMALL AND GREAT, RICH AND POOR, FREE AND BOND, TO RECEIVE A MARK IN THEIR RIGHT HAND, OR IN THEIR FOREHEADS: 17 AND THAT NO MAN MIGHT BUY OR SELL, SAVE HE THAT HAD THE MARK, OR THE NAME OF THE BEAST, OR THE NUMBER OF HIS NAME. 18 HERE IS WISDOM. LET HIM THAT HATH UNDERSTANDING COUNT THE NUMBER OF THE BEAST: FOR IT IS THE NUMBER OF A MAN; AND HIS NUMBER [IS] SIX HUNDRED THREESCORE [AND] SIX.**

[Rev 14:8-12 KJV] 8 And there followed another angel, saying, **BABYLON IS FALLEN, IS FALLEN, THAT GREAT CITY, BECAUSE SHE MADE ALL NATIONS DRINK OF THE WINE OF THE WRATH OF HER FORNICATION.** 9 And the third angel followed them, saying with a loud voice, **IF ANY MAN WORSHIP THE BEAST AND HIS IMAGE, AND RECEIVE [HIS] MARK IN HIS FOREHEAD, OR IN HIS HAND, 10 THE SAME SHALL DRINK OF THE WINE OF THE WRATH OF GOD, WHICH IS POURED OUT WITHOUT MIXTURE INTO THE CUP OF HIS INDIGNATION; AND HE SHALL BE TORMENTED WITH FIRE AND BRIMSTONE IN THE PRESENCE OF THE HOLY ANGELS, AND IN THE PRESENCE OF THE LAMB: 11 AND THE SMOKE OF THEIR TORMENT ASCENDETH UP FOR EVER AND EVER: AND THEY HAVE NO REST DAY NOR NIGHT, WHO WORSHIP THE BEAST AND HIS IMAGE, AND WHOSOEVER RECEIVETH THE MARK OF HIS NAME. 12 HERE IS THE PATIENCE OF THE SAINTS: HERE [ARE] THEY THAT KEEP THE COMMANDMENTS OF GOD, AND THE FAITH OF JESUS.**

(I think the insertion of verse twelve at this point in the prophecy, which states that the saints will be those who keep the faith of Yeshua AND keep the commandments of God, is to remind us that WORSHIPPING THE BEAST WILL BE BREAKING THE FIRST COMMANDMENT OF YEHOVAH ELOHIM AND BOWING TO THE GRAVEN IMAGE OF THE BEAST WILL BE BREAKING THE SECOND COMMANDMENT! ONLY THOSE WHO RESPECT AND

KNOW TO KEEP THE COMMANDMENTS OF GOD WILL NOT DO THESE!!!)

[Dan 8:23-25 KJV] 23 And in the latter time of their kingdom, WHEN THE TRANSGRESSORS ARE COME TO THE FULL, a KING OF FIERCE COUNTENANCE, and UNDERSTANDING DARK SENTENCES, shall stand up. 24 And HIS POWER SHALL BE MIGHTY, BUT NOT BY HIS OWN POWER: and he shall destroy wonderfully, and shall prosper, and practise, and SHALL DESTROY THE MIGHTY AND THE HOLY PEOPLE. 25 And through his policy also HE SHALL CAUSE CRAFT TO PROSPER in his hand; and he shall magnify [himself] in his heart, and by peace shall destroy many: HE SHALL ALSO STAND UP AGAINST THE PRINCE OF PRINCES; BUT HE SHALL BE BROKEN WITHOUT HAND.

(These verses show that the king/beast of this kingdom will be empowered by satan! Witchcraft will prosper. Also, we know it will be when there are many "transgressors"!) We also know that it is in the last days because, although he comes against the Prince of Princes (Yeshua), Yeshua will destroy him!

Thank goodness, it will be worth whatever we have to go through to not worship the "beast" or bow down to his graven image, **EVEN IF WE DIE – BECAUSE YESHUA WILL DEFEAT HIM AND RESURRECT US!!! (Daniel 12 and Revelation 19-20).**

SO, TO REITERATE, ALTHOUGH NOT MENTIONED IN ACTS 15:20, THE SECOND COMMANDMENT TO NOT BOW DOWN TO GRAVEN IMAGES IS VERY IMPORTANT TO KNOW AND KEEP – FOR JEW AND GENTILE BELIEVERS IT SEEMS – I CERTAINLY WOULDN'T TAKE A CHANCE ON THINKING IT DIDN'T PERTAIN TO ME IF I WERE A GENTILE BELIEVER!!!

It is important to know that, when Christians, which are predominantly completely gentile believers, say they are not "under the law", we need to understand that **THEY WERE NEVER "UNDER THE LAW"** because **THE GENTILES WERE NOT PART OF THE 1ST COVENANT** and **THE 10 COMMANDMENTS ALONG WITH THE STATUTES AND JUDGMENTS ARE THE COVENANT.** They **ARE** what we refer to as the **MOSAIC COVENANT**, because it was given from Yehovah to Moses, on Mount Sinai when the children of Israel came out of Egypt. It promised blessings to Israel if they kept the written commandments, statutes, and judgments and it promised curses if they didn't. It is an extension of the covenant that Yehovah Elohim made with Abraham, Isaac, and Jacob (Israel), the Fathers. (See **Exodus chapters 20-23** for the 10 Commandments and many of the statutes and judgments, but there are more all through Exodus, Leviticus, Numbers and Deuteronomy too – called the five books of Moses.)

All of the commandments are very important, but I am going to digress again and discuss the Fourth Commandment to keep the Sabbath holy.

THE KEEPING OF THE TRUE SABBATH FROM SUNDOWN FRIDAY EVENING TO SUNDOWN SATURDAY EVENING IS THE ONLY ONE OF THE 10 COMMANDMENTS THAT HAS BEEN ALTERED BY, FIRST, THE ROMAN CATHOLIC CHURCH AND HAS CONTINUED TO BE KEPT AS ALTERED BY THE PROTESTANT CHRISTIAN CHURCH! It has been changed to Sunday. However, since that was handed down to us so many hundreds of years ago, approximately 321-325 A.D., by the Emperor Constantine , most Believers are just not aware of it. **(See Appendix III Constantine the Great and Sun-God Worship).** I believe the Father has been merciful to our ignorance. Possibly, even Constantine's purpose was to make sure that Yeshua's Resurrection, (what Catholics termed "the Lord's Day") which was on a Sunday, was honored. **The problem is that Sunday is the first day of the week. THE SABBATH IS THE SEVENTH DAY AND WAS FIRST SANCTIFIED BY YEHOVAH ELOHIM AT CREATION AND HE HAS NEVER CHANGED IT!!!**

[Gen 2:1-3 KJV] 1 Thus the heavens and the earth were finished, and all the host of them. 2 And on the seventh day God ended his work which he had made; and he rested on the seventh day from all his work which he had made. 3 **And GOD BLESSED THE SEVENTH DAY, AND SANCTIFIED IT**: because that in it HE had rested (shabbatted or kept Sabbath - #7673 in the Strong's Concordance) from all his work which God created and made.

God later made it a commandment of the Written Torah to the children of Israel as part of the Mosaic covenant made at Mount Sinai. It was to be a day of rest and a day of worship, a "holy convocation" (a holy meeting together of the congregation - a sacred assembly) according to Exodus 20:9-11 and Leviticus 23:1-3 and special offerings were to be made.

IF YOU THINK ABOUT IT, IT IS ABOUT THE HEIGHT OF HUMAN ARROGANCY TO THINK WE COULD CHANGE EVEN ONE OF YEHOVAH ELOHIM'S COMMANDMENTS!!!

There are many instances in the New Testament that show Yeshua healing on the Sabbath and being condemned by the Pharisees for doing so. Yeshua explained that it was not unlawful to do good on the Sabbath. The Church has taken these instances to infer that Yeshua did not honor the Sabbath. However, many scriptures say that it was Yeshua's practice to go to the synagogue on the Sabbath:

[Luk 4:16 KJV] 16 And he came to Nazareth, where he had been brought up: and, **AS HIS CUSTOM WAS, HE WENT INTO THE SYNAGOGUE ON THE SABBATH DAY**, and stood up for to read.

Its worth noting, too, that you never hear that Yeshua told anyone to do their normal weekday business on the Sabbath – I doubt that Yeshua worked in the "carpenter" shop on the Sabbath!!!

For gentile believers, the fact that the Sabbath was established at Creation, before the Written Torah, should make us realize that The Father's desire is that even we should rest on the Seventh Day, not the First Day, **as The Father did**. I say that because **the day of Yeshua's resurrection is actually a fulfillment of an ANNUAL feast, not a weekly one.** It is the Day of First Fruits of the Barley Harvest (Leviticus 23:9-14) that Yehovah commanded Israel to keep. Yeshua fulfilled it when he became the First Fruits of those risen from the dead (I Corinthians 15:20):

[1Co 15:20 KJV] 20 But now is Christ risen from the dead, [and] become the firstfruits of them that slept.

That did happen on a first day of the week according to Leviticus, which started at the end of the Sabbath at sundown and went until sundown on the First Day of the week (Sunday.) But, worship on every Sunday celebrates it as a weekly feast. Although it is always good to celebrate Yeshua's resurrection, even every day, worship every Sunday evolved into a substitution for the Sabbath. But, Sunday, the first day of the week, is not the Sabbath!!

SO, NOT RESTING ON THE SEVENTH DAY, THE TRUE SABBATH, IS BREAKING YEHOVAH ELOHIM'S FOURTH COMMANDMENT!!!

Although I know that Constantine was known as the first Christian Emperor, and he did do **MANY** wonderful things to make life more tolerable for Christians, unfortunately, history records he is the one who made it a government policy to rest and worship on Sunday instead of Sabbath, possibly because of the prevalence of sun-god worship:

> Later in 321, Constantine instructed that **Christians and non-Christians alike** should be united in observing **THE VENERABLE DAY OF THE SUN, REFERRING TO THE SUN-WORSHIP THAT AURELIAN HAD**

> **ESTABLISHED AS AN OFFICIAL CULT**. Furthermore, and long after his oft alleged conversion to Christianity, Constantine's coinage continued to carry the symbols of the sun. Even after the pagan gods had disappeared from the coinage, Christian symbols appeared only as Constantine's *personal* attributes: the chi rho between his hands or on his labarum, but never on the coin itself. Even when Constantine dedicated the new capital of Constantinople, which became the seat of Byzantine Christianity for a millennium, he did so wearing the Apollonian sun-rayed Diadem; no Christian symbols were present at this dedication. (Wikipedia contributors, "Constantine the Great")

(For much more information on this subject, see also Appendix III - Constantine the Great and Sun-God Worship).

The book, Constantine's Sword: The Church and the Jews: A History by James Carroll has a description of the conversion of Constantine to Christianity in chapter 19, entitled "The Vision of Constantine" that is worth reading. It describes the emperor's rise to power and (what seems to me was apparently a gradual) conversion to Christianity from 312 A.D. to 324 A.D. and his decision to become not only emperor but head (Pope) of the entire Church, establishing the Roman Catholic Church.

Actually, the entire distancing of Christianity from its original Jewish roots seems to have been started by Constantine.

Constantine's Christian Creed had Christians to say this:

> I renounce all customs, rites, legalisms, unleavened breads and sacrifices of lambs of the Hebrews, and all the other feasts of the Hebrews, sacrifices, prayers, aspirations, purifications, sanctifications, and propitiations, and fasts and new moons, and **SABBATHS**, and superstitions, and hymns and chants, and observances and synagogues. **ABSOLUTELY EVERYTHING JEWISH, EVERY LAW**, rite and custom and if afterwards I shall wish to deny and return to Jewish superstition, or shall be found eating with Jews, or feasting with them, or secretly conversing and condemning the Christian religion instead of openly confuting them and condemning their vain faith, then let the trembling of Cain and the leprosy of Gehazi cleave to me, as well as the legal punishments to which I acknowledge myself liable. And may I be an anathema in the world to come, and may my soul be set down with Satan and the devils. (Stefano Assemani 105)

Additionally, in approximately 365 AD, the Catholic Council of Laodicea wrote, in one of their canons, that Christians must not judaize by **RESTING ON THE SABBATH**, but **MUST WORK ON THAT DAY,** rather honoring the Lord's Day. But if any were found to be Judaizers, they were to be anathema (against) from Christ.

Think about this carefully. **A COUNCIL** of the Christian Church **DECIDED THAT THEY COULD CHANGE GOD'S FOURTH COMMANDMENT**, commanding people to work on the true seventh day Sabbath, ordained by God from Creation, and confirmed in the Written Torah in Exodus 20 as a day of rest!!!

Constantine is responsible, as well, for changing the timing of the annual celebration of Yeshua's resurrection to a pagan date of "Easter":

> Constantine enforced the prohibition of the First Council of Nicaea against celebrating the Lord's Supper on the day before the Jewish Passover (14 *Nisan*) (see Quartodecimanism and Easter controversy). This marked a definite break of Christianity from the Judaic tradition. From then on the Roman Julian Calendar, a solar calendar, was given precedence over the lunar Hebrew Calendar among the Christian churches of the Roman Empire. Constantine made new laws regarding the Jews. They were forbidden to own Christian slaves or to circumcise their slaves. (Wikipedia contributors, "Constantine the Great")

Also, consider this concerning the parting of the ways between Jews and Christians:

> ....is reflected in the ways that the Church father , well into the fourth century, warn against Christian participation in Jewish observances. **FOR CENTURIES, CHRISTIANS' CELEBRATION OF EASTER COINCIDED EXACTLY WITH PASSOVER, AND THEIR OBSERVANCE OF SABBATH CONTINUED TO TAKE PLACE ON SATURDAY. IT TOOK AN ORDER OF CONSTANTINE, REFERRED TO EARLIER, AND DECREES OF THE FOURTH-CENTURY CHURCH COUNCILS TO DRAW FAST DISTINCTIONS BETWEEN JEWISH AND CHRISTIAN OBSERVANCES...Ultimately, both Jews and Christians rejected the middle group of believers who sought to honor the organic link between the religion of Jesus and the religion of Jews - what Jesus, his mother, and his first followers, including Paul, all took for granted. JEWISH CHRISTIANS, LIKE THOSE WHO CELEBRATED THE EUCHARIST AS A PASSOVER MEAL, AND CHRISTIAN JEWS, LIKE THOSE WHO CONTINUED WORSHIPPING IN THE TEMPLE UNTIL ITS DESTRUCTION OR REVERING JERUSALEM UNTIL ITS FINAL OBLITERATION, DISAPPEARED FROM THIS STORY AND HISTORY, IF ONLY OVER A VERY LONG TIME.** Their fate is common in history for groups holding the middle ground once a dispute has been polarized.....those who refuse to identify with the polar extremes are in grave danger.
>
> Despite the gradual nature of the Jewish-Christian split, it is still possible

to detect, **EARLY IN THE SECOND CENTURY**, a definitive event that in effect set the course. Within a few decades of the composition of John, the last canonical gospel, and within a few years of the final Roman destruction of Jerusalem, in 135, **A CHRISTIAN PREACHER NAMED MARCION (85-160) CARRIED THE IDEA OF SUPERSESSIONIST "FULFILLMENT" TO ITS LOGICAL CONCLUSION, ARGUING THAT THE JEWISH SCRIPTURES NO LONGER HAD VALIDITY AS THE REVEALED WORD OF GOD.** As Jesus replaced the Temple, and as a God of love replaced a God of Law, the foundational writings of the kerygma – **MARCION PROPOSED THE GOSPEL OF LUKE AND A DE-JUDAIZED VERSION OF PAUL'S LETTERS – REPLACED THE TORAH AND OTHER BOOKS OF THE BIBLE.** This was a new Bible for a new Israel. A great debate ensued, and a crisis, too. What did Christians believe about Israel and its Scriptures? If the denigrations were true, why not abandon those texts, as God had abandoned those people? **EVENTUALLY MARCION'S OPPONENTS – CLEMENT OF ROME, JUSTIN MARTYR, IRANAEUS, AND OTHERS – CARRIED THE DAY. THE JEWISH SCRIPTURES, AS THE SOURCE OF THE PROPHECIES THAT JESUS FULFILLED, WERE NECESSARY FOR CHRISTIAN FAITH…IN THE SECOND CENTURY, MARCION WON HALF THE BATTLE, FOR HIS IDEA OF A CANONICAL SET OF CHRISTIAN SCRIPTURES WAS ACCEPTED. THE CREATION OF A NEW TESTAMENT TO STAND PERMANENTLY IN TENSION WITH WHAT IS NOW DESIGNATED AS THE OLD TESTAMENT CRYSTALLIZED THE FORETELL-FULFILL STRUCTURE. THE TAGS "OLD" AND "NEW" INSTITUTIONALIZED THE CHRISTIAN HABIT OF JEWISH DENIGRATION.** (Carroll 145-146)

I PERSONALLY BELIEVE THE FATHER IS OPENING OUR EYES TO ALL OF THIS IN OUR TIME SO WE CAN CHANGE AND BECOME OBEDIENT TO HIS DESIRES. There are **MANY** other practices in the Christian Church today that have pagan, idolatrous roots that The Father is revealing so that we can get rid of them and go back to the original pure Written Torah. The practices that have pagan roots that were (and still are) incorporated into the Catholic Church are so vast (and to some extent) are still in the Protestant Churches , and they are discussed partially in **APPENDIX I - AUTHORITY IN THE CHURCH.** However, this is a subject that I believe you will want to discover for yourself and make changes as you see that **THE WRITTEN TORAH IS STILL VALID!!**

Continuing now concerning the decisions of the first Jerusalem Council, my belief is that Acts 15:21 explains much more than we have understood for the gentile believers!:

<u>Act 15:21 KJV - For MOSES of old time hath in every city them that preach him, BEING READ IN THE SYNAGOGUES EVERY SABBATH DAY.</u>

I believe that this could have meant that THE APOSTLES knew that the completely gentile believers in Yeshua were coming out of completely pagan culture and had not grown up learning the Torah the way the Jewish believers had. THEY WERE LIKE CHILDREN, THAT YOU DON'T HOLD RESPONSIBLE TO DO THINGS THAT THEY HAVEN'T LEARNED YET!

SO, IF THEY JUST KEPT THE FOUR TORAH COMMANDMENTS IN ACTS 15: 20, THEY COULD THEN GO TO THE SYNAGOGUE ON THE SABBATH AND LEARN THE REST OF THE WRITTEN TORAH (REFERRED TO AS "MOSES"). MY BELIEF IS THAT ONCE THEY LEARNED MORE AND MORE OF THE TORAH, THEN THE FATHER, YEHOVAH ELOHIM, WOULD HOLD THEM RESPONSIBLE TO DO IT, JUST LIKE WE AS GOOD PARENTS EXPECT OUR CHILDREN TO START PUTTING INTO PRACTICE THE THINGS THAT THEY LEARN AS THEY GROW. JUST IMAGINE A TEENAGER THAT STILL WANTS SOMEONE TO FEED HIM INSTEAD OF FEEDING HIMSELF AND YOU WILL GET THE IDEA! THIS IS A VERY IMPORTANT PRINCIPLE THAT WE DON'T CONSIDER.

Honestly, if the HOLY SPIRIT were not referenced by James in verse 28 as partial author, along with the Apostles, of giving the gentile believers only these four commandments to keep, I wouldn't even consider believing it. Why? Because of all the other scriptures that uphold the keeping of ALL OF THE WRITTEN TORAH by not only the tribes of Israel, but also those gentiles (strangers) that joined themselves to Israel!!!

CHAPTER 11

The Obligation to Keep the Written Torah – Completely Gentile Believers – According to the Holy Spirit in the Written Torah and the Prophets

WE MUST NOTE THAT THE SAME HOLY SPIRIT OF YEHOVAH GIVEN IN THE BOOK OF ACTS IS THE AUTHOR OF ALL THE FORMER SCRIPTURES – THE WRITTEN TORAH AND THE PROPHETS!!!

REMEMBER THAT THE HOLY SPIRIT IS THE SPIRIT OF TRUTH AND BRINGS CLARITY, NOT CONFUSION!!

ONE PROPHECY BY THE PROPHET ISAIAH, UNDER INSPIRATION OF THE HOLY SPIRIT OF YEHOVAH, SAYS THAT THE SONS OF THE STRANGER THAT JOIN THEMSELVES TO ISRAEL SHOULD KEEP, NOT ONLY THE SABBATH, BUT ALL OF THE COVENANT (ISAIAH 56:6-8 quoted below)!!!

SINCE THE HOLY SPIRIT OF YEHOVAH IS REFERENCED BY JAMES IN THE JERUSALEM COUNCIL'S DECISION IN ACTS 15, THEN MY OPINION IS THAT HE MUST HAVE MEANT THAT THE GENTILES WERE TO START WITH THESE BASIC COMMANDS AND THEN START LEARNING THE REST OF THE WRITTEN TORAH. OTHERWISE, IT MAY NOT HAVE BEEN THE HOLY SPIRIT...

(See Appendix I about later Church Councils that CLAIM that the Holy Spirit inspired them to change Yehovah's Sabbath!)

I believe we have to always judge any "spirit" by the Words of Yeshua and the Written Torah, even if someone is claiming that they have heard from the Holy Spirit!

REMEMBER THAT MANY HOLY SPIRIT INSPIRED SCRIPTURES IN THE WRITTEN TORAH ALSO STATE THAT ANY GENTILES THAT WANT TO

WORSHIP YEHOVAH **MUST KEEP THE COMMANDMENTS** AND THEY ARE ACTUALLY GRAFTED INTO THE TRUE ISRAEL OF GOD! :

[Exo 12:49 KJV] 49 **ONE LAW** SHALL BE TO HIM THAT IS HOMEBORN, **AND UNTO THE STRANGER THAT SOJOURNETH AMONG YOU.**

[Lev 18:26 KJV] 26 YE SHALL THEREFORE KEEP MY STATUTES AND MY JUDGMENTS, AND SHALL NOT COMMIT [ANY] OF THESE ABOMINATIONS: **[NEITHER] ANY OF YOUR OWN NATION, NOR ANY STRANGER THAT SOJOURNETH AMONG YOU:**

[Lev 24:22 KJV] 22 YE SHALL HAVE **ONE MANNER OF LAW, AS WELL FOR THE STRANGER, AS FOR ONE OF YOUR OWN COUNTRY:** FOR I [AM] THE LORD YOUR GOD.

****[Num 15:15-16 KJV] 15 **ONE ORDINANCE [SHALL BE BOTH] FOR YOU OF THE CONGREGATION, AND ALSO FOR THE STRANGER THAT SOJOURNETH [WITH YOU], AN ORDINANCE FOR EVER IN YOUR GENERATIONS: AS YE [ARE], SO SHALL THE STRANGER BE BEFORE THE LORD. 16 ONE LAW AND ONE MANNER SHALL BE FOR YOU, AND FOR THE STRANGER THAT SOJOURNETH WITH YOU.******

THE ABOVE VERSES FROM THE WRITTEN TORAH LET US KNOW THAT IT WAS ALWAYS THE FATHER'S IDEA THAT THE STRANGERS COULD JOIN THEMSELVES TO ISRAEL, BUT THEY WERE TO KEEP THE SAME COVENANT (COMMANDMENTS)!!! We all have always heard Yehovah say that he does not change!:

[Mal 3:6 KJV] 6 **FOR I [AM] THE LORD, I CHANGE NOT**; therefore ye sons of Jacob are not consumed.

[Isa 56:1-8 KJV] 1 Thus saith the LORD, Keep ye judgment, and do justice: for my salvation [is] near to come, and my righteousness to be revealed. 2 Blessed [is] the man [that] doeth this, and the son of man [that] layeth hold

on it; that keepeth the sabbath from polluting it, and keepeth his hand from doing any evil. 3 NEITHER LET THE SON OF THE STRANGER, THAT HATH JOINED HIMSELF TO THE LORD, SPEAK, SAYING, THE LORD HATH UTTERLY SEPARATED ME FROM HIS PEOPLE: neither let the eunuch say, Behold, I [am] a dry tree. 4 For thus saith the LORD unto the eunuchs that keep my sabbaths, and CHOOSE [THE THINGS] THAT PLEASE ME, and take hold of my covenant; 5 Even unto them will I give in mine house and within my walls a place and a name better than of sons and of daughters: I will give them an everlasting name, that shall not be cut off. 6 ALSO THE SONS OF THE STRANGER, THAT JOIN THEMSELVES TO THE LORD, TO SERVE HIM, AND TO LOVE THE NAME OF THE LORD, TO BE HIS SERVANTS, EVERY ONE THAT KEEPETH THE SABBATH FROM POLLUTING IT, AND TAKETH HOLD OF MY COVENANT; 7 Even them will I bring to my holy mountain, and make them joyful in my house of prayer: their burnt offerings and their sacrifices [shall be] accepted upon mine altar; for mine house shall be called an house of prayer for all people. 8 The Lord GOD which gathereth the outcasts of Israel saith, YET WILL I GATHER [OTHERS] TO HIM, beside those that are gathered unto him.

The context of these scriptures, when you read the previous chapters, in my opinion, are obviously concerning the time that The Father sends Yeshua back the second time to rule and reign from Zion, His holy mountain, in Jerusalem for 1000 years. It seems clear to me that he is talking about former complete gentiles joined to Israel by the New Covenant made available by the blood of Yeshua. They will also be making sacrifices on his altar, for his house will be called a house of prayer FOR ALL PEOPLE. But, remember they will be keeping His Sabbath holy (not polluting it) and taking hold of His Covenant (keeping his commandments) and keeping their hands from doing any evil (vs. 2). If the completely gentile believers will be keeping the Written Torah then, why would they not now???

THIS IS ALSO GOOD PLACE TO SEE SOMETHING ELSE INTERESTING YESHUA SAYS ABOUT THIS MATTER: [Jhn 10:16 KJV] 16 And other sheep I have, which are not of this fold: them also I must bring, and they shall hear my voice; and THERE SHALL BE ONE FOLD, [AND] ONE SHEPHERD.

IT SOUNDS TO ME LIKE YESHUA IS SAYING THAT THE GENTILES THAT WILL BELIEVE IN HIM WILL COME AND BE PART OF HIS JEWISH FOLD AND THEY WILL BECOME ONE – NOT DIVIDED INTO TWO DIFFERENT GROUPS WITH TWO DIFFERENT SETS OF RULES....WE ALL WILL LISTEN TO THAT ONE SHEPHERD.

Think about it. What other organization do you know of that doesn't expect ALL the members to keep the same rules! **WE CERTAINLY WANT TO EXPECT THE SAME PRIVILEGES (PROMISES) GIVEN TO ISRAEL! IF WE WANT THE SAME PRIVILEGES, WHY SHOULD WE NOT EXPECT TO (AT LEAST EVENTUALLY) HAVE THE SAME RESPONSIBILITIES? Should we be trying to NOT obey the Written Torah Yehovah has said is His Will for his children, Israel? I DON'T THINK SO! Not if we really LOVE and WANT TO PLEASE our Father!**

I PERSONALLY HAVE DECIDED THAT, IF I AM GRAFTED INTO ISRAEL BY MY FAITH IN YESHUA, THEN I FIND MY IDENTITY IN ISRAEL – I AM NOW AN ISRAELITE! I have chosen to align myself with Israel and **KEEP THE SAME COMMANDMENTS, STATUTES, AND JUDGMENTS THAT THE FATHER HAS MADE CLEAR THAT HE WANTS NATURAL ISRAEL TO KEEP.** According to Isaiah 44:5, I have "surnamed myself by the name of Israel":

[Isa 44:5 KJV] 5 One shall say, I [am] the LORD'S; and another shall call [himself] by the name of Jacob; and another shall subscribe [with] his hand unto the LORD, and SURNAME [HIMSELF] BY THE NAME OF ISRAEL.

So, complete gentiles CAN still do this today – go to our Congregations on the Sabbath and learn the Written Torah!!!

Remember that I posted on the first of this treatise, in the section called "THE END OF THE MATTER", **THAT THERE ARE MORE TORAH LAWS THAN THOSE LISTED IN ACTS 15:20 THAT THE FATHER EXPECTS EVEN THE COMPLETELY GENTILE BELIEVERS TO KEEP IN ORDER TO BE ABLE TO GO INTO THE NEW JERUSALEM – SO, OBVIOUSLY WE MUST KEEP LEARNING!!!**

COULD IT REALLY BE GOOD FOR COMPLETELY GENTILE BELIEVERS TO LEARN ALL OF THE REST OF THE WRITTEN TORAH AND TO KEEP IT?

YES!!!

How do we know?

Because Yeshua told his JEWISH DISCIPLES not to think that he came to get rid of the Written Torah and that if they would keep it, even the least of the commandments (not just the ten commandments but the statutes and judgments too!) and TEACH THEM TO OTHERS they would be great in the Kingdom of God! If they didn't, they wouldn't! ISRAEL WAS ENTRUSTED WITH PRESERVING THE WRITTEN TORAH! Thank Yehovah they have done that through the millennia, so we could learn it from them! Yeshua said in

Matthew 5:17-20:

Mat 5:17 KJV - **THINK NOT THAT I AM COME TO DESTROY THE LAW, OR THE PROPHETS**: I am not come to destroy, but to fulfill. Mat 5:18 KJV - For verily I say unto you, **TILL HEAVEN AND EARTH PASS, ONE JOT OR ONE TITTLE SHALL IN NO WISE PASS FROM THE LAW, TILL ALL BE FULFILLED. MATTHEW5:19 KJV - WHOSOEVER THEREFORE SHALL BREAK ONE OF THESE LEAST COMMANDMENTS, AND SHALL TEACH MEN SO, HE SHALL BE CALLED THE LEAST IN THE KINGDOM OF HEAVEN: BUT WHOSOEVER SHALL DO AND TEACH [THEM], THE SAME SHALL BE CALLED GREAT IN THE KINGDOM OF HEAVEN.**

Mat 5:20 KJV - For I say unto you, That except your righteousness shall exceed [the righteousness] of the scribes and Pharisees, ye shall in no case enter into the kingdom of heaven.

******That verse, Matthew 5:19, almost NEVER gets preached!**

I can honestly say I have never heard any pastor or evangelist or bible teacher preach or teach on this verse in a regular Christian church, denominational or non-denominational, catholic or evangelical. I have only heard it taught in the Messianic or Hebrew Roots congregations!

BUT YESHUA SAID IT!

SO, IF YOU WANT TO BE GREAT IN THE KINGDOM OF HEAVEN, EVEN AS A COMPLETELY GENTILE BELIEVER, LEARN AND KEEP GOD'S COMMANDMENTS, EVEN THE LEAST OF THEM - AND THEN TEACH THEM TO OTHERS!!!

CHAPTER 12

What Yeshua Really Meant About His "Fulfilling" the Torah and the Prophets

[Mat 5:17-18 KJV] 17 Think not that I am come to destroy the law, or the prophets: I AM NOT COME TO DESTROY, BUT TO FULFIL. 18 For verily I say unto you, Till heaven and earth pass, one jot or one tittle shall in no wise pass from the law, till all be fulfilled.

The argument in Christianity that "Yeshua fulfilled the Torah, so we don't have to", has been around for almost two thousand years! But it is completely false, as I have hopefully shown in this book up to this point! Remember, he had just said NOT to think he came to destroy the Torah or the prophets! Heaven and earth have not passed away!!

I believe **Yeshua explains definitively what He meant by "fulfill" in Luke 24: 44-49.** After His resurrection, He appeared to His disciples, and said this in what I have come to refer to as **The Balanced Gospel:**

[Luk 24:44-49 KJV] 44 And he said unto them, These [are] the words which I spake unto you, while I was yet with you, that ALL THINGS MUST BE FULFILLED, WHICH WERE WRITTEN IN THE LAW OF MOSES, AND [IN] THE PROPHETS, AND [IN] THE PSALMS, CONCERNING ME. 45 Then opened he their understanding, that they might understand the scriptures, 46 And said unto them, THUS IT IS WRITTEN, AND THUS IT BEHOVED CHRIST TO SUFFER, AND TO RISE FROM THE DEAD THE THIRD DAY: 47 AND THAT REPENTANCE AND REMISSION OF SINS SHOULD BE PREACHED IN HIS NAME AMONG ALL NATIONS, beginning at Jerusalem. 48 And ye are witnesses of these things. 49 And, behold, I SEND THE PROMISE OF MY FATHER UPON YOU: but tarry ye in the city of Jerusalem, until YE BE ENDUED WITH POWER FROM ON HIGH.

Here Yeshua makes it clear that HE WAS FULFILLING THE SCRIPTURES CONCERNING HIS LIFE, HIS BURIAL AND HIS RESURRECTION THAT ARE IN THE WRITTEN TORAH AND THE PROPHETS!!!

(I call this The Balanced Gospel because EVERYTHING THAT YESHUA WANTS PREACHED IS HERE IN ONE PLACE: Repentance (the turning away from sins and starting to keep Yehovah's Written Torah) and forgiveness of those sins is to be preached in His Name! He says to receive the promise of the power of the Holy Spirit before preaching, though, so people will believe us like they believed him!)

SO, IN HIS FIRST COMING, YESHUA FULFILLED VERSES THAT ARE WRITTEN ABOUT HIMSELF THAT ARE SCATTERED, ALMOST HIDDEN, THROUGHOUT THE WRITTEN TORAH AND THE PROPHETS! He FULFILLED Micah 5:2 by being born in Bethlehem. He was The Prophet like Moses that we are to hear and obey, FULFILLING Deuteronomy 18:15-19. He FULFILLED Zechariah 9:9 by riding into Jerusalem humbly on a donkey while being hailed as the King by the Jewish people. He FULFILLED the prophecies in Psalm 22 concerning his crucifixion. He FULFILLED Isaiah 53 as "the arm of the Lord" who died to become the complete sacrifice for sin. He FULFILLED Psalm 110:1 by his resurrection, being raised up to heaven to sit at the right hand of Yehovah until he is sent back to finish the rest of this Psalm . These and many, many other prophecies Yeshua FULFILLED in his first coming!

He WILL FULFILL the rest of the prophecies about himself in His Second Coming on "the Day of the Lord (Yehovah)"! Just as He came "in the Name of Yehovah" in his first coming, He will come "in the Name of Yehovah" at his second coming (Psalm 118:26, Micah 5:4). This is why in many of the prophecies about how Yehovah will come and save His people, Yeshua will be the one who comes "in His Name" to actually carry it out!!! He is referred to in Isaiah 40:10 of the King James version of the Bible as "the arm of the Lord (Yehovah)" that will rule for Him! In Isaiah 52:13–16, Yehovah describes how Yeshua will be shown to all the world as the Exalted King at his second coming, while acknowledging how he was brutally tortured at his first coming:

[Isa 52:13-15 KJV] 13 BEHOLD, MY SERVANT SHALL DEAL PRUDENTLY, HE SHALL BE EXALTED AND EXTOLLED, AND BE VERY HIGH. 14 AS MANY WERE ASTONIED AT THEE; HIS VISAGE WAS SO MARRED MORE THAN ANY MAN, AND HIS FORM MORE THAN THE SONS OF MEN: 15 SO SHALL HE SPRINKLE MANY NATIONS; THE KINGS SHALL SHUT THEIR MOUTHS AT HIM: FOR [THAT] WHICH HAD NOT BEEN TOLD THEM SHALL THEY SEE; AND [THAT] WHICH THEY HAD NOT HEARD SHALL THEY CONSIDER.

SO YESHUA WILL RETURN and WILL FULFILL ALL OF THE PROPHECIES OF THE DAY OF THE LORD (YEHOVAH) and REIGN FOR 1000 YEARS!

OBVIOUSLY, ALL OF THE WRITTEN TORAH AND THE PROPHETS HAVE NOT YET BEEN FULFILLED!!!

CHAPTER 13

Christianity's Need to Understand the Difference Between the Oral Torah and the Written Torah

MATTHEW 5:20 EXPLAINS A LOT OF WHAT HAS BEEN CHRISTIANITY'S PROBLEM. WE HAVE NOT UNDERSTOOD THAT YESHUA WAS NOT COMING AGAINST OR BREAKING THE WRITTEN TORAH, EVEN WITH HIS HEALING ON THE SABBATH. IT WAS ALWAYS THE ORAL LAWS THAT WERE ADDED TO THE WRITTEN TORAH BY THE PHARISEES AND THE SADDUCEES THAT YESHUA CONDEMNED!!

[Mat 5:20 KJV] 20 For I say unto you, That except your righteousness shall exceed [the righteousness] of the scribes and Pharisees, ye shall in no case enter into the kingdom of heaven.

I HAVE ALREADY WRITTEN ABOUT THIS EARLIER , BUT I AM GOING TO ADDRESS IT HERE AGAIN BECAUSE THE MISUNDERSTANDING ABOUT IT HAS BEEN SO GREAT. The Pharisees had added so many rules (thousands!) to the Written Torah, saying that these additions were extra laws that Yehovah had told Moses that he did not write down. Jewish tradition says Moses passed them to Joshua, Joshua to the elders, the elders to the prophets, and the prophets handed it down to the men of the Great Assembly , according to the opening statement in Mishnaic tractate Pirkei Avot ("Sayings of the Fathers") and were called the "Oral Torah." Eventually, after many years (AT THE TIME OF YESHUA, THEY STILL WERE NOT WRITTEN DOWN!), they did write them down and they are now embodied in documents such as The Mishnah and The Talmud (of which there are various versions). There are even more documents that I am not familiar with. A research into the "Oral Torah" in different encyclopedias will give a more complete understanding of how these laws have come down through the centuries. THE POINT IS, THEY MADE KEEPING THE TRUE WRITTEN TORAH SOMETIMES IMPOSSIBLE AND DEFINITELY BURDENSOME, ACCORDING TO YESHUA - and YEHOVAH HAD SAID TO NOT ADD ANYTHING TO THE WRITTEN TORAH NOR TAKE ANYTHING AWAY FROM IT!:

[DEU 12:32 KJV] 32 WHAT THING SOEVER I COMMAND YOU, OBSERVE TO DO IT: THOU SHALT NOT ADD THERETO, OR DIMINISH FROM IT.

BUT THE ORAL TORAH DID ADD TO THE WRITTEN TORAH!!!:

Because **CHRISTIANITY** is comprised of mostly completely gentile believers, Christians have been **SO IGNORANT OF THE DIFFERENCE BETWEEN THE ORAL TORAH AND THE WRITTEN TORAH, WHICH HAS CAUSED SO MUCH CONFUSION FOR OVER 2000 YEARS OF HISTORY. I AM GOING TO REPEAT THIS QUOTATION THAT EXPLAINS THE ORAL TORAH WITH NO CONCERN FOR BEING REDUNDANT. We must begin to understand this!!!**:

> According to Rabbinic Judaism, the **Oral Torah** or **Oral Law** (Hebrew: תורה שבעל פה, *Torah she-be-`al peh*, lit "**Torah that is spoken**") represents those laws, statutes, and legal interpretations that **were not recorded in the Five Books of Moses, the "Written Torah" (Hebrew: תורה שבכתב, *Torah she-bi-khtav*, lit. "Torah that is written")**, but **NONETHELESS ARE REGARDED BY ORTHODOX JEWS AS PRESCRIPTIVE and CO-GIVEN.** This holistic Jewish code of conduct encompass a wide swath of ritual, worship, God-man and interpersonal relationships, from dietary laws to Sabbath and festival observance to marital relations, agricultural practices, and civil claims and damages.
>
> According to Jewish tradition, the Oral Torah was passed down orally in an unbroken chain from generation to generation until its contents were finally committed to writing following the destruction of the Second Temple in 70 CE, when Jewish civilization was faced with an existential threat.
>
> The major repositories of the Oral Torah are the *Mishnah*, compiled between 200–220 CE by Rabbi Yehudah haNasi, and the *Gemara*, a series of running commentaries and debates concerning the Mishnah, which together are the *Talmud*, the preeminent text of Rabbinic Judaism. In fact, two "versions" of the Talmud exist: one produced in Jerusalem c. 300–350 CE (the Jerusalem Talmud), and second, more extensive Talmud compiled in Babylonia and published c. 450–500 CE (the Babylonian Talmud).

Belief that the Oral Torah was transmitted orally from God to Moses on Mount Sinai during the Exodus from Egypt is a fundamental tenet of faith of Orthodox Judaism, and was recognized as one of the Thirteen Principles of Faith by Maimonides. However, not all branches of Rabbinic Judaism accept the divine provenance of the Oral Torah, such that Conservative and (to a greater extent) Reform Jews give deference to the Talmudic sages while empowering themselves to formulate and adopt their own rulings and interpretations.

There have also been historical dissenters to the Oral Torah in its entirety, including adherents to Karaite Judaism, who attempt to derive their religious practice strictly from the Written Torah, using Scripture's most natural meaning to form their basis of Jewish law. (Wikipedia contributors, "Oral Torah")

(SEE APPENDIX IV – ORAL TORAH)

(You also may want to do more of your own research in other sources such as the Encyclopedia Judaica and the Jewish Encyclopedia.)

This Oral Torah is one reason Yeshua said, " Come to me, you who are weary and heavy laden and I will give you rest!" We have been so concerned that we weren't being "legalists" that we have completely misunderstood this. Legalism isn't a bad word when it is legalism (keeping of the law) based on the Written Torah!!! MAN-MADE LEGALISM is a term that probably could describe this Oral Torah that was added to the Written Torah which was weighing down the people, NOT THE WRITTEN TORAH! THESE EXTRA ADDITIONAL LAWS DID ADD TO THE WRITTEN TORAH AND WERE REFERRED TO AS THE "TRADITIONS OF THE ELDERS." IN HEBREW, THE WORD USUALLY IS A "TAKKANAH" (PLURAL *TAKKANOT*), WHICH IS A MAJOR LEGISLATIVE ENACTMENT WITHIN "HALAKHA" (JEWISH ORAL LAW) WHICH COULD ACTUALLY CHANGE THE WRITTEN TORAH! THESE ARE WHAT YESHUA CAME AGAINST EVERY TIME HE COULD! HE CALLED THE SCRIBES AND PHARISEES OF THAT DAY HYPOCRITES BECAUSE THEY PLACED THEM HIGHER THAN THE WRITTEN TORAH AND/OR THEY DIDN'T EVEN KEEP THEM BECAUSE THEY HAD DEVISED WAYS TO GET AROUND KEEPING THEM THEMSELVES! (See all of Matthew 23).

Mat 15:1 KJV – Then came to Jesus scribes and Pharisees, which were of Jerusalem, saying,

Mat 15:2 KJV – Why do thy disciples <u>TRANSGRESS THE TRADITION OF THE ELDERS? For they wash not their hands when they eat bread.</u>

Mat 15:3 KJV – But he answered and said unto them, <u>WHY DO YE ALSO TRANSGRESS THE COMMANDMENT OF GOD BY YOUR TRADITION?</u>

Mat 15:4 KJV – <u>FOR GOD COMMANDED, saying, HONOUR THY FATHER AND MOTHER: and, HE THAT CURSETH FATHER OR MOTHER, LET HIM DIE THE DEATH.</u>

<u>***NOTE THAT HE UPHELD THE WRITTEN TORAH HERE – EVEN THE DEATH PENALTY! !*****</u>**

<u>THIS IS EXODUS 20:12, DEUTERONOMY 27:16 AND LEVITICUS 20:9.</u>

<u>[Exo 20:12 KJV] 12 Honour thy father and thy mother: that thy days may be long upon the land which the LORD thy God giveth thee.</u>

<u>[Deu 27:16 KJV] 16 Cursed [be] he that setteth light by his father or his mother. And all the people shall say, Amen.</u>

<u>[Lev 20:9 KJV] 9 FOR EVERY ONE THAT CURSETH HIS FATHER OR HIS MOTHER SHALL BE SURELY PUT TO DEATH: HE HATH CURSED HIS FATHER OR HIS MOTHER; HIS BLOOD [SHALL BE] UPON HIM.</u>

<u>Remember that these are Yeshua's words and not mine!! It certainly looks like Yeshua is saying that even the death penalty for the many sins that require it should be administered (although only in accordance with the administration prescribed in the Written Torah). The murderer that was beside him on the cross, was not told he didn't have to die for his sin, but he was given the promise of being with Yeshua in Paradise because he believed in Him (Luke 23:43). We know that Yeshua did not condemn "the woman caught in adultery" [John 8:3-11], but what is not taken into account is that, according to the Written Torah, Yeshua could not have condemned her since He was NOT A WITNESS to her adultery:</u>

<u>Exo 20:14 KJV] 14 Thou shalt not commit adultery.</u>

<u>[Lev 20:10 KJV] 10 And the man that committeth adultery with [another] man's wife, [even he] that committeth adultery with his neighbour's wife, the adulterer and the adulteress shall surely be put to death.</u>

[Deu 17:6-7 KJV] 6 AT THE MOUTH OF TWO WITNESSES, OR THREE WITNESSES, shall he that is worthy of death be put to death; [but] at the mouth of one witness he shall not be put to death. 7 THE HANDS OF THE WITNESSES SHALL BE FIRST UPON HIM TO PUT HIM TO DEATH.

Also, we need to remember that the Pharisees were trying to trick Yeshua to break the Written Torah and He wasn't about to let them. If he had told them not to stone the woman, it is possible that they could justly say he was advising people to break the Written Torah. But he didn't – he just worked on their consciences by telling those supposed witnesses that the one without sin (maybe even that same sin....?) should cast the first stone.

HOWEVER, REMEMBER THAT HE TOLD HER TO "GO AND SIN NO MORE!" (REPENT!)

Back to the death penalty, though, it is important to note that The Father is the one who, from just after the flood, made murder a death penalty sin (LONG before the Written Torah was given):

[**GEN 9:5-6 KJV**] 5 And surely your blood of your lives will I require; at the hand of every beast will I require it, and at the hand of man; at the hand of every man's brother will I require the life of man. 6 **WHOSO SHEDDETH MAN'S BLOOD, BY MAN SHALL HIS BLOOD BE SHED: FOR IN THE IMAGE OF GOD MADE HE MAN**.

I don't claim to know how the death penalty should be applied according to the Written Torah at this point in time. There are many laws in the Written Torah that are not able to be performed properly without the Temple, the priesthood, the officers and judges, etc. being in place in Israel. But, that does not take away from Yeshua's words endorsing the keeping of the Written Torah. We should remember that most of the original laws of the United States have their root in the Written Torah, particularly Deuteronomy, including the death penalty for murder. Our Constitution is based largely, though not completely, on the Written Torah.

Personally, I am very thankful that Yeshua said there is not one sin that could not be forgiven, when we repent, EXCEPT FOR BLASPHEMY OF THE HOLY SPIRIT! King DAVID ASKED FOR MERCY in Psalm 51 although he had committed adultery and had a man

murdered, and THE FATHER SOVEREIGNLY DECIDED to forgive him:

[2Sa 12:13 KJV] 13 And David said unto Nathan, I have sinned against the LORD. And Nathan said unto David, THE LORD ALSO HATH PUT AWAY THY SIN; THOU SHALT NOT DIE.

I have broken many of the commandments that would require the death penalty, and so have most of the people I know. Breaking the TRUE SEVENTH DAY SABBATH is not the least of them [Exodus 31:14-16] and not honoring my Mother and Father properly is another. BREAKING THE SABBATH IS CONDEMNED AS A DEATH PENALTY SIN TWICE IN THE SCRIPTURES BELOW:

[Exo 31:12-17 KJV] 12 And the LORD spake unto Moses, saying, 13 Speak thou also unto the children of Israel, saying, Verily my sabbaths ye shall keep: for it [is] a sign between me and you throughout your generations; that [ye] may know that I [am] the LORD that doth sanctify you. 14 YE SHALL KEEP THE SABBATH THEREFORE; FOR IT [IS] HOLY UNTO YOU: EVERY ONE THAT DEFILETH IT SHALL SURELY BE PUT TO DEATH: for whosoever doeth [any] work therein, that soul shall be cut off from among his people. 15 Six days may work be done; but in the SEVENTH [is] the sabbath of rest, holy to the LORD: WHOSOEVER DOETH [ANY] WORK IN THE SABBATH DAY, HE SHALL SURELY BE PUT TO DEATH. 16 Wherefore the children of Israel shall keep the sabbath, to observe the sabbath throughout their generations, [for] a perpetual covenant. 17 It [is] a sign between me and the children of Israel for ever: for [in] six days the LORD made heaven and earth, and on the seventh day he rested, and was refreshed.

BLASPHEMY OF GOD; ADULTERY; MURDER; SERVING OTHER GODS (IDOLATRY) AND WORSHIPING THE SUN,MOON, OR STARS; HOMOSEXUALITY/SODOMY; BESTIALITY; LYING WITH A WOMAN AND HER MOTHER; AND WITCHCRAFT/SORCERY ALSO ALL HAVE DEATH PENALTIES ACCORDING TO THE WRITTEN TORAH. So, until the Holy Spirit reveals more on how these laws should be administered at this time, I think it would, at the least, behoove us to start learning and becoming very aware of Yehovah's Holy Written Torah and repent, change quickly, and pray for mercy if we find ourselves in any of these sins!

Now, continuing with Yeshua's condemnation of the "Oral Torah" (the commandments of men-the traditions of the elders):

Mat 15:5 KJV - But ye say, Whosoever shall say to [his] father or [his] mother, [It is] a gift, by whatsoever thou mightest be profited by me;

Mat 15:6 KJV - And honour not his father or his mother, [he shall be free]. <u>THUS HAVE YE MADE THE COMMANDMENT OF GOD OF NONE EFFECT BY YOUR TRADITION.</u>

Mat 15:7 KJV - [Ye] hypocrites, well did Esaias prophesy of you, saying,

Mat 15:8 KJV - This people draweth nigh unto me with their mouth, and honoureth me with [their] lips; but their heart is far from me.

Mat 15:9 KJV - <u>BUT IN VAIN THEY DO WORSHIP ME, TEACHING [FOR] DOCTRINES THE COMMANDMENTS OF MEN.</u>

Read Isaiah 29:13-14 below to see the prophecy that Yeshua was referring to:

<u>[Isa 29:13-14 KJV] 13 Wherefore the Lord said, Forasmuch as this people draw near [me] with their mouth, and with their lips do honour me, but have removed their heart far from me, and THEIR FEAR TOWARD ME IS TAUGHT BY THE PRECEPT OF MEN: 14 Therefore, behold, I will proceed to do a marvellous work among this people, [even] a marvellous work and a wonder: for the wisdom of their wise [men] shall perish, and the understanding of their prudent [men] shall be hid.</u>

<u>NOTICE THAT YESHUA WAS UPHOLDING THE WRITTEN TORAH, THE COMMANDMENTS YEHOVAH GAVE TO MOSES, BUT NOT THE ORAL TORAH, THEIR TRADITIONS, THE COMMANDMENTS OF MEN!</u>

This also brings up another point I alluded to earlier. **MANY TIMES THESE TRADITIONS, THIS ORAL TORAH, ACTUALLY WOULD MAKE YOU VIOLATE THE WRITTEN TORAH IF YOU KEPT THEM!** – as Yeshua brought out in Matthew 15:3-6 above. **I have had experience with Orthodox Jewish people who do revere the Oral Torah <u>ABOVE</u> the Written Torah, <u>possibly not completely realizing that is what they are doing</u>**. But, as I persisted in asking questions to make sure I understood, they confirmed that they did believe the Oral Torah **HAD TO BE OBSERVED** – that they were binding commandments!

Unfortunately, there are also some Messianic Jews, as well as some Gentile Believers (usually those who have come to the understanding of the Hebrew Roots of the Christian faith), who come to the conclusion that we **ARE TO KEEP THE ORAL TORAH** based on Matthew 23:1-3! In the King James version of the Bible, Yeshua **SEEMS** to be supporting the Oral Torah in this one scripture only. This is in direct contradiction to everything else he taught.

[Mat 23:1-4 KJV] 1 Then spake **Jesus** to the multitude, and to his disciples, 2 Saying, **The scribes and the Pharisees sit in Moses' seat**: 3 **All therefore whatsoever they bid you observe, [that] observe and do; but do not ye after their works: for they say, and do not.** 4 For they bind heavy burdens and grievous to be borne, and lay [them] on men's shoulders; but they [themselves] will not move them with one of their fingers.

According to Michael Rood in The Chronological Gospels, the "seat of Moses" was a literal seat in the synagogue in which the sages and the Pharisees sat to proclaim their Oral Torah, which became binding law upon anyone who willingly submitted to their self-proclaimed authority (209).

He also states in his commentary on these verses:

> {Mt. 23:3.1} Hebrew Gospel of Matthew , George Howard, Mercer University Press, Pg. 112, Matthew 23:3 The ancient Hebrew text of Matthew's Gospel states plainly that the followers of Yeshua are commanded to not follow the ***takanot* and *ma'asim* of the Pharisees oral torah**, but that they should "do what *he* (Moses) says to do" in clear opposition to what the Pharisees teach. The Greek texts, which were translated from the Aramaic text, which was translated from the Hebrew original, missed the entire point of Yeshua's admonition; each of these translations read: do what *they* (the Pharisees) command you to do. In the Hebrew texts of Matthew's Gospel, the difference between obeying what *he* < yod –aleph-mim-resh – *yomar* > says to do, and what *they* < yod-aleph-mim-resh-vav – *yomru* > say to do, is just a single small jot of the scribe's quill. In the original Hebrew text there is no *vav* at the end of the word yomar (he) and without the *vav* there is no word *yomru* (they). Hebrew scholars who work with ancient texts understand how Aramaic and Greek translators could have easily missed that pen stroke – and that profound significance of that pen stroke, especially when the translators theology may have already pre-determined how they were going to transmit the text. Translating the text as if there were a *vav* on the end of the word may seem like a very small difference on the surface. In reality,

the absence of that small stroke of the quill is the difference between being obedient to the commandments of the Almighty, which no man has the authority to either add or to diminish (Deuteronomy 4:2, 12:32), and living under a man-made system of religion that by its very nature is in violation of the commandments given to us at Mount Sinai.

The Encyclopedia Judaica defines *takanot* as *rules enacted by the Pharisees which change or negate biblical law*, while *ma'asim* are *acts of the rabbis that serve as a legal precedent for righteous behavior.* Yeshua clearly and pointedly commanded his disciples, "Do not follow the *takanot* and *ma'asim* of the Pharisees!"....If we miss this one single stroke of the pen, which is the difference between following Moses or following the religious system of the Pharisees, we have missed the entire teaching ministry of the Messiah. He came to declare the truth that sets men free from the bondage of religion – every man-made religion that populates the planet. In George Howard's translation of the Hebrew Matthew, he adds the word [they] in brackets when his Hebrew text clearly reads < yod-aleph-mim-resh – *yomar* > *he* [Moses]. (Rood 209)

SO, WE CAN JUSTLY CONCLUDE THAT YESHUA WAS COMPLETELY AGAINST THE ORAL TORAH!

(It is imperative to know this or else we would all be in big trouble, since <u>we all</u>, Jew or Gentile believers, would be needing to learn and keep the Oral Torah in order to keep all of Yeshua's instructions!!!)

<u>Remember, Yehovah Elohim said concerning the written Torah:</u>

<u>**DEU 12:32 KJV - WHAT THING SOEVER I COMMAND YOU, OBSERVE TO DO IT: THOU SHALT NOT ADD THERETO, NOR DIMINISH FROM IT.****</u>**

<u>A SIMPLE DEDUCTION FROM ALL MY RESEARCH IS THAT SIN IS MAN DOING THINGS HIS OWN WAY, NOT GOD'S WAY!!!</u>

This is shown, from the beginning of creation, with **<u>CAIN</u>** offering a sacrifice to Yehovah Elohim **<u>IN HIS OWN WAY, NOT GOD'S WAY!</u>** This was rebellion. Obviously, Adam and Eve had taught him what was an acceptable sacrifice to Yehovah. Since he did it his own way, God called it sin. **<u>IN FACT, THIS IS THE FIRST PLACE THE WORD SIN IS USED IN THE BIBLE!</u> SO SIN IS REBELLION TO YEHOVAH'S WAYS, EXPRESSED BY NOT DOING <u>EXACTLY</u> WHAT HE SAID IN HIS WRITTEN TORAH– EITHER BY TAKING AWAY FROM HIS COMMANDMENTS OR BY ADDING TO THEM, MAKING THEM OUR OWN**

WAYS.....

<u>**ANOTHER SIMPLE OBSERVATION IS THAT, GENERALLY, THE ORTHODOX JEWS HAVE ADDED TO THE WRITTEN TORAH AND THE CHRISTIAN CHURCH HAS DIMINISHED FROM THE WRITTEN TORAH! ****</u>**

CHAPTER 14

Yeshua Condemns the Doctrine of the Sadducees Also – Did They Develop an "Oral Temple Service"?

I am not a scholar in Judaism, so I know that I am making simplistic generalizations about the many different sects of Judaism. However, I am perfectly aware that **YESHUA** included two of the sects prevalent at the time, **THE PHARISEES AND THE SADDUCEES**, in his list of **THOSE WHOSE LEAVEN (DOCTRINE OR TEACHING) BELIEVERS ARE TO BEWARE OF:**

[Mat 16:12 KJV] 12 Then understood they how that he bade [them] not beware of the leaven of bread, but **OF THE DOCTRINE OF THE PHARISEES AND OF THE SADDUCEES.**

(He also said beware of the doctrine of Herod! See Mark 8:15. This is possibly an inference to Rome - part of which I think we have covered previously with the Roman paganism that, unfortunately, **did** get very incorporated into Christianity!)

I have spoken about the Pharisees and their obvious additions to the Written Torah. **BUT, THE ERROR IN THE SADDUCEES' DOCTRINE HAS BEEN A LITTLE HARDER TO PINPOINT FOR ME.** My understanding is that the word "Sadducee" actually comes from the term "tzadokim" which means "righteous ones". Most sources even say that they originally were the "sons of Zadok" referred to in the Book of Ezekiel (Ezekiel 44) who were the priests and in charge of the temple down to the 2nd century B.C. called Zadokites. However, by the time of Yeshua, they had already degenerated under the influence of Hellenism and the party name was retained long after the Zadokite high priests had made way for the Hasmonean house. (In fact, at the time of Yeshua, I have heard that the High Priest's office was being sold by the Roman government to the highest bidder, although I have no documentation for that.) Generally, though, the Sadducees still did not agree with the additions to the Written Torah that the Pharisees subscribed to. **HOWEVER, THEY WERE IN CHARGE OF THE TEMPLE SERVICE AND IT SEEMS TO ME THAT MANY OF THE RITUALS IN THE TEMPLE SERVICE I READ ABOUT IN THE JEWISH ENCYCLOPEDIA CAN ONLY BE FOUND IN THE**

TALMUD AND/OR MISHNAH AND <u>MAY ACTUALLY ALSO BE ADDITIONS TO THE VERY SPECIFIC COMMANDS FOR THE PRIESTS THAT THE FATHER YEHOVAH ELOHIM INSTITUTED IN THE WRITTEN TORAH.</u> (See Appendix V – Temple, Administration and Service of).

I have heard it said that these temple service rituals were given by King David, given to him by a vision in which he saw the temple in heaven and Yehovah Elohim told him how to conduct various services. However, in searching for reference to any of this in the books of the Bible, I could only find **<u>I CHRONICLES CHAPTERS 21 THROUGH 28</u> DETAILING <u>IN WRITING</u> <u>EVERYTHING</u> THAT <u>KING DAVID SAID</u> THE FATHER GAVE HIM PROPHETICALLY BY THE HOLY SPIRIT**! See I Chronicle 28:11-21 below as a summary:

[1Ch 28:11-21 KJV] 11 Then David gave to Solomon his son the pattern of the porch, and of the houses thereof, and of the treasuries thereof, and of the upper chambers thereof, and of the inner parlours thereof, and of the place of the mercy seat, 12 And **<u>THE PATTERN OF ALL THAT HE HAD BY THE SPIRIT, of the courts of the house of the LORD, and of all the chambers round about, of the treasuries of the house of God, and of the treasuries of the dedicated things: 13 Also for the courses of the priests and the Levites, and for all the work of the service of the house of the LORD, and for all the vessels of service in the house of the LORD</u>.** 14 [He gave] of gold by weight for [things] of gold, for all instruments of all manner of service; [silver also] for all instruments of silver by weight, for all instruments of every kind of service: 15 Even the weight for the candlesticks of gold, and for their lamps of gold, by weight for every candlestick, and for the lamps thereof: and for the candlesticks of silver by weight, [both] for the candlestick, and [also] for the lamps thereof, according to the use of every candlestick. 16 And by weight [he gave] gold for the tables of shewbread, for every table; and [likewise] silver for the tables of silver: 17 Also pure gold for the fleshhooks, and the bowls, and the cups: and for the golden basons [he gave gold] by weight for every bason; and [likewise silver] by weight for every bason of silver: 18 And for the altar of incense refined gold by weight; and gold for the pattern of the chariot of the cherubims, that spread out [their wings], and covered the ark of the covenant of the LORD. 19 **ALL [THIS, SAID DAVID], <u>THE LORD</u> MADE ME UNDERSTAND <u>IN WRITING BY [HIS] HAND UPON ME</u>, [EVEN] ALL THE WORKS OF THIS PATTERN**. 20 And David said to Solomon his son, Be strong and of good courage, and do [it]: fear not, nor be dismayed: for the LORD God, [even] my God, [will be] with thee; he will not fail thee, nor forsake thee, until thou hast finished all the work for the service of the house of the LORD. 21 And, behold, the courses of the priests and the Levites, [even they shall be with thee] for all the service of the house of God: and [there shall be] with thee for all manner of workmanship every willing skilful man, for any manner of service: also the princes and all the people [will be] wholly at thy commandment.

HOWEVER, <u>DAVID'S WRITTEN ACCOUNT</u> DOES NOT GO INTO ALL THE DETAIL THAT THE TEMPLE SERVICE RITUALS IN THE MISHNAH AND THE TALMUD DO!!! Remember, the Talmud and the Mishnah were originally oral and were not written down until after the first century AD. So, **IF** the temple service rituals listed in the Jewish Encyclopedia, or the Talmud and the Mishnah are **OVER AND ABOVE WHAT YEHOVAH ACTUALLY SHOWED KING DAVID BY THE SPIRIT** that he recorded **IN WRITING** in I Chronicles 21-28 and what was already written in The Torah, **THE PRIESTS, THE SADDUCEES IN YESHUA'S TIME**, would fall under the same prophecy of **ISAIAH 29:13-14 CONDEMNING MAN-MADE LAWS** that Yeshua quotes in Matthew 15:6-9. **<u>You might could even call these additions the ORAL TEMPLE SERVICE!</u>**

I did more searching to see if David actually thought he was a Priest and able to add to Yehovah's laws on his own and I don't believe he did. This is what I found:

[1Ch 15:1-15 KJV] 1 And [David] made him houses in the city of David, and prepared a place for the ark of God, and pitched for it a tent. 2 THEN DAVID SAID, <u>NONE</u> OUGHT TO CARRY THE ARK OF GOD BUT THE LEVITES: FOR <u>THEM</u> HATH THE LORD CHOSEN TO CARRY THE ARK OF GOD, AND TO MINISTER UNTO HIM FOR EVER. 3 And David gathered all Israel together to Jerusalem, to bring up the ark of the LORD unto his place, which he had prepared for it. 4 And David assembled the children of Aaron, and the Levites: 5 Of the sons of Kohath; Uriel the chief, and his brethren an hundred and twenty: 6 Of the sons of Merari; Asaiah the chief, and his brethren two hundred and twenty: 7 Of the sons of Gershom; Joel the chief, and his brethren an hundred and thirty: 8 Of the sons of Elizaphan; Shemaiah the chief, and his brethren two hundred: 9 Of the sons of Hebron; Eliel the chief, and his brethren fourscore: 10 Of the sons of Uzziel; Amminadab the chief, and his brethren an hundred and twelve. 11 And <u>DAVID CALLED FOR ZADOK AND ABIATHAR THE PRIESTS, and for the Levites</u>, for Uriel, Asaiah, and Joel, Shemaiah, and Eliel, and Amminadab, 12 And said unto them, Ye [are] the chief of the fathers of the Levites: sanctify yourselves, [both] ye and your brethren, that ye may bring up the ark of the LORD God of Israel unto [the place that] I have prepared for it. 13 <u>FOR BECAUSE YE [DID IT] NOT AT THE FIRST, THE LORD OUR GOD MADE A BREACH UPON US, FOR THAT WE SOUGHT HIM NOT AFTER THE DUE ORDER</u>. 14 So <u>the priests and the Levites sanctified themselves to bring up the ark of the LORD God of Israel</u>. 15 And

<u>THE CHILDREN OF THE LEVITES BARE THE ARK OF GOD</u> UPON THEIR SHOULDERS WITH THE STAVES THEREON, <u>AS MOSES COMMANDED ACCORDING TO THE WORD OF THE LORD.</u>

[1Ch 15:25-27 KJV] 25 So David, and the elders of Israel, and the captains over thousands, went to bring up the ark of the covenant of the LORD out of the house of Obededom with joy. 26 And it came to pass, <u>WHEN GOD HELPED THE LEVITES THAT BARE THE ARK OF THE COVENANT OF THE LORD, THAT THEY OFFERED SEVEN BULLOCKS AND SEVEN RAMS.</u> 27 And David [was] clothed with a robe of fine linen, and all the Levites that bare the ark, and the singers, and Chenaniah the master of the song with the singers: David also [had] upon him an ephod of linen.

[1Ch 16:37-40 KJV] 37 So he left there before the ark of the covenant of the LORD Asaph and his brethren, to minister before the ark continually, as every day's work required: 38 And Obededom with their brethren, threescore and eight; Obededom also the son of Jeduthun and Hosah [to be] porters: 39 <u>AND ZADOK THE PRIEST, AND HIS BRETHREN THE PRIESTS, BEFORE THE TABERNACLE OF THE LORD IN THE HIGH PLACE THAT [WAS] AT GIBEON, 40 TO OFFER BURNT OFFERINGS UNTO THE LORD UPON THE ALTAR OF THE BURNT OFFERING CONTINUALLY MORNING AND EVENING, AND [TO DO] ACCORDING TO ALL THAT IS WRITTEN IN THE LAW OF THE LORD, WHICH HE COMMANDED ISRAEL</u>;

I have heard that the fact that David wore a ephod of linen put him in the category of a priest, but I believe he obviously did not see himself as that, as he had the priests and the Levites fulfill <u>their</u> Yehovah Elohim ordained duties here.

I have also heard that there are those who believe that David was a priest "in the order of the Melech Zadik." They base this on Psalm 110 where David prophesied this:

[Psa 110:1-7 KJV] 1 [[A Psalm of David.]] <u>The LORD</u> said unto <u>MY LORD</u>, Sit thou at my right hand, until I make thine enemies thy footstool. 2 The LORD shall send the rod of thy strength out of Zion: rule thou in the midst of thine enemies. 3 Thy people [shall be] willing in the day of thy power, in the beauties of holiness from the womb of the morning: <u>THOU hast the dew of thy youth</u>. 4 <u>The LORD hath sworn, and will not repent, THOU [art] a priest for ever after the order of Melchizedek</u>. 5 The Lord at thy right hand shall strike through kings in the day of his wrath. 6 He shall judge among the

heathen, he shall fill [the places] with the dead bodies; he shall wound the heads over many countries. 7 He shall drink of the brook in the way: therefore shall he lift up the head.

But, if you read the entire Psalm, it is obvious that this prophecy is about the resurrected Messiah – Yeshua ha Mashiach – who is coming to rule from Zion as a Righteous King and Priest. The first verse would have read, with some Hebrew left in it, "Yehovah said unto my Adon…" or my Master. See the Strong's Concordance #H113:

אָדוֹן 'âdôwn, aw-done'; or (shortened) אָדֹן 'âdôn; from an unused root (meaning to rule); sovereign, i.e. controller (human or divine):—lord, master, owner. Compare also names beginning with 'Adoni-'.

Yeshua Himself quotes this and clarifies that the Messiah is the Lord that David was referring to in this Psalm. Only the Messiah is the Priest after the order of the Melech Zadik, not David:

[Mar 12:35-37 KJV] 35 And Jesus answered and said, while he taught in the temple, How say the scribes that Christ is the Son of David? 36 For David himself said by the Holy Ghost, The LORD (YEHOVAH)said to my Lord (MASTER), Sit thou on my right hand, till I make thine enemies thy footstool. 37 David therefore himself calleth him Lord (MASTER); and whence is he [then] his son? And the common people heard him gladly.

WE SHOULD NOTE, ALSO, THAT YESHUA CONFIRMED THE WRITTEN TORAH AND THE PROPHETS AND THE PSALMS IN MATTHEW 5:17-19 AND IN LUKE 24:44-49, BUT HE NEVER CONFIRMED THE ORAL TORAH OR THIS (POSSIBLY) ORAL TEMPLE SERVICE THAT HAS BEEN SUBSCRIBED TO KING DAVID! I BELIEVE THAT IF YESHUA HAD NOT BEEN IN AGREEMENT WITH THE WRITTEN PROPHECY GIVEN TO KING DAVID IN I CHRONICLES 21 THROUGH 28 CONCERNING THE BUILDING OF THE TEMPLE AND ITS SERVICE, HE WOULD HAVE NEGATED IT WHILE HE WAS HERE ON EARTH. BUT HE DID NOT! BUT, HE DID CONDEMN THE DOCTRINE OF THE SADDUCEES!

SO, THE SADDUCEES SEEM TO HAVE SUBSCRIBED AN "ORAL TEMPLE SERVICE" TO KING DAVID… IF SO, THEY WOULD HAVE COMMITTED THE SAME ERROR THAT THE PHARISEES DID IN THEIR SUBSCRIBING THE "ORAL TORAH" TO MOSES, WHICH WAS OVER AND ABOVE THE WRITTEN TORAH THAT THE FATHER ACTUALLY DID GIVE HIM AND CAUSED THEM TO INCUR THE FATHER'S ANGER!

[Isa 29:13-14 KJV] 13 Wherefore the Lord said, Forasmuch as this people draw near [me] with their mouth, and with their lips do honour me, but HAVE REMOVED THEIR HEART FAR FROM ME, and THEIR FEAR TOWARD ME IS TAUGHT BY THE PRECEPT OF MEN: 14 Therefore, behold, I will proceed to do a marvellous work among this people, [even] a marvellous work and a wonder: for the wisdom of their wise [men] shall perish, and the understanding of their prudent [men] shall be hid.

In my cursory study of these two groups, I noticed that the Sadducees basically rejected the Pharisees' Oral Torah and the Pharisees rejected much of the Sadducees' Oral Temple Service. One example from the Jewish Encyclopedia states: "The Sadducees opposed the popular festivity of the water libation and the procession preceding the same on each night of the Sukkot feast, as well as the closing festivity, on which the Pharisees laid much stress, of the beating of the willow-trees" (Kohler,"Sadducees").

They had differing views on the determination of the feast days too. Concerning the Sadducees:

> They contended that the seven weeks from the first barley-sheaf-offering ("omer") to Pentecost should, according to Lev. xxiii. 15-16, be counted from "the day after Sabbath," and, consequently, that Pentecost should always be celebrated on the first day of the week (Meg. Ta'an. i.; Men. 65a). In this they obviously followed the old Biblical view which regards the festival of the firstlings as having no connection whatsoever with the Passover feast; whereas the Pharisees, connecting the festival of the Exodus with the festival of the giving of the Law, interpreted the "morrow after the Sabbath" to signify the second day of Passover (see Jubilees, Book of)...They opposed the Pharisaic idea of the 'Erub, the merging of several private precincts into one in order to admit of the carrying of food and vessels from one house to another on the Sabbath ('Er. vi. 2). (Kohler, "Sadducees")

There are so many more examples of their differences, as well as each of their differences with other Jewish groups, such as the Essenes, Herodians, and Boethusians. (However, I would venture to say that mainstream Christianity has them beat with the number of different denominations, all created because of different beliefs and practices!)

My personal opinion is that neither the Pharisees nor the Sadducees used

the pure written word of Yehovah, the Written Torah, as their plumb-line, so they could both be wrong.

A thought that occurred to me as I pondered all of this is **HOW RIDICULOUS IT IS TO THINK THAT THE FATHER YEHOVAH WOULD EXPECT THE PRIESTS TO PERFECTLY REMEMBER EXTRA ORAL INSTRUCTIONS OF HOW TO WORSHIP HIM IN THE TEMPLE**, especially **WHEN HE HAD DETAILED IT SO SPECIFICALLY IN THE WRITTEN TORAH and in DAVID'S PROPHECY.** (Re-read Numbers chapter 7 and **NOTE THE DETAIL WRITTEN** of the offerings each of the twelve tribes brought to the tabernacle of Moses. The offerings are all the same, but they are **REITERATED TWELVE TIMES** for each of the tribes!) So, if He had wanted the priests to observe more rules, would He not have made sure those instructions were written as well??? **YAH FORBID IF THE PRIEST HAD DEMENTIA OR ALZHEIMERS DISEASE!** A quote I heard a long time ago is "**THE PALEST INK IS BETTER THAN THE BEST MEMORY**" and **IT IS CERTAINLY TRUE IN MY LIFE!!** To confirm this thought, we should again note that **YESHUA ONLY RESPONDED** to satan's temptations with, **"IT IS WRITTEN!!!!"**

IT IS POSSIBLE that sometimes the priests simply came up with a protocol/tradition that filled in the blanks where THE FATHER DID NOT SPECIFICALLY SAY how particular services should be accomplished. THE FATHER EVIDENTLY WANTED TO LEAVE SOME FLEXIBILITY IN THE SERVICE. There is nothing necessarily wrong with adding a protocol, as long as it does not cause Yehovah's written commandments to be violated. However, THAT PROTOCOL/TRADITION SHOULD NOT BE CALLED A COMMANDMENT SINCE IT WOULD BE NOT BE SINFUL TO CHANGE IT!!!

THE PROBLEM WITH US HUMANS IS THAT WE LOVE TRADITIONS!!

IF WE EVER DO SOMETHING MORE THAN ONCE, WE WANT TO MAKE A TRADITION OUT OF IT!

THEN, WE WANT TO MAKE IT A COMMANDMENT!!!!

As I researched the Second Temple Service, it seemed to me that this tendency is obvious there. **(SEE APPENDIX V- TEMPLE, ADMINISTRATION AND SERVICE OF).**

However, this is a vast subject that I have not been able to research thoroughly. Although I do know that the Sadducees (the chief priests and captains of the temple) along with the Pharisees, were **constantly trying to entangle Yeshua in his words** and were the ones who actually captured him and condemned him in their council with the High Priest Caiaphas, taking him to Pilate, the Roman governor, to have him executed. **OBVIOUSLY, SOMETHING WAS AMISS IN THEIR HEARTS... SO WHY WOULD WE THINK THEY WERE BEING CAREFUL TO MAKE SURE THEY KEPT THE FATHER'S <u>WRITTEN TORAH</u> PROPERLY WITH THEIR TEMPLE SERVICE...?**

Yeshua, in relating the parable of the Good Samaritan, says the Priest and the Levite just passed by their brother, a Jewish man from Jerusalem who was overtaken by robbers....<u>they had no compassion in their hearts</u>. Something was definitely amiss in the hearts of <u>THIS GENERATION of Priests and Levites</u>... (see Luke 10:29-37).

Yeshua said when He was arrested:

[Luk 22:52-53 KJV] 52 Then Jesus said unto the **CHIEF PRIESTS, AND CAPTAINS OF THE TEMPLE, AND THE ELDERS**, which were come to him, Be ye come out, as against a thief, with swords and staves? 53 When I was daily with you in the temple, ye stretched forth no hands against me: but **<u>THIS IS YOUR HOUR, AND THE POWER OF DARKNESS</u>.**

Even after Yeshua's resurrection, the High Priest and the chief priests were threatened by the apostles' preaching and miracles, and so continued to threaten them with punishment and prison if they continued. **<u>Acts 5:17 substantiates this and substantiates the fact that they were the sect of the Sadducees Yeshua had warned his apostles about</u>:**

[Act 5:17-20 KJV] 17 Then **<u>THE HIGH PRIEST</u> ROSE UP, AND <u>ALL THEY THAT WERE WITH HIM</u>, (<u>WHICH IS THE SECT OF THE SADDUCEES</u>,)** and were filled with indignation, 18 And laid their hands on the apostles, and put them in the common prison. 19 But the angel of the Lord by night opened the prison doors, and brought them forth, and said, 20 Go, stand and speak in the temple to the people all the words of this life.

The temple did come down in 70 A.D. (possibly 68 A.D. according to some reports) just as Yeshua prophesied in Matthew 24. However, by referencing back to the prophet Daniel (Daniel 9:27), Yeshua also let us know that at the very end of this age, there will be a temple again that the king of the north/the beast/the anti-messiah will desecrate with the abomination that causes desolation.

THE INTERESTING THING IS THAT THIS TEMPLE AND THE DAILY SACRIFICES ON ITS BIBLICALLY DEDICATED ALTAR HAVE TO BE ACCEPTABLE TO YEHOVAH PRIOR TO THAT POINT IN TIME. DANIEL 11 SAYS THERE WILL BE THOSE WHO ARE KEEPING THE HOLY COVENANT!!!:

(Yeshua said)[Mat 24:15 KJV] 15 When ye therefore shall see the abomination of desolation, spoken of by Daniel the prophet, **STAND IN THE HOLY PLACE**, (whoso readeth, let him understand:)

[Dan 9:27 KJV] 27 And **he shall confirm the covenant with many for one week**: and **in the midst of the week he shall cause the sacrifice and the oblation to cease, and for the overspreading of abominations he shall make [it] desolate**, even until the consummation, and that determined shall be poured upon the desolate.

[Dan 11:29-35 KJV] 29 At the time appointed he shall return, and come toward the south; but it shall not be as the former, or as the latter. 30 For the ships of Chittim shall come against him: therefore he shall be grieved, and return, and have indignation against **THE HOLY COVENANT**: so shall he do; he shall even return, and have intelligence with them that forsake the holy covenant. 31 And arms shall stand on his part, and **THEY SHALL POLLUTE THE SANCTUARY OF STRENGTH**, and **SHALL TAKE AWAY THE DAILY [SACRIFICE], AND THEY SHALL PLACE THE ABOMINATION THAT MAKETH DESOLATE**. 32 And such as do wickedly against the covenant shall he corrupt by flatteries: but **THE PEOPLE THAT DO KNOW THEIR GOD SHALL BE STRONG, AND DO** [exploits]. 33 And **THEY THAT UNDERSTAND AMONG THE PEOPLE SHALL INSTRUCT MANY**: yet they shall fall by the sword, and by flame, by captivity, and by spoil, [many] days. 34 Now when they shall fall, they shall be holpen with a little help: but many shall cleave to them with flatteries. 35 And [some] of them of understanding shall fall, to try them, and to purge, and to make [them] white, [even] to the time of the end: because [it is] yet for a time appointed.

SO, WHO ARE THESE HOLY PRIESTS MAKING THE DAILY SACRIFICES? THAT IS THE QUESTION.... ARE THEY TZADOKIM, SONS OF ZADOK - SADDUCEES? I DON'T KNOW. BUT, I DO KNOW THEY MUST BE KEEPING THE HOLY COVENANT (THE WRITTEN TORAH) IN A WAY ACCEPTABLE TO YEHOVAH FOR A PERIOD JUST BEFORE THE ANTI-MESSIAH DESECRATES THE TEMPLE.

Because I am questioning the validity of the plethora of Jewish traditions, this book may sound like I am bashing the Jewish people. I absolutely am

<u>not</u>! MY GOODNESS, YESHUA HIMSELF IS JEWISH! Also, I actually have researched my family name "Collins" and have found the root of it "Coll" on <u>www.Sephardim.com</u> (the Spanish Jews are called Sephardim) as most probably of Jewish origin. (I have actually heard that I might share that root with Chrisopher Columbus, who actually was Jewish. His real last name was Colon' with the Hebrew root of "Col". I am not citing this but you can look up references yourself.) **REGARDLESS, THOUGH, AS I SAID EARLIER, EVEN IF I AM OF COMPLETELY GENTILE LINEAGE, I HAVE SURNAMED MYSELF BY THE NAME OF "ISRAEL" AND CONSIDER MYSELF AN ISRAELITE BY THE BLOOD OF YESHUA! I WANT TO BE COMPLETELY ALIGNED WITH ISRAEL, YEHOVAH'S FAMILY - MY FAMILY! I WANT TO BE OBEDIENT TO YEHOVAH, KEEPING HIS WRITTEN TORAH, JUST AS HE CALLS THE STRANGERS WHO JOIN THEMSELVES TO YEHOVAH TO DO IN ISAIAH 56: 6-8, LEVITICUS 24:22, NUMBERS 15:15-16, LEVITICUS 19:33-34, AND ALL THE OTHER SCRIPTURES I HAVE QUOTED.**

<u>HOWEVER, I AM BASHING THE TRADITIONS OF MEN, BECAUSE YESHUA DID, AND I AM STANDING FOR THE TRUTH!</u>

LET US <u>COMPLETE THE REFORMATIONS</u> – NOT JUST ELIMINATING ALL OF THE MAN-MADE CHRISTIAN CHURCH TRADITIONS BUT ALL OF <u>THE MAN-MADE JEWISH TRADITIONS TOO</u>!

THAT IS WHAT YESHUA WAS DOING AND PREACHING!!!

CHAPTER 15

How Yeshua Lived and What He Preached

SO, HOW DID YESHUA ACTUALLY LIVE?

YESHUA, BEING THE PERFECT SON OF YEHOVAH ELOHIM, JUST DID WHAT WAS RIGHT ACCORDING TO THE WRITTEN TORAH PERFECTLY FROM HIS HEART- NOT MORE AND NOT LESS:

[Psa 40:7-8 KJV] 7 Then said I, Lo, I come: in the volume of the book [it is] written of me, 8 I DELIGHT TO DO THY WILL, O MY GOD: YEA, THY LAW [IS] WITHIN MY HEART.

(The word "Law" in the above verse is "TORAH" in the original Hebrew.)

HE COULD BE THAT SINLESS, PERFECT OFFERING AS THE LAMB OF GOD FOR US, AND DIDN'T WORRY ABOUT PLEASING THE PHARISEES OR THE SADDUCEES WHO WERE CONDEMNING HIS ACTIONS AND ACCUSING HIM OF SINNING BECAUSE HE DIDN'T FOLLOW THEIR "TRADITIONS ."

To further show he **UPHELD** the keeping of **ALL OF THE WRITTEN TORAH**, see what Yeshua said about keeping the weighter, or more important parts of the Written Torah, but not leaving out the least, or less important, of those commandments, statutes, and judgments :

[Mat 23:23 KJV] 23 Woe unto you, scribes and Pharisees, hypocrites! for ye pay tithe of mint and anise and cummin, and **have omitted the weightier [matters] of the law, judgment, mercy, and faith: these ought ye to have done, and NOT TO LEAVE THE OTHER UNDONE**.

SO, THE POINT BEING MADE NOW IS THAT YESHUA DID SAY IT IS GOOD TO KEEP ALL OF THE WRITTEN TORAH – EVERY JOT AND TITTLE OF IT AND EVEN THE VERY LEAST COMMANDMENT! DON'T LEAVE OUT ANY OF IT!

When Yeshua first started his public ministry, just as he came out of the 40 days of testing in the Desert, he preached exactly what John the Baptist had been preaching:

Mat 3:1 KJV - In those days came **John the Baptist**, preaching in the wilderness of

Judaea,

Mat 3:2 KJV - And saying, **<u>REPENT YE</u>: FOR THE KINGDOM OF HEAVEN IS AT HAND**.

Mat 4:17 KJV - From that time **<u>JESUS BEGAN TO PREACH</u>**, and to say, **<u>REPENT:</u> FOR THE KINGDOM OF HEAVEN IS AT HAND.**

<u>REPENT</u> IS THE HEBREW WORD "TESHUVAH" – IT MEANS "TURN AROUND." Turn around or back to what? **<u>TURN BACK TO YEHOVAH'S TRUE WRITTEN TORAH</u>, (<u>STOP SINNING</u>) AND <u>QUIT KEEPING THE COMMANDMENTS OF MEN</u>!**

An example of what Yeshua preached is here, where he had healed a lame man at the Pool of Bethesda: [Jhn 5:14 KJV] 14 Afterward Jesus findeth him in the temple, and said unto him, BEHOLD, THOU ART MADE WHOLE: <u>SIN NO MORE</u>, LEST A WORSE THING COME UNTO THEE.

<u>WHY DID YESHUA PREACH TO REPENT? FOR THE KINGDOM OF HEAVEN IS JUST AROUND THE CORNER! THAT SHOULD STILL BE OUR MESSAGE - YESHUA SAID TO WATCH AND BE READY ALWAYS BECAUSE HE IS RETURNING AT AN HOUR WE DON'T KNOW!!!</u>

<u>"REPENT - TURN BACK TO THE WRITTEN TORAH" IS WHAT EVERY PROPHET OF ISRAEL HAD PREACHED!!!</u>

<u>Think about how many parables Yeshua gave about how The Father had sent the prophets before, but at the last sent His Beloved Son – being sure they would listen to him! (Luke 20:1-19). Remember, all the Prophets always were sent to turn the people back to Yehovah to keep His Laws and Yeshua, being the Beloved Son, was finally sent preaching that same message too!</u>

SO, YESHUA PREACHED "REPENT – TURN BACK TO THE WRITTEN TORAH," <u>JUST LIKE THE PREVIOUS PROPHETS</u>, BECAUSE HE ACTUALLY IS "<u>THE PROPHET</u>" THAT MOSES SPOKE OF IN DEUTERONOMY 18:18. YEHOVAH SAID HE WOULD RAISE UP ONE THAT WAS LIKE MOSES THAT THE CHILDREN OF ISRAEL WERE TO LISTEN TO:

[Deu 18:15-19 KJV] 15 The LORD thy God will raise up unto thee a Prophet from the midst of thee, of thy brethren, like unto me; unto him ye shall hearken; 16
According to all that thou desiredst of the LORD thy God in Horeb in the day of the assembly, saying, Let me not hear again the voice of the LORD my God, neither let me see this great fire any more, that I die not. 17 And the LORD said unto me, They

have well [spoken that] which they have spoken. 18 **<u>I will raise them up a Prophet from among their brethren, like unto thee, and will put my words in his mouth;</u>** and **<u>he shall speak unto them all that I shall command him.</u>** 19 **<u>And it shall come to pass, [that] whosoever will not hearken unto my words which he shall speak in my name, I will require [it] of him</u>.**

Peter confirmed that Yeshua was The Prophet that Moses spoke of:

[Act 3:22-23 KJV] 22 For Moses truly said unto the fathers, A prophet shall the Lord your God raise up unto you of your brethren, like unto me; him shall ye hear in all things whatsoever he shall say unto you. 23 **And it shall come to pass, [that] every soul, which will not hear <u>that prophet</u>, shall be destroyed from among the people.**

YESHUA COULD NOT HAVE BEEN "THE PROPHET LIKE UNTO MOSES" IF HE HAD LED PEOPLE AWAY FROM KEEPING THE WRITTEN TORAH, EVEN THOUGH HE WAS WORKING MIRACLES- HE WOULD HAVE BEEN A FALSE PROPHET AND SHOULD HAVE BEEN PUT TO DEATH!!! READ DEUTERONOMY 13:1-5.

Yeshua, as the Beloved Son of God and as The Prophet that the Father sent, said:

[Jhn 12:44-50 KJV] 44 Jesus cried and said, He that believeth on me, believeth not on me, but on him that sent me. 45 And he that seeth me seeth him that sent me. 46 I am come a light into the world, that whosoever believeth on me should not abide in darkness. 47 And if any man hear my words, and believe not, I judge him not: for I came not to judge the world, but to save the world. 48 <u>He that rejecteth me, and receiveth not my words, hath one that judgeth him: the word that I have spoken, the same shall judge him in the last day. 49 For I have not spoken of myself; but the Father which sent me, he gave me a commandment, what I should say, and what I should speak.</u> 50 And I know that his commandment is life everlasting: whatsoever I speak therefore, even as the Father said unto me, so I speak.

Yeshua also said:

Mat 7:13 KJV - Enter ye in at the strait gate: for wide [is] the gate, and broad [is] the way, that leadeth to destruction, and many there be which go in thereat:

Mat 7:14 KJV - Because strait [is] the gate, and <u>narrow [is] the way, which</u>

leadeth unto life, and few there be that find it.

Mat 7:15 KJV - Beware of false prophets, which come to you in sheep's clothing, but inwardly they are ravening wolves.

Mat 7:16 KJV - Ye shall know them by their fruits. Do men gather grapes of thorns, or figs of thistles?

Mat 7:17 KJV - Even so every good tree bringeth forth good fruit; but a corrupt tree bringeth forth evil fruit.

Mat 7:18 KJV - A good tree cannot bring forth evil fruit, neither [can] a corrupt tree bring forth good fruit.

Mat 7:19 KJV - Every tree that bringeth not forth good fruit is hewn down, and cast into the fire.

Mat 7:20 KJV - Wherefore by their fruits ye shall know them.

Mat 7:21 KJV - NOT EVERY ONE THAT SAITH UNTO ME, LORD, LORD, SHALL ENTER INTO THE KINGDOM OF HEAVEN; BUT HE THAT DOETH THE WILL OF MY FATHER WHICH IS IN HEAVEN.

Mat 7:22 KJV - Many will say to me in that day, Lord, Lord, have we not prophesied in thy name? and in thy name have cast out devils? and in thy name done many wonderful works?

Mat 7:23 KJV - And then will I profess unto them, I never knew you: DEPART FROM ME, YE THAT WORK INIQUITY.

Except for the great white throne judgment by the Father at the end of the 1000 year reign of Mashiach, I think these may be the scariest words in the Bible!

I think it would be wise to know for sure what the word "iniquity" means, then:

INIQUITY, IN THE GREEK LANGUAGE, IS "ANOMIA" OR IN ENGLISH, CAN ALSO BE TRANSLATED "LAWLESSNESS" (BREAKING THE WRITTEN TORAH)! Anomia is G458 in the Strong's Concordance in the online Blue Letter Bible Lexicon and means **1)"THE CONDITION OF WITHOUT LAW" AND 2) "CONTEMPT AND VIOLATION OF LAW, INIQUITY, WICKEDNESS."**

THESE WORDS OF YESHUA'S ARE ENOUGH TO MAKE ME WANT TO NOT BE "LAWLESS!"

Think about this carefully – Yeshua basically **SEEMS** to be saying that you could believe in him (you are calling him "Lord")and **use the power of attorney given to believers to use His Name to do miracles, cast out demons, and heal people** – but, because you did not **REPENT and turn back to the Written Torah** (the law) and **turn away from "lawlessness," he will reject you** and not allow you into the kingdom!!! **SO, IS REPENTANCE IMPORTANT???**

******(HERE, I WILL INSERT WHAT I STATED AT THE BEGINNING OF THIS SECTION OF THE OBLIGATION OF THE COMPLETELY GENTILE BELIEVERS TO KEEP THE WRITTEN TORAH)******

<u>BUT, you say, he was talking only to Jews</u>! That is true. AT THAT TIME. <u>However, remember, after His resurrection , he told those same Jewish Apostles to go into all the world and teach the gentiles about him and to teach the gentiles to observe everything that he had told his Jewish Apostles to do!:</u>

Mat 28:18 KJV - And Jesus came and spake unto them, saying, All power is given unto me in heaven and in earth.

Mat 28:19 KJV - <u>Go ye therefore</u>, and <u>teach all nations</u>, baptizing them in the name of the Father, and of the Son, and of the Holy Ghost:

Mat 28:20 KJV - <u>Teaching THEM to observe ALL THINGS whatsoever I have commanded YOU:</u> and, lo, I am with you alway, [even] unto the end of the world. Amen.

Remember in <u>Matthew 5:19</u>, Yeshua had said to his disciples, "**whosoever**" would keep the commandments and teach them to others would be great in the Kingdom! **If we can believe that the "whosoever" in John 3:16 concerning salvation is for us gentiles, <u>when he was talking to Jews</u>, we should believe that this "whosoever" applies to us gentiles as well!**

Jhn 3:16 KJV - For God so loved the world, that he gave his only begotten Son, that **<u>whosoever</u>** believeth in him should not perish, but have everlasting life.

SO, EVEN IF COMPLETELY GENTILE BELIEVERS ARE NOT "<u>OBLIGATED</u>" TO KEEP ALL OF THE WRITTEN TORAH (<u>AT LEAST AT THE BEGINNING OF THEIR JOURNEY AS CHRISTIANS</u>), IF YOU WANT YOUR FATHER TO SEE YOU AS GREAT IN THE KINGDOM OF GOD, <u>YOU WILL</u>! <u>IT'S YOUR CHOICE</u>!

CHAPTER 16

The DESIRE to Keep the Written Torah to Please The Father is Given by the Holy Spirit!

WHEN YOU KNOW THAT IT WOULD PLEASE YOUR FATHER IF YOU WERE TO LEARN THE WRITTEN TORAH AND DO IT, WOULDN'T YOU WANT TO?

I THINK YOU WOULD, IF YOU ARE TRULY BORN AGAIN OF THE HOLY SPIRIT!!!

In fact, that is what I think The Father meant when he said that he would "write THE LAW upon their hearts" Jeremiah 31:33 that describes the New Covenant. THE WORD TRANSLATED LAW HERE IS THE HEBREW WORD TORAH!! ITS NOT A DIFFERENT LAW!! He said he would actually cause the House of Judah and the House of Israel and the Gentiles on Whom His Name Is Called to have a DESIRE (the "WANT TO"!) TO OBEY HIM by POURING OUT HIS HOLY SPIRIT INTO THEIR HEARTS. Remember that He had cast the House of Israel out of the land and divorced them because they WOULD NOT keep the Torah – they didn't have it in their heart to obey him. They didn't want to. They were REBELLIOUS AND STIFFNECKED! They could have kept the Written Torah – I repeat, THEY COULD HAVE KEPT THE WRITTEN TORAH - THEY DIDN'T WANT TO!!!

HOW DO I KNOW THEY COULD KEEP THE TORAH?

BECAUSE THE FATHER IS NOT SCHIZOPHRENIC!!! HE WOULD NOT HAVE GIVEN THEM LAWS THEY COULD NOT KEEP AND THEN PUNISH THEM FOR NOT KEEPING THEM!!!

Let me say that again slowly.

THE FATHER IS NOT SCHIZOPHRENIC!!!

The Father WOULD NOT HAVE GIVEN Israel THE 10 COMMANDMENTS, STATUTES, AND JUDGMENTS if they COULD NOT keep them and then PUNISH THEM FOR NOT KEEPING THEM!

No, they WOULD NOT keep them!!!

[Isa 30:8-11 KJV] 8 Now go, write it before them in a table, and note it in a book, that it may be for the time to come for ever and ever: 9 That THIS [IS] A REBELLIOUS PEOPLE, LYING CHILDREN, CHILDREN [THAT] WILL NOT HEAR THE LAW OF THE LORD: 10 Which say to the seers, See not; and to the prophets, Prophesy not unto us right things, speak unto us smooth things, prophesy deceits: 11 Get you out of the way, turn aside out of the path, cause the Holy One of Israel to cease from before us.

[Isa 42:21, 23-24 KJV] 21 The LORD is well pleased for his righteousness' sake; he will magnify the law, and make [it] honourable. ... 23 Who among you will give ear to this? [who] will hearken and hear for the time to come? 24 Who gave Jacob for a spoil, and Israel to the robbers? did not the LORD, he against whom we have sinned? for they WOULD NOT walk in HIS WAYS, NEITHER WERE THEY OBEDIENT UNTO HIS LAW.

[Isa 48:18-19 KJV] 18 O THAT THOU HADST HEARKENED TO MY COMMANDMENTS! THEN HAD THY PEACE BEEN AS A RIVER, AND THY RIGHTEOUSNESS AS THE WAVES OF THE SEA: 19 Thy seed also had been as the sand, and the offspring of thy bowels like the gravel thereof; his name should not have been cut off nor destroyed from before me.

[Zec 7:8-14 KJV] 8 And the word of the LORD came unto Zechariah, saying, 9 Thus speaketh the LORD of hosts, saying, Execute true judgment, and shew mercy and compassions every man to his brother: 10 And oppress not the widow, nor the fatherless, the stranger, nor the poor; and let none of you imagine evil against his brother in your heart. 11 But they refused to hearken, and pulled away the shoulder, and stopped their ears, that they should not hear. 12 Yea, THEY MADE THEIR HEARTS [as] AN ADAMANT STONE, LEST THEY SHOULD HEAR THE LAW, AND THE WORDS WHICH THE LORD OF HOSTS HATH SENT IN HIS SPIRIT BY THE FORMER PROPHETS: therefore came a great wrath from the LORD of hosts. 13 Therefore it is come to pass, [that] as he cried, and they would not hear; so they cried, and I would not hear, saith the LORD of hosts: 14 But I scattered them with a whirlwind among all the nations whom they knew not. Thus the land was desolate after them, that no man passed through nor returned: for they laid the pleasant land desolate.

Israel HAD MADE their heart hard as a stone. They could have circumcised

their own hearts themselves but they didn't. They desperately needed a HEART CHANGE and The Father decided to graciously just give them one through the New Covenant! This HEART CHANGE is what I think THE NEW BIRTH (BEING BORN OF THE HOLY SPIRIT OF YEHOVAH) gave them (and US)!

(IF YOU DON'T HAVE A HEART THAT "WANTS TO" OBEY GOD, EVEN TO THE POINT OF LEARNING AND OBEYING THE WRITTEN TORAH AFTER BEING SHOWN THAT HE DESIRES FOR YOU TO, YOU MIGHT BETTER QUESTION IF YOU HAVE REALLY BEEN BORN AGAIN!!!)

Note below that Yehovah says **THEY** are the ones who broke the covenant, **EVEN THOUGH HE KEPT IT**. The House of Israel and the House of Judah broke the covenant by not keeping his commandments, statutes, and judgments! **So, He says He is going to write those laws on their hearts.** I believe this is so that they will **WANT TO** keep them! **It's not a different set of laws – He still calls it "My Law! My Torah! "**

[Jer 31:31-34 KJV] 31 Behold, the days come, saith the LORD, that I will make a NEW COVENANT with THE HOUSE OF ISRAEL, AND WITH THE HOUSE OF JUDAH: 32 Not according to the covenant that I made with their fathers in the day [that] I took them by the hand to bring them out of the land of Egypt; which MY COVENANT THEY BRAKE, although I was an husband unto them, saith the LORD: 33 But this [shall be] the covenant that I will make with the house of Israel; After those days, saith the LORD, I will put MY LAW in their inward parts, and WRITE IT IN THEIR HEARTS; and will be their God, and they shall be my people. 34 And they shall teach no more every man his neighbour, and every man his brother, saying, Know the LORD: for they shall all know me, from the least of them unto the greatest of them, saith the LORD: for I will forgive their iniquity, and I will remember their sin no more.

THIS WOULD EXPLAIN WHY WE DON'T, ALL OF A SUDDEN, JUST KNOW ALL OF THE LAW WITHOUT STUDYING IT, WHICH WE HAVE THOUGHT HAVING "THE LAW WRITTEN ON OUR HEARTS" MEANT . WE NOW HAVE THE HEART, THE DESIRE TO OBEY GOD, BUT MAYBE NOT THE KNOWLEDGE!

Why else would Yeshua say not only to keep the least of the commandments

but TEACH THEM TO OTHERS? (Matthew 5: 19)

I CAN SAY THIS FROM EXPERIENCE. I HAVE LEARNED MANY OF THE FATHER'S LAWS SINCE I HAVE BEEN STUDYING THE WRITTEN TORAH (GENESIS THROUGH DEUTERONOMY.) MOST OF THEM I HAD NEVER HEARD BEFORE, EVEN THOUGH I WAS A CHRISTIAN THAT LOVED YEHOVAH AND HAD THE DESIRE (THE HEART) TO OBEY AND PLEASE HIM!!!

For example, since I have started studying the Written Torah, I have found that reading horoscopes and astrology were sinful (I actually found that out about 20 years ago in Deuteronomy and stopped doing it – I just didn't understand why we Christians acknowledged that doing these particular things were wrong, but didn't pay any attention to other commandments a few verses down!) So, now I have also found that anything to do with wizardry (think not only "The Wizard of Oz" but the many current movies and computer games), sorcery (think Harry Potter movies and books, anything to do with witchcraft), tattoos, wearing wool and linen together, among many others things, are wrong too. Many Christians that I know love God participate in these things. BUT WE HAVE BEEN DECEIVED BY SATAN TO THINK THAT IT WOULDN'T PLEASE HIM FOR US TO STUDY, OBEY AND KEEP THE WRITTEN TORAH!! SATAN HAS DECEIVED US INTO THINKING THAT WE WOULD BE TRYING "TO BE SAVED BY KEEPING THE LAW" IF WE STUDIED IT AND TRIED TO KEEP IT! I KNOW SOME BELIEVERS THINK THAT ONLY WHAT WE RECEIVE BY "REVELATION" FROM THE HOLY SPIRIT SHOULD WE KEEP. I KNOW THAT SOMETIMES THE HOLY SPIRIT DOES REVEAL DIRECTLY TO SOME PEOPLE THINGS THAT ARE IN HIS WRITTEN TORAH. BUT, I BELIEVE THAT IS JUST MERCY! I BELIEVE HE WOULD MUCH RATHER US BE DILIGENT TO STUDY IT FOR OURSELVES – SINCE HE WAS SO FAITHFUL TO MAKE SURE IT WAS WRITTEN FOR US! SATAN HAS DECIEVED THE BELIEVERS IN YESHUA FOR MILLENIA THAT GOD WOULD BE DISPLEASED IF WE KEPT THE WRITTEN TORAH! BUT, HOPEFULLY, YOU ARE BEGINNING TO SEE THAT THAT IS NOT THE CASE!

Read Psalm 119 – obedience to the Torah is good and, as Yeshua said concerning the Psalms, "the scripture cannot be broken"! John 10:35 KJV says, "If he called them gods, unto whom the word of God came, and THE SCRIPTURE CANNOT BE BROKEN..." In this verse, Yeshua was referring to a passage in PSALMS: Psa 82:6 KJV – "I have said, Ye [are] gods; and all of you [are] children of the most High." SO, PSALM 119, THE LONGEST CHAPTER IN THE BIBLE AND THAT CONFIRMS IN EVERY SINGLE VERSE HOW GOOD THE COMMANDMENTS, STATUTES, AND JUDGMENTS ARE, IS SCRIPTURE THAT

CANNOT BE BROKEN TOO! Just a sampling of the verses say:

Psa 119:7 KJV - I will praise thee with uprightness of heart, when I shall have learned thy righteous judgments.

Psa 119:48 KJV - My hands also will I lift up unto thy commandments, which I have loved; and I will meditate in thy statutes.

Psa 119:98 KJV - Thou through thy commandments hast made me wiser than mine enemies: for they [are] ever with me.

ALSO, LISTEN TO MORE OF THE FATHER'S HEART:

PSA 81:13 KJV - OH THAT MY PEOPLE HAD HEARKENED UNTO ME, [AND] ISRAEL HAD WALKED IN MY WAYS!

PSA 81:14 KJV - I SHOULD SOON HAVE SUBDUED THEIR ENEMIES, AND TURNED MY HAND AGAINST THEIR ADVERSARIES.

Psa 1:1 KJV - Blessed [is] the man that walketh not in the counsel of the ungodly, nor standeth in the way of sinners, nor sitteth in the seat of the scornful.

Psa 1:2 KJV - BUT HIS DELIGHT [IS] IN THE LAW OF THE LORD; AND IN HIS LAW DOTH HE MEDITATE DAY AND NIGHT.

Psa 1:3 KJV - And he shall be like a tree planted by the rivers of water, that bringeth forth his fruit in his season; his leaf also shall not wither; and whatsoever he doeth shall prosper.

Psa 1:4 KJV - The ungodly [are] not so: but [are] like the chaff which the wind driveth away.

Psa 1:5 KJV - Therefore the ungodly shall not stand in the judgment, nor sinners in the congregation of the righteous.

Psa 1:6 KJV - For the LORD knoweth the way of the righteous: but the way of the ungodly shall perish.

CHAPTER 17

Negating Other False Beliefs Concerning "Keeping the Law"

We Christians have heard erroneous teaching so long through the years that we do not question it ourselves. **WE HAVE HEARD "NO ONE COULD KEEP THE LAW - THAT IT WAS GIVEN ONLY TO SHOW EVERYONE THAT THEY COULD NOT KEEP IT AND SO NEEDED A SAVIOR - ONLY JESUS COULD KEEP THE LAW ." But the New Testament itself says differently! IT SAYS THAT THE PARENTS OF JOHN THE BAPTIST (YOCHANON THE IMMERSER) KEPT THE WRITTEN TORAH -THE LAW - BLAMELESSLY AND WERE RIGHTEOUS BEFORE YEHOVAH!!!**

Luk 1:5 KJV - There was in the days of Herod, the king of Judaea, **a certain priest named Zacharias**, of the course of Abia: and **his wife [was] of the daughters of Aaron, and her name [was] Elisabeth.**

LUK 1:6 KJV - **AND THEY WERE BOTH RIGHTEOUS BEFORE GOD, WALKING IN ALL THE COMMANDMENTS AND ORDINANCES OF THE LORD BLAMELESS.**

THIS DOES NOT MEAN THAT THEY NEVER SINNED. But, the Written Torah, the Law, had provisions right there in it for sacrifices that were to be made if you broke one of the laws from which you could be forgiven and then be right with Yehovah again - counted righteous! Those sacrifices to be made were actually part of the Torah! Obviously, Zacharias and Elizabeth must not have broken any laws that required the death penalty. **BUT THE POINT IS, THAT, OF COURSE, YEHOVAH EXPECTED ISRAEL TO KEEP THE LAW - HIS COMMANDMENTS, STATUTES AND JUDGMENTS! HE SAID IT OVER AND OVER AND OVER!!! THEY COULD HAVE KEPT IT!!!** There are so many places he says it, that I am not even going to try to list them all. But read again the verses in Deuteronomy 30:15-18:

Deu 30:15 KJV - See, I have set before thee this day life and good, and death and evil;

Deu 30:16 KJV - In that **I COMMAND THEE** this day **TO LOVE THE LORD THY GOD, TO WALK IN HIS WAYS, AND TO KEEP HIS COMMANDMENTS AND HIS STATUTES AND HIS JUDGMENTS**, that thou mayest live and multiply: and the

LORD thy God shall bless thee in the land whither thou goest to possess it.

Deu 30:17 KJV - But **IF THINE HEART TURN AWAY**, so **THAT THOU WILT NOT HEAR**, but shalt be drawn away, and worship other gods, and serve them;

Deu 30:18 KJV - **I DENOUNCE UNTO YOU THIS DAY, THAT YE SHALL SURELY PERISH, [AND THAT] YE SHALL NOT PROLONG [YOUR] DAYS UPON THE LAND, WHITHER THOU PASSEST OVER JORDAN TO GO TO POSSESS IT.**

*******(This certainly DOES NOT sound like Yehovah " was just trying to show them that they COULD NOT keep it" to me, as we have heard a thousand times!!! No, THEY were responsible to turn their heart towards Yehovah and keep His Written Torah–but they WOULD NOT, as we know from history.)*******

Another cliché which we have heard in the Christian church so long is, **"If you break one of God's laws, you've broken them all."** People say this with a sense of resignation, concluding that there is no use to try – that if we even try, we are assuming that we can achieve salvation by our efforts. Although I agree that only Yeshua kept the Written Torah perfectly without sinning, I do not agree that we should not **TRY** to keep God's commandments, statutes, and judgments. It makes no sense to me to think that, if I have not mastered keeping one of the least of Yehovah's laws, such as not wearing wool and linen together, means that I should give up and go ahead and steal !!! We need to use common sense. To me, it makes sense that we should be in a continual state of growing in holiness.

While I'm at it, another argument believers use against keeping the Written Torah, is that **"only the commandments that are spoken about in the New Testatment are valid." HOWEVER, WHERE DO WE THINK THESE COMMANDMENTS CAME FROM? THEY CAME FROM THE WRITTEN TORAH!! Thank goodness, there are a lot of them in the New Covenant or we would not have been walking in as much holiness as we have throughout the last two thousand years!!!** We just need to go ahead and study the Written Torah and learn the rest of them! (Unfortunately, as I have stated, many Christians today are even abandoning the commandments listed in the New Covenant –no fornication, homosexuality, sorcery, murder (abortion)being a few.)

Yes, Yeshua is the only one who kept the Torah perfectly, from His heart, and never had to make any sacrifice for sin to be forgiven. That is why He is the Spotless, Pure, Lamb of God who was able to come and take away the sin

of the world by sacrificing Himself! But he didn't come to take away the Written Torah of God!

Another argument we have all heard against learning and keeping the Written Torah is that we don't have to if we just keep the commandment to "Love." Yeshua did say that loving God and loving your neighbor as yourself were the 1st and 2nd greatest commandments in the Law. But, remember, **THEY WERE IN THE LAW – THE WRITTEN TORAH!:**

1st and greatest commandment:

Deu 6:1 KJV - Now these [are] the commandments, the statutes, and the judgments, which the LORD your God commanded to teach you, that ye might do [them] in the land whither ye go to possess it:

Deu 6:2 KJV - That thou mightest fear the LORD thy God, to keep all his statutes and his commandments, which I command thee, thou, and thy son, and thy son's son, all the days of thy life; and that thy days may be prolonged.

Deu 6:3 KJV - Hear therefore, O Israel, and observe to do [it]; that it may be well with thee, and that ye may increase mightily, as the LORD God of thy fathers hath promised thee, in the land that floweth with milk and honey.

Deu 6:4 KJV - Hear, O Israel: The LORD our God [is] one LORD:

Deu 6:5 KJV - And thou shalt love the LORD thy God with all thine heart, and with all thy soul, and with all thy might.

2nd Greatest Commandment:

Lev 19:17 KJV - Thou shalt not hate thy brother in thine heart: thou shalt in any wise rebuke thy neighbour, and not suffer sin upon him.

Lev 19:18 KJV - Thou shalt not avenge, nor bear any grudge against the children of thy people, **but thou shalt love thy neighbour as thyself: I [am] the LORD.**

Yeshua said on these two commandments hang all the law and the prophets. Again, satan's deception tries to make us think, then, that we will just **KNOW** how to love God and love our neighbor automatically. But, when you study the Written Torah, you see that **THE FATHER IS ACTUALLY SHOWING US CONCRETE WAYS OF HOW HE WANTS US TO LOVE HIM (such as the first four commandments - by not having any other gods before Him, by not making graven images (which is idolatry), by not using His name in vain, and by honoring His**

Sabbaths - and other statutes and judgments too many to list!) and <u>CONCRETE WAYS OF HOW HE WANTS US TO LOVE OUR NEIGHBOR (the last six commandments , such as not stealing, murdering, etc. and other statutes and judgments too many to list!).</u>

I DO BELIEVE, SIMPLY PUT, THAT FROM THE VERY BEGINNING, THE FATHER HAS WANTED A FAMILY THAT LOVES HIM AND LOVES EACH OTHER! JUST LIKE WE WANT IN OUR FAMILIES!! AS PARENTS, WE WANT TO BE LOVED, HONORED, AND OBEYED AND FOR OUR CHILDREN TO LOVE EACH OTHER AND GET ALONG WELL. WE INHERITED THAT DESIRE FROM HIM!!

Note that verse 17 states that part of not hating your brother and loving him, is to rebuke him when he is obviously in sin, and possibly oblivious to it, and not allowing sin to be upon him. In other words, we do need to hold each other accountable to a point, but, of course, not in a hypocritical way, and not in a mean and hurtful way, but in a truly loving, but firm, manner.

CHAPTER 18

Yeshua Used the Written Torah to Resist the Temptations of Satan

Recently, I have even had a revelation about Yeshua and the Written Torah!

In reading the story of Yeshua, right after he was baptized in the Jordan River by John the Baptist (the Immerser), I saw that he was DRIVEN BY THE HOLY SPIRIT INTO THE WILDERNESS (DESERT) FOR 40 DAYS TO BE TEMPTED OF THE DEVIL. I SAW THAT YESHUA HIMSELF, WHO WAS BORN OF THE HOLY SPIRIT, THE VERY SON OF GOD, WHO WAS FILLED WITH THE POWER OF THE HOLY SPIRIT, USED THE WRITTEN TORAH TO RESIST THE TEMPTATIONS OF THE DEVIL TO TRY TO MAKE HIM SIN!! (Read Luke 4:1-13 for entire story). EVERYTHING THE DEVIL TEMPTED YESHUA WITH, HE ANSWERED BACK WITH A COMMANDMENT FROM THE BOOK OF DEUTERONOMY!! I have actually heard that Deuteronomy, the last of the 5 books of Moses, is commonly called "the book of the law", as it was given by Yehovah to Moses to command the Israelites right before he actually allowed them to go into The Promised Land occupied by the Canaanites, after their 40 year trek in the wilderness. It seems to be a re-compilation of all that He had said previously. So, Yeshua said to the devil "IT IS WRITTEN"! Well, where was it written? There was no New Testament! The commandments he quoted to the devil were: DEUTERONOMY 8:3, DEUTERONOMY 10:20, AND DEUTERONOMY 6:16 - THEY ALL WERE FROM THE BOOK OF DEUTERONOMY -THE WRITTEN TORAH! SO, I SAW THAT IF YESHUA HIMSELF USED THE WRITTEN TORAH TO COMBAT THE ENEMY AND RESIST THE DEVIL'S TEMPTATIONS TO SIN! SATAN EVEN USED PSALM 91 OUT OF CONTEXT TO TRY TO DECEIVE YESHUA. IF YESHUA DID THIS, WHO ARE WE TO THINK THAT WE SHOULD NOT USE THE WRITTEN TORAH TO DISCERN RIGHT FROM WRONG, TRUTH FROM ERROR, RIGHTEOUSNESS FROM SIN, THE TRUE HOLY SPIRIT FROM A DECIEVING DEMONIC SPIRIT, WHEN WE ARE TEMPTED BY THE DEVIL TO SIN!!!

CHAPTER 19

Yehovah's Perfect Torah

BUT, you say, Yeshua did speak about certain laws in Matthew chapters 5 – 7 (what we call The Sermon on the Mount) that sound like he was changing them. Many times people point to these verses and say, "see, Jesus did change the Written Torah so we don't need to keep it!"

Actually, even here, I believe that much of what Yeshua is addressing is the Oral Torah! Some of the admonitions in The Sermon on the Mount **SOUND LIKE** the Written Torah, but **He prefaces his statements with, words like, "you have heard it said of them of old time" (I think a reference to the sages), not with "it is written", in other words, not the Written Torah. WHEN HE REFERENCES THE WRITTEN TORAH, HE USUALLY CALLS IT "MOSES" OR JUST SAYS, "IT IS WRITTEN". Remember, He had just, a few verses above in Matthew 5:17, said NOT to think He was coming to destroy the Written Torah!!!**

BUT, IT'S ALSO POSSIBLE THAT HE WAS SHOWING US THAT YEHOVAH'S PERFECT TORAH IS EVEN STRICTER THE WRITTEN TORAH!!! Yeshua did make a distinction between Yehovah Elohim's intentions "from the beginning" (or creation) about some issues and what He gave as commandments, statutes and judgments to Moses in Writing for Israel to observe. Also, some of what Yeshua addressed dealt with our heart motives. IN MY OBSERVATION, THE WRITTEN TORAH ONLY DESIGNATES PUNISHMENT FOR PEOPLE'S ACTIONS, but YESHUA WAS SHOWING US THAT, BEYOND JUST OUR ACTIONS, THE FATHER IS LOOKING AT OUR HEARTS! (However, this does not mean that He is not looking at our actions too!!!) I believe He always did consider their heart motives and whether He was **pleased** with their service or not was based on their heart. Consider this:

1Ch 28:9 KJV - And thou, Solomon my son, know thou the God of thy father, and **SERVE HIM WITH A PERFECT HEART AND WITH A WILLING MIND: FOR THE LORD SEARCHETH ALL HEARTS, AND UNDERSTANDETH ALL THE IMAGINATIONS OF THE THOUGHTS: if thou seek him, he will be found of thee; but if thou forsake him, he will cast thee off for ever**.

So, for example, Yeshua says that a man is committing adultery **in his heart** if he looks with lust on a woman, even if he doesn't physically go through with the act, which is all the Written Torah judged and punished. I think he was letting us in on what Yehovah's judgment bar really is and it tells us that this higher standard is what The Father will judge by now! **So, obviously, now, with THE GIFT OF A CHANGED HEART, we must be able to keep both or He wouldn't tell us to!** **AGAIN, THE FATHER IS NOT SCHIZOPHRENIC! JUST AS WITH THE WRITTEN TORAH, HE WOULDN'T TELL US TO DO SOMETHING IF WE WERE NOT ABLE, AND THEN PUNISH US IF WE DIDN'T DO IT! THANK YEHOVAH WE CAN REPENT EVEN OF SINS OF THE HEART!** I believe Yeshua did overcome every temptation to sin, even in his heart, and was perfectly sinless. Think about that: he could have sinned since he was tempted in all points, just as we are, the scripture says! **BUT HE OVERCAME SIN, EVEN IN HIS HEART, AND WAS ABLE TO BE THE LAMB OF GOD SACRIFICED FOR SIN FOR US!**

I don't have a complete understanding of all this, and I don't think anyone else does either. However, **I do believe Yehovah desires for us to keep this Perfect Torah** because Yeshua says, in **Mat 5:48 KJV- " BE YE THEREFORE PERFECT, even as your Father which is in heaven is perfect." So why are we not perfect? WOULD YESHUA TELL US TO BE PERFECT IF IT WERE NOT A POSSIBILITY NOW, WITH A HEART TRANSFORMED BY THE LOVE OF GOD COMING INTO US BY HIS HOLY SPIRIT BIRTHING OUR SPIRITS AGAIN, CHANGING OUR DESIRES TO WANT TO OBEY GOD?**

BELIEVERS IN YESHUA ARE CONCEIVED BY THE HOLY SPIRIT, TOO, JUST LIKE YESHUA! MIRACLE OF MIRACLES!!!

(I will say that I think The Father shows us that it is not how we start, but how we end up! Remember the Prodigal Son. We may not be perfect , we may fall, but we ARE supposed to be being perfected!)

We now have **THE DESIRE** to follow all of Yehovah's Torah by His Spirit being poured out into our hearts. **We now not only CAN KEEP HIS WRITTEN TORAH AND THE WORDS OF YESHUA (WHICH TEACHES US OF YEHOVAH'S PERFECT TORAH), but WE HAVE THE DESIRE TO!** So it seems like we would always, from our hearts, live life perfectly, but we still don't always do it!

WE OBVIOUSLY STILL HAVE A CHOICE!!! WE CAN STILL CHOOSE TO SIN – to break His Written Torah that we've learned and also to follow lust, selfishness, pride and other **SINS OF THE HEART.** Many times **WE CHOOSE** wrongly and sin. **HOWEVER, WE ALSO CAN CHOOSE TO FOLLOW THE HOLY SPIRIT IN OUR HEARTS THAT LEADS US TO KEEP YEHOVAH'S WRITTEN TORAH AND HIS**

PERFECT TORAH.

As an example, "LOVING OUR ENEMIES" is possible for us to do or Yeshua wouldn't have told us to do it. But, I for one, do not always choose to. **In fact, I think that this is the hardest commandment for me to do <u>from my heart</u>.** I am not just talking about those who do me wrong on some minor issue. But, I know there may be coming a day when I have real enemies that want not only to hurt me but to kill me, probably because I serve Yehovah and His Son Yeshua. **QUITE HONESTLY, ONLY WHEN I REMEMBER THAT YEHOVAH REALLY IS GOING TO TAKE VENGEANCE ON THE WICKED ONE DAY, DO I THINK I WILL BE ABLE TO DECIDE THAT I DON'T HAVE TO DO IT NOW MYSELF!!** Reading all the Prophets and the Book of Revelation, Revelation 6:9-11, Psalm 37 and Psalm 73, and many more scriptures, make it abundantly clear that there is a payday for the wicked!! I can trust My Father to avenge me in His time and in His way. Consider what the Prophet Isaiah says about Yeshua, the Messiah, when he returns:

[Isa 63:1-6 KJV] 1 Who [is] this that cometh from Edom, with dyed garments from Bozrah? this [that is] glorious in his apparel, travelling in the greatness of his strength? **I THAT SPEAK IN RIGHTEOUSNESS, MIGHTY TO SAVE.** 2 Wherefore [art thou] red in thine apparel, and thy garments like him that treadeth in the winefat? 3 I have trodden the winepress alone; and of the people [there was] none with me: for I will tread them in mine anger, and trample them in my fury; and their blood shall be sprinkled upon my garments, and I will stain all my raiment. **4 FOR THE DAY OF VENGEANCE [IS] IN MINE HEART, AND THE YEAR OF MY REDEEMED IS COME.** 5 And I looked, and [there was] none to help; and I wondered that [there was] none to uphold: therefore mine own arm brought salvation unto me; and my fury, it upheld me. 6 And I will tread down the people in mine anger, and make them drunk in my fury, and I will bring down their strength to the earth.

So, when I really consider the wrath of God, and the horrors of hell and then the Eternal Lake of Fire, **EVEN I can at least pray for my enemies to REPENT AND BELIEVE IN YESHUA so they don't have to go there!** That is as far as I may have come in loving my enemies... but it may be the best way...

<u>MY POINT IS, THOUGH, THAT JUST BECAUSE ITS OBVIOUS THAT WE DO NOT KEEP YEHOVAH'S PERFECT TORAH AT ALL TIMES, THAT CERTAINLY DOESN'T MEAN WE SHOULDN'T TRY!!</u>

<u>***I ABSOLUTELY THINK WE BETTER TRY! WHEN WE FAIL, WE NEED TO</u>**

RECOGNIZE THAT WE HAVE SINNED, SINCERELY REPENT, ASK FOR FORGIVENESS BASED ON THE BLOOD SACRIFICE OF YESHUA, RECEIVE THAT FORGIVENESS THANKFULLY, AND GET UP AND TRY AGAIN!!!***

BUT, UNLESS YESHUA SPECIFICALLY ADDRESSED THE RAISING OF THE BAR CONCERNING A CERTAIN COMMANDMENT, STATUTE, OR JUDGMENT, THEN WE SHOULD TRY TO LEARN AND KEEP THE WRITTEN TORAH. IT IS NOT TOO HARD FOR US TO KEEP! IN FACT, KEEPING YEHOVAH'S WRITTEN TORAH IS A PIECE OF CAKE COMPARED TO KEEPING HIS PERFECT TORAH IN OUR HEARTS!!!

HOWEVER, WE STILL SHOULD NOT ADD ANYTHING TO THE WRITTEN TORAH THAT YESHUA DIDN'T INSTRUCT US TO, EITHER. HE CAME TO SHOW US YEHOVAH'S WILL AND HE DID. HIS WORDS ARE SUFFICIENT. ONE MORE TIME, REMEMBER, YESHUA SAID TO DO AND TEACH EVEN THE LEAST OF THE WRITTEN COMMANDMENTS TO BE CALLED GREAT IN THE KINGDOM OF GOD!!! THIS IS PART OF HIS INSTRUCTION TO US, TOO!

Actually, I believe that commandment to even love our enemies is the hardest commandment Yeshua gave us. **But, I think it was already in the Written Torah to a point – The Father has told us concrete ways of how we are to love our enemies:**

[Exo 23:4-5 KJV] 4 If thou meet thine enemy's ox or his ass going astray, thou shalt surely bring it back to him again. 5 If thou see the ass of him that hateth thee lying under his burden, and wouldest forbear to help him, thou shalt surely help with him.

Also, the Proverbs, which is the wisdom Yehovah, our Father, gave to Solomon and **SHOWS HIS (THE FATHER'S) HEART**, already said:

[Pro 24:17 KJV] 17 Rejoice not when thine enemy falleth, and let not thine heart be glad when he stumbleth:

[Pro 25:21 KJV] 21 If thine enemy be hungry, give him bread to eat; and if he be thirsty, give him water to drink.

Yeshua came to give us Yehovah's words, like Moses did, remember? Yehovah's heart did not change! He knows what awaits those who won't turn to him.... [Psa

37:20 KJV] 20 But the wicked shall perish, and the enemies of the LORD [shall be] as the fat of lambs: they shall consume; into smoke shall they consume away.

So, we must love even our enemies...

CHAPTER 20

The Continued Validity of the Dietary Laws of the Written Torah

We need to continue eliminating the arguments against all the believers in Yeshua learning and keeping **ALL** of the Written Torah! A big stumbling block for completely gentile believers is believing that we are actually to keep the statutes to not eat unclean foods! The misunderstanding is based on Acts 10 (entire chapter) where Peter had a vision of unclean animals. However, a careful reading of the account shows that The Father was showing Peter that **NO MAN** was to be called common or unclean, being a gentile, if HE, Yehovah Elohim, had cleansed him. **This was like a parable – it wasn't really about the animals. If it had been, why would we not have seen the rest of the story being about Peter going to tell all the rest of the apostles that they no longer needed to keep the Torah dietary laws from Leviticus 11??? No, the rest of the story was about Peter being confronted with the decision to go with the gentiles who had just come to ask him to go with them to Cornelius's home.** As there is no Written Torah commandment that would have prohibited it, the Oral Torah from the Pharisees obviously would have prohibited Peter from going if Yehovah had not convinced him that it was all right (remember our discussion of the fact that Cornelius was a "devout" gentile and probably should have been treated as part of Israel already).

After about 10 years of my keeping these Biblically kosher laws, **I decided to ask The Holy Spirit to show me absolutely the truth**, **so I would know without a doubt that these laws really do still apply after Peter's vision. IMMEDIATELY,** He brought to my consciousness **Revelation 18: 1-2** which describes events at the end of the age!:

Rev 18:1 KJV - And after these things I saw another angel come down from heaven, having great power; and the earth was lightened with his glory.

Rev 18:2 KJV - And he cried mightily with a strong voice, saying, Babylon the great is fallen, is fallen, and is become the habitation of devils, and the hold of every foul spirit, and a cage of **every UNCLEAN and hateful bird.**

I had never even thought of that verse before! It had to have come to me by

__The Holy Spirit!__ **THIS VERSE DECLARES THAT THERE WILL STILL BE UNCLEAN BIRDS AT THE END OF THE AGE – HE EVEN CALLS THEM HATEFUL!** So, I am satisfied that there are still unclean animals! Consequently, I don't eat them, as the Written Torah says:

Deu 14:3 KJV - Thou shalt not eat any abominable thing.

__The entire chapter of Leviticus 11 details the clean and unclean meats.__

In conclusion, it states:

Lev 11:46 KJV - This [is] the law of the beasts, and of the fowl, and of every living creature that moveth in the waters, and of every creature that creepeth upon the earth:

Lev 11:47 KJV - **To make a difference between the unclean and the clean, and between the beast that may be eaten and the beast that may not be eaten.**

Actually, most people do not realize that Noah, __long before the Written Torah was given,__ was fully aware of the difference between clean and unclean animals. Noah was told to bring seven sets of clean animals into the ark and only two sets of unclean animals! :

[Gen 7:1-3 KJV] 1 And the LORD said unto Noah, Come thou and all thy house into the ark; for thee have I seen righteous before me in this generation. 2 OF EVERY __CLEAN BEAST__ THOU SHALT TAKE TO THEE BY SEVENS, THE MALE AND HIS FEMALE: AND OF BEASTS THAT [ARE] __NOT CLEAN__ BY TWO, THE MALE AND HIS FEMALE. 3 Of fowls also of the air by sevens, the male and the female; to keep seed alive upon the face of all the earth.

You can also see __Isaiah 65:1-7, Isaiah 66:14-17__, which describes __WHEN YESHUA RETURNS AND PUNISHES THOSE WHO ARE EATING SWINE'S FLESH, THE MOUSE, AND THE BROTH OF THE ABOMINABLE!:__

[Isa 65:2-4 KJV] 2 I have spread out my hands all the day unto a rebellious people, which walketh in a way [that was] not good, after their own thoughts; 3 A people that provoketh me to anger continually to my face; that sacrificeth in gardens, and burneth incense upon altars of brick; 4 Which remain among the graves, and lodge in the monuments, __WHICH EAT SWINE'S FLESH, AND BROTH OF ABOMINABLE [THINGS IS IN] THEIR VESSELS__;

[Isa 66:14-17 KJV] 14 And when ye see [this], your heart shall rejoice, and your bones shall flourish like an herb: and the hand of the LORD shall be

known toward his servants, and [his] indignation toward his enemies. 15 For, behold, the LORD will come with fire, and with his chariots like a whirlwind, to render his anger with fury, and his rebuke with flames of fire. 16 For by fire and by his sword will the LORD plead with all flesh: and the slain of the LORD shall be many. 17 They that sanctify themselves, and purify themselves in the gardens behind one [tree] in the midst, <u>EATING SWINE'S FLESH, AND THE ABOMINATION, AND THE MOUSE, SHALL BE CONSUMED TOGETHER</u>, SAITH THE LORD.

It is unfortunate that I know for a fact from listening to some respected ministers' teaching concerning the subject of clean and unclean food, that **the reason they hold that we are not to learn and keep all of the Written Torah is because <u>they DO NOT WANT TO HAVE TO KEEP THESE FOOD LAWS</u>. In other words, their fleshly desires for these meats, because they are so tasty, rules them. IN OTHER WORDS, THEIR STOMACHS RULE!** I have heard many people ask, "Why would Yehovah not want us to eat them when they taste so good?" They **DO** taste good!! However, that is irrelevant. **<u>Could it be that it is a test for us, whether we will be faithful to keep his commandments or not? Yehovah will do that.</u> <u>When the children of Israel were in the desert, Yehovah said he was testing them as to whether they would keep his commandments or not:</u>**

<u>[Deu 8:2-3 KJV] 2 And thou shalt remember all the way which the LORD thy God led thee these forty years in the wilderness, TO HUMBLE THEE, [AND] TO PROVE THEE, TO KNOW WHAT [WAS] IN THINE HEART, WHETHER THOU WOULDEST KEEP HIS COMMANDMENTS, OR NO. 3 And he humbled thee, and suffered thee to hunger, and fed thee with manna, which thou knewest not, neither did thy fathers know; that he might make thee know that man doth not live by bread only, but by every [word] that proceedeth out of the mouth of the LORD doth man live.</u>

Also, many things that are ungodly satisfy our flesh, like unbiblical sex. Just because it feels good does not make it right! **Just like he has given us the pleasure of biblical marital sex, The Father has given us many good meats we can eat that taste wonderful. Can't we be grateful for that? Think of Adam and Eve in the garden of Eden – they could eat of ANY tree of the garden, but that ONE tree! Could it be that The Father placed that tree there as a test to see if they would keep His command? <u>THE WHOLE WORLD FELL BECAUSE ADAM AND EVE DECIDED THAT YEHOVAH ELOHIM DID NOT MEAN WHAT HE SAID CONCERNING FOOD AND THEIR STOMACHS RULED!!!</u>**

<u>THINK ABOUT THAT!!!</u>

Chapter 21

The Written Torah Will Be Kept in the Kingdom of God on Earth During the 1000 Year Reign of Mashiach with the Saints

MOVING FORWARD, WE'LL NOW SEE WHAT YESHUA SAID CONCERNING THE KINGDOM OF GOD ON EARTH – THE 1000 YEAR REIGN OF MASHIACH!:

After Yeshua had been resurrected for many years and residing in heaven with the Father, he evidently felt the need to straighten out some things that had gotten off track in the churches:

YESHUA said in Rev 3:19 KJV **- As many as I love, I rebuke and chasten: be zealous therefore, and REPENT!**

Yeshua confirmed a few of the things that were commanded to the completely gentile believers at the Jerusalem Council when he gave the Apostle John the letters to the seven churches in Asia recorded in the Book of the Revelation of Yeshua ha Mashiach (chapters 1-3.) Yeshua said specifically that he was rebuking any of these churches who had in them those that taught that it was permissible to eat meats (food) sacrificed to idols and to fornicate, two commandments listed in Acts 15. He rebuked those congregations that had those in them that taught the doctrine of Balaam (who caused Israel to sin by fornication with Moabite women). However, he also spoke against the ones who taught the doctrine of the Nicolaitines (there are differing ideas about what this was, but one theory is that it was the practice of setting up a hierarchical structure in the church – the Greek words "niko" meaning "to conquer" and "laity" meaning "the people").

(Possibly, Yeshua gave these instructions to the seven churches because they already had in them those who were teaching that the Written Torah was null and void)! However, notice that **the Apostle John almost always differentiates between and includes both "the testimony of Jesus" and "the Word of God" throughout the Book of the Revelation:**

[Rev 1:1-2 KJV] 1 **THE REVELATION OF JESUS CHRIST**, which God gave unto him, to shew unto his servants things which must shortly come to pass; and he sent and signified [it] **by his angel unto his servant John:** 2 **WHO BARE RECORD OF THE WORD OF GOD, AND OF THE TESTIMONY OF JESUS CHRIST,** and **OF ALL THINGS THAT HE SAW.**

Then, we have a description of many who have made it to heaven!

Rev 7:9 KJV - After this I beheld, and, lo, **a great multitude, which no man could number, of all nations, and kindreds, and people, and tongues, stood before the throne, and before the Lamb, clothed with white robes, and palms in their hands;**

Rev 7:10 KJV - And cried with a loud voice, saying, Salvation to our God which sitteth upon the throne, and unto the Lamb. (Remember, Yeshua is the Lamb)

Rev 7:11 KJV - And all the angels stood round about the throne, and [about] the elders and the four beasts, and fell before the throne on their faces, and worshipped God,

Rev 7:12 KJV - Saying, Amen: Blessing, and glory, and wisdom, and thanksgiving, and honour, and power, and might, [be] unto our God for ever and ever. Amen.

Rev 7:13 KJV - And one of the elders answered, saying unto me, **What are these which are arrayed in white robes? and whence came they?**

Rev 7:14 KJV - And I said unto him, Sir, thou knowest. And he said to me, **These are they which came out of great tribulation, and have washed their robes, and made them white in the blood of the Lamb.**

Rev 7:15 KJV - Therefore are **they before the throne of God**, and serve him day and night in his temple: and he that sitteth on the throne shall dwell among them.

Rev 7:16 KJV - They shall hunger no more, neither thirst any more; neither shall the sun light on them, nor any heat.

Rev 7:17 KJV - For the Lamb which is in the midst of the throne shall feed them, and shall lead them unto living fountains of waters: and God shall wipe away all tears from their eyes.

I believe the Holy Spirit brought to my attention that THESE PEOPLE ARE STANDING BEFORE THE THRONE OF GOD AND BEFORE THE LAMB, WHICH MEANS THEY ARE PRESENT IN THE NEW JERUSALEM WHILE IT IS STILL IN HEAVEN! Then they cannot be people who were committing those particular sins that Yehovah Elohim says will keep people from entering the New Jerusalem!!! They are not fearful, unbelieving, abominable, murderers, whoremongers, idolaters, sorcerers, or liars!! (See Revelation 21:1-8). They have **washed their robes** and **made them white in the blood of the Lamb**, so they had to have **REPENTED** of breaking (at least these categories of) Written Torah commandments, if they had ever committed them, and kept their faith in Yeshua! (They may not have been keeping all of the Written Torah, although we know that it is always The Father's will that we do.)

LATER, THE "SAINTS" ARE SPECIFICALLY CALLED IN THE BOOK OF THE REVELATION (REVELATION 14:12) THOSE PEOPLE WHO KEEP THE COMMANDMENTS OF YEHOVAH ELOHIM AND HAVE THE TESTIMONY OF YESHUA.

IT COULD BE THAT KEEPING THESE EIGHT CATEGORIES OF COMMANDMENTS ARE THE ONLY ONES REQUIRED TO BE CALLED A SAINT (BELIEF IN YESHUA IS ONE OF THESE COMMANDMENTS). I SAY THAT BECAUSE YESHUA SAID THAT THERE WILL BE ONLY ONE FOLD AND ONE SHEPHERD. HOWEVER, THERE MAY BE MORE REWARDS IF YOU KEPT NOT ONLY THESE BUT ALSO EVEN THE LEAST OF THE COMMANDMENTS AND TAUGHT THEM TO OTHERS, BECAUSE YESHUA SAID YOU WOULD BE GREAT IN THE KINGDOM OF HEAVEN IF YOU DID AND YOU WOULD BE LEAST IN THE KINGDOM OF HEAVEN IF YOU DIDN'T (MATTHEW 5:19).

There are numerous places that **all believers in Yeshua** are referred to as this same word, "**saints.**" **EVERY TIME** the word saints is used in the New Testament, it comes from the same Greek word, the Strong's Concordance G40:

ἅγιος hágios, hag'-ee-os; from ἅγος hágos (an awful thing) (compare G53, G2282); sacred (physically, pure, morally blameless or religious, ceremonially, consecrated):—(most) holy (one, thing), saint.

This word is translated in the King James Version of the Bible **as "saints" 61 times**, and **"holy" 161 times**, and **"holy one" 4 times**.

Revelation 14:12 states emphatically:

*****Rev 14:12 KJV - **Here is the patience of the SAINTS: here [are] THEY THAT KEEP THE COMMANDMENTS OF GOD, AND THE FAITH OF JESUS.*******

Another place it is stated as well:

****Rev 12:17 KJV - And the dragon was wroth with **the woman**, and went to make war with **the remnant of her seed, WHICH KEEP THE COMMANDMENTS OF GOD, AND HAVE THE TESTIMONY OF JESUS CHRIST**.

(OBVIOUSLY, THEN, THE WRITTEN TORAH IS NOT NULL AND VOID AND YESHUA IS ALIVE!)

Note in the verses below that these must be **"Saints"** that **have victoriously made it to heaven, probably by death**, because they would not worship the Beast, his image, or take his mark. They are singing **THE SONG OF MOSES (WHO REPRESENTS THE WRITTEN TORAH-THE COMMANDMENTS OF GOD)** and **THE SONG OF THE LAMB (WHO REPRESENTS THE FAITH OF JESUS)**, just as Revelation 14:12 says about the saints. They continue worshipping Yehovah Elohim El Shaddai, calling Him the King of **SAINTS**!

[Rev 15:2-4 KJV] 2 And I saw as it were a sea of glass mingled with fire: and **THEM THAT HAD GOTTEN THE VICTORY OVER THE BEAST, AND OVER HIS IMAGE, AND OVER HIS MARK, [AND] OVER THE NUMBER OF HIS NAME**, stand on the sea of glass, having the harps of God. 3 And **THEY SING THE SONG OF MOSES THE SERVANT OF GOD, AND THE SONG OF THE LAMB**, saying, Great and marvellous [are] thy works, **LORD GOD ALMIGHTY; just and true [are] thy ways, thou KING OF SAINTS**. 4 Who shall not fear thee, O Lord, and glorify thy name? for [thou] only [art] holy: for all nations shall come and worship before thee; for thy judgments are made manifest.

(Even after this scene in heaven, there are still believers still on the earth, because they are admonished by Yeshua. They must be the ones that are gathered together from all over the earth when Yeshua returns, changed into immortal bodies in an instant, if they keep and don't defile their garments!:

[Rev 16:15 KJV] 15 Behold, I come as a thief. Blessed [is] he that watcheth, and **KEEPETH HIS GARMENTS**, **lest he walk naked**, and they see his shame.

Obviously, you can lose your garments!!)

The saints seem to be equated with THE BRIDE OF MASHIACH. NOTE THAT THE SAINTS ARE GRANTED TO BE CLOTHED IN FINE LINEN, CLEAN AND WHITE!!

[Rev 19:7-9 KJV] 7 Let us be glad and rejoice, and give honour to him: FOR THE MARRIAGE OF THE LAMB is come, and HIS WIFE HATH MADE HERSELF READY. 8 And TO HER was granted that she should be arrayed in FINE

LINEN, CLEAN AND WHITE: FOR THE FINE LINEN IS THE RIGHTEOUSNESS OF SAINTS. 9 And he saith unto me, Write, Blessed [are] they which are called unto the MARRIAGE supper of the Lamb. And he saith unto me, These are the true sayings of God.

The saints, who are The Lamb's wife, are called to the marriage supper of the Lamb. That happens when Yeshua returns and takes vengeance on the wicked for The Father, Yehovah Elohim. Those "**ARMIES**" in heaven that are **clothed in fine linen are the ones who return with him**, which seem to be **THE SAINTS .** **Remember they are the ones who have been given fine linen to wear based on their righteousness, which must be their keeping those commandments of God and their faith in Yeshua. They get to assist Him in defeating the wicked!** The **marriage supper of the Lamb** is **the great supper provided to the fowls of heaven to feast on the slain wicked**:

[Rev 19:11-21 KJV] 11 And I saw heaven opened, and behold a white horse; and HE THAT SAT UPON HIM [WAS] CALLED FAITHFUL AND TRUE, AND IN RIGHTEOUSNESS HE DOTH JUDGE AND MAKE WAR. 12 His eyes [were] as a flame of fire, and on his head [were] many crowns; and he had a name written, that no man knew, but he himself. 13 And he [was] clothed with a vesture dipped in blood: and his name is called The Word of God. 14 And THE ARMIES [WHICH WERE] IN HEAVEN FOLLOWED HIM UPON WHITE HORSES, CLOTHED IN FINE LINEN, WHITE AND CLEAN. 15 And out of his mouth goeth a sharp sword, that with it he should smite the nations: and he shall rule them with a rod of iron: and HE TREADETH THE WINEPRESS OF THE FIERCENESS AND WRATH OF ALMIGHTY GOD. 16 And he hath on [his] vesture and on his thigh a name written, KING OF KINGS, AND LORD OF LORDS. 17 And I SAW AN ANGEL STANDING IN THE SUN; AND HE CRIED WITH A LOUD VOICE, SAYING TO ALL THE FOWLS THAT FLY IN THE MIDST OF HEAVEN, COME AND GATHER YOURSELVES TOGETHER UNTO THE SUPPER OF THE GREAT GOD; 18 THAT YE MAY EAT THE FLESH OF KINGS, AND THE FLESH OF CAPTAINS, AND THE FLESH OF MIGHTY MEN, AND THE FLESH OF HORSES, AND OF THEM THAT SIT ON THEM, AND THE FLESH OF ALL [MEN, BOTH] FREE AND BOND, BOTH SMALL AND GREAT. 19 And I saw the beast, and the kings of the earth, and their armies, gathered together to make war against him that sat on the horse, and against his army. 20 And THE BEAST was taken, and with him THE FALSE PROPHET THAT WROUGHT MIRACLES BEFORE HIM, WITH WHICH HE DECEIVED THEM THAT HAD RECEIVED THE MARK OF THE BEAST, AND THEM THAT WORSHIPPED HIS IMAGE. These both were cast alive into a lake of fire burning with brimstone.

21 And <u>THE REMNANT WERE SLAIN WITH THE SWORD OF HIM THAT SAT UPON THE HORSE, WHICH [SWORD] PROCEEDED OUT OF HIS MOUTH</u>: and <u>ALL THE FOWLS WERE FILLED WITH THEIR FLESH</u>.

This is prophesied in Psalm 149 also (Note that <u>all</u> the saints are referred to as Israel and as the children of Zion! There is only one Israel!):

[Psa 149:1-9 KJV] 1 Praise ye the LORD. Sing unto the LORD a new song, [and] his praise in the **CONGREGATION OF SAINTS**. 2 Let **ISRAEL** rejoice in him that made him: let the **CHILDREN OF ZION** be joyful in their King. 3 Let them praise his name in the dance: let them sing praises unto him with the timbrel and harp. 4 For the LORD taketh pleasure in his people: he will beautify the meek with salvation. 5 **Let the SAINTS be joyful in glory**: let them sing aloud upon their beds. 6 **[Let] the high [praises] of God [be] in their mouth, and A TWOEDGED SWORD IN THEIR HAND; 7 TO EXECUTE VENGEANCE UPON THE HEATHEN, [AND] PUNISHMENTS UPON THE PEOPLE; 8 TO BIND THEIR KINGS WITH CHAINS, AND THEIR NOBLES WITH FETTERS OF IRON; 9 <u>TO EXECUTE UPON THEM THE JUDGMENT WRITTEN: THIS HONOUR HAVE ALL HIS SAINTS.</u> Praise ye the LORD.**

The word translated in this verse as "saints" from the Hebrew, according to the Strong's Exhaustive Concordance of the Bible, is very interesting too:

חָסִיד châçîyd, khaw-seed'; from <u>H2616</u>; properly, <u>kind</u>, i.e. (<u>religiously</u>) <u>pious</u> (a saint):—<u>godly</u> (man), <u>good</u>, <u>holy</u> (one), <u>merciful</u>, <u>saint</u>, (un-) godly

IT SOUNDS LIKE THE SAINTS ARE GODLY AND HOLY TO YEHOVAH AS WELL AS KIND AND MERCIFUL TO OTHERS.....

They are honored to help Yeshua finally carry out the vengeance on the wicked at the end of the age.

So that means they are there with Yeshua, in their immortal bodies, having been part of the first resurrection, and **<u>RULE WITH HIM</u>** for a thousand years (until they are attacked again)!

[Rev 20:4 KJV] 4 AND I SAW THRONES, AND THEY SAT UPON THEM, AND JUDGMENT WAS GIVEN UNTO THEM: and [I saw] <u>the souls of them that were beheaded for the witness of Jesus, and for the word of God, and which had not worshipped the beast, neither his image, neither had received [his] mark upon their foreheads, or in their hands</u>; and they lived and reigned with Christ a thousand years.

[Rev 20:5 KJV] 5 But the rest of the dead lived not again until the thousand years were finished. This [is] the first resurrection.

[Rev 20:6 KJV] 6 Blessed and holy [is] he that hath part in the <u>first resurrection</u>: on such the second death hath no power, BUT THEY SHALL BE PRIESTS OF GOD AND OF CHRIST, AND SHALL REIGN WITH HIM A THOUSAND YEARS.

There are **many prophecies** in the Bible about the hope of a resurrection, including Psalm 71:20 (KJV) where David says, **"<u>THOU, which hast shewed me great and sore troubles, SHALT QUICKEN ME AGAIN, and SHALT BRING ME UP AGAIN FROM THE DEPTHS OF THE EARTH</u>."**

But, exactly who is going to be in the kingdom of God for that 1000 year reign is entirely in The Father's sovereignty. We know Abraham, Isaac, and Jacob will be there, along with many who come from the east and west (Matthew 8:11-12), Daniel (Daniel 12:13), and all of the twelve apostles who will be ruling the twelve tribes of Israel (Luke 22:28-30). Of course, this is just a sampling of who will be there.

However, that they will be the "SAINTS" was also prophesied in Daniel chapter 7. You should read the entire chapter for the whole story, but verses 23 to 28 synopsizes it:

[Dan 7:15, 23-28 KJV] 15 I Daniel was grieved in my spirit in the midst of [my] body, and the visions of my head troubled me. ... 23 Thus he said, The fourth beast shall be the fourth kingdom upon earth, which shall be diverse from all kingdoms, and shall devour the whole earth, and shall tread it down, and break it in pieces. 24 And the ten horns out of this kingdom [are] ten kings [that] shall arise: and another shall rise after them; and he shall be diverse from the first, and he shall subdue three kings. 25 And he shall speak [great] words against the most High, and <u>shall wear out THE SAINTS OF THE MOST HIGH</u>, and think to change times and laws: and <u>they shall be given into his hand until a time and times and the dividing of time.</u> 26 BUT the judgment shall sit, and <u>THEY</u> SHALL TAKE AWAY HIS DOMINION, TO CONSUME AND TO DESTROY [IT] UNTO THE END. 27 And THE KINGDOM AND DOMINION, AND THE GREATNESS OF THE KINGDOM UNDER THE WHOLE HEAVEN, SHALL BE GIVEN TO THE PEOPLE OF <u>THE SAINTS OF THE MOST HIGH</u>, WHOSE KINGDOM [IS] AN EVERLASTING KINGDOM, AND ALL DOMINIONS SHALL SERVE AND OBEY HIM. 28 Hitherto [is] the end of the matter. As for me Daniel, my cogitations much troubled me, and my

countenance changed in me: but I kept the matter in my heart.

WHATEVER IT TAKES TO BE IN THAT NUMBER OF THE SAINTS, IT WILL BE WORTH IT!

It has generally been assumed that those who are part of a church (congregation) will make it to heaven. But, let's think about that. Revelation 3 speaks to the "church" at Laodecia, people who said they believed in Yeshua, but His harsh words to them includes speaking to them of their nakedness. He counsels them to buy "white raiment" from him so they can be clothed and the shame of their nakedness would not appear. It sounds like they have a choice. **Since the true saints are granted clean, white, fine linen to wear, because of their righteousness (possibly keeping at least those eight categories of commandments of Yehovah, including belief in Yeshua), and the people in this church are naked, then they don't meet the criteria to obtain that status...** remember, this really was a church or he wouldn't have been writing to them. They were one of the candlesticks (menorahs) – lights in this part of Asia Minor!!!

[Rev 3:14-22 KJV] 14 And unto the angel of **THE CHURCH OF THE LAODICEANS** write; **THESE THINGS SAITH THE AMEN, THE FAITHFUL AND TRUE WITNESS, THE BEGINNING OF THE CREATION OF GOD**; 15 I know thy works, that thou art neither cold nor hot: I would thou wert cold or hot. 16 So then **BECAUSE THOU ART LUKEWARM, AND NEITHER COLD NOR HOT, I WILL SPUE THEE OUT OF MY MOUTH.** 17 **Because thou sayest, I am rich, and increased with goods, and have need of nothing; and knowest not that thou art wretched, and miserable, and poor, and blind, and NAKED**: 18 **I COUNSEL THEE TO BUY OF ME** gold tried in the fire, that thou mayest be rich; and **WHITE RAIMENT, THAT THOU MAYEST BE CLOTHED, AND [THAT] THE SHAME OF THY NAKEDNESS DO NOT APPEAR**; and anoint thine eyes with eyesalve, that thou mayest see. 19 **AS MANY AS I LOVE, I REBUKE AND CHASTEN: BE ZEALOUS THEREFORE, AND REPENT.** 20 Behold, I stand at the door, and knock: if any man hear my voice, and open the door, I will come in to him, and will sup with him, and he with me. 21 **TO HIM THAT OVERCOMETH WILL I GRANT TO SIT WITH ME IN MY THRONE, EVEN AS I ALSO OVERCAME, AND AM SET DOWN WITH MY FATHER IN HIS THRONE.** 22 He that hath an ear, let him hear what the Spirit saith unto the churches.

WHAT AN AWESOME PROMISE TO THOSE WHO WOULD REPENT!!!

I have just heard recently, although I can't verify it, from a Messianic teacher that I respect, that **NONE OF THOSE SEVEN ASIAN CHURCHES TO WHOM THESE ADMONITIONS WERE WRITTEN IN REVELATION 1-3 IS STILL FUNCTIONING AFTER THESE TWO THOUSAND YEARS!** If so, that should be a wake up call to all believers that we must do our part to **OVERCOME** to **be in that number of the saints, the Bride of Yeshua Ha Mashiach! Be zealous and repent!**

During Yeshua's reign as King of Kings during the last 1000 years of this earth (the MILLENNIAL OR MESSIANIC KINGDOM as it is called), ALL PEOPLE THAT ARE SAVED ALIVE, EVEN GENTILES, WILL COME UP TO JERUSALEM TO HEAR ALL THE WRITTEN TORAH OF YEHOVAH ELOHIM AND DO IT!

IT SOUNDS LIKE PEOPLE CAN LEARN IT NOW OR LEARN IT LATER! BUT, WE WILL LEARN IT!

Isaiah 2 states:

Isa 2:1 KJV - The word that Isaiah the son of Amoz saw concerning Judah and Jerusalem.

Isa 2:2 KJV - And it shall come to pass **IN THE LAST DAYS**, [that] **THE MOUNTAIN OF THE LORD'S HOUSE** shall be established in the top of the mountains, and shall be exalted above the hills; and **ALL NATIONS** shall flow unto it. (This word translated as nations means ethnic groups, or tribes, in Hebrew.)

Isa 2:3 KJV - And **MANY PEOPLE** shall go and say, Come ye, and let us go up to the mountain of the LORD, **TO THE HOUSE OF THE GOD OF JACOB**; and **he will teach us of HIS WAYS, and we will walk in HIS PATHS: for out of Zion shall go forth THE LAW [The Hebrew word is TORAH – Strong's Concordance Hebrew #8451] and THE WORD OF THE LORD from Jerusalem.**

Isa 2:4 KJV - And he shall **JUDGE AMONG THE NATIONS**, and shall **REBUKE MANY PEOPLE**: and they shall beat their swords into plowshares, and their spears into pruninghooks: **NATION SHALL NOT LIFT UP SWORD AGAINST NATION, NEITHER SHALL THEY LEARN WAR ANY MORE.**

FROM THESE VERSES, WE CAN SEE THAT IN THE MILLENIAL KINGDOM OF THE MESSIAH, THE WRITTEN TORAH AND YESHUA'S WORDS WILL LEAD PEOPLE TO GET ALONG WELL WITH EACH OTHER AND NOT BE AT WAR WITH EACH OTHER!!! OF COURSE, THEY WILL BE RULED BY A PERFECT KING OF KINGS WITH A ROD OF IRON AT THAT POINT!

This is even reiterated in Micah 4:

Mic 4:1 KJV - But **IN THE LAST DAYS** it shall come to pass, [that] the mountain of the house of the LORD shall be established in the top of the mountains, and it shall be exalted above the hills; and people shall flow unto it.

Mic 4:2 KJV - And **MANY NATIONS shall come, and say, Come, and let us go up to the mountain of the LORD, and TO THE HOUSE OF THE GOD OF JACOB; and he will teach us of HIS WAYS, and we will walk in HIS PATHS: for THE LAW shall go forth of Zion, and THE WORD OF THE LORD from Jerusalem.**

Mic 4:3 KJV - And he shall **JUDGE AMONG MANY PEOPLE**, and **REBUKE** strong nations afar off; and they shall beat their swords into plowshares, and their spears into pruninghooks: **NATION SHALL NOT LIFT UP A SWORD AGAINST NATION, NEITHER SHALL THEY LEARN WAR ANY MORE.**

Also, as brought out before, in Isaiah 56:1-8, The Father states that He will bring even the "sons of the stranger", the completely gentiles, that keep His Sabbaths and keep His Covenant (His Commandments), to His Holy Mountain of Zion and accept their sacrifices during the Messianic Kingdom as it will be a House of Prayer for all peoples. Yeshua confirmed this prophecy.

EVEN THE FEASTS OF YEHOVAH AS ORDAINED IN THE WRITTEN TORAH (SEE LEVITICUS 23, NUMBERS 28 AND 29, DEUTERONOMY 16) WILL STILL BE KEPT – EVEN BY THE GENTILES! SEE ZECHARIAH 14:

Zec 14:16 KJV - And it shall come to pass, [that] EVERY ONE that is left of all the nations which came against Jerusalem shall even go up from year to year to worship the King, the LORD of hosts, and to keep THE FEAST OF TABERNACLES.

Zec 14:17 KJV - And it shall be, [that] whoso will not come up of [ALL] THE FAMILIES OF THE EARTH unto Jerusalem to worship the King, the LORD of hosts, even upon them shall be no rain.

Zec 14:18 KJV - And if the family of Egypt go not up, and come not, that [have] no [rain]; there shall be the plague, WHEREWITH THE LORD WILL SMITE THE HEATHEN THAT COME NOT UP TO KEEP THE FEAST OF TABERNACLES.

Zec 14:19 KJV - This shall be the punishment of Egypt, and THE PUNISHMENT OF ALL NATIONS THAT COME NOT UP TO KEEP THE FEAST OF TABERNACLES.

Ezekiel 37:15-25 ALSO CONFIRMS THAT THE WRITTEN TORAH WILL BE ADHERED TO AGAIN IN THE LAND OF ISRAEL UNDER THE KINGSHIP OF

YESHUA HA MASHIACH, THE SON OF DAVID!

Eze 37:15 KJV - The word of the LORD came again unto me, saying,

Eze 37:16 KJV - Moreover, thou son of man, take thee one stick, and write upon it, For Judah, and for the children of Israel his companions: then take another stick, and write upon it, For Joseph, the stick of Ephraim, and [for] all the house of Israel his companions:

Eze 37:17 KJV - And join them one to another into one stick; and they shall become one in thine hand.

Eze 37:18 KJV - And when the children of thy people shall speak unto thee, saying, Wilt thou not shew us what thou [meanest] by these?

Eze 37:19 KJV - Say unto them, Thus saith the Lord GOD; Behold, I will take the stick of Joseph, which [is] in the hand of Ephraim, and the tribes of Israel his fellows, and will put them with him, [even] with the stick of Judah, and make them one stick, and they shall be one in mine hand.

Eze 37:20 KJV - And the sticks whereon thou writest shall be in thine hand before their eyes.

Eze 37:21 KJV - And say unto them, Thus saith the Lord GOD; Behold, I will take the children of Israel from among the heathen, whither they be gone, and will gather them on every side, and bring them into their own land:

Eze 37:22 KJV - And I will make them one nation in the land upon the mountains of Israel; and one king shall be king to them all: and they shall be no more two nations, neither shall they be divided into two kingdoms any more at all:

Eze 37:23 KJV - NEITHER SHALL THEY DEFILE THEMSELVES ANY MORE WITH THEIR IDOLS, NOR WITH THEIR DETESTABLE THINGS, NOR WITH ANY OF THEIR TRANSGRESSIONS: but I will save them out of all their dwellingplaces, wherein they have sinned, and WILL CLEANSE THEM: so shall they be my people, and I will be their God.

Eze 37:24 KJV - and DAVID MY SERVANT [SHALL BE] KING OVER THEM; AND THEY ALL SHALL HAVE ONE SHEPHERD: THEY SHALL ALSO WALK IN MY JUDGMENTS, AND OBSERVE MY STATUTES, AND DO THEM.

Eze 37:25 KJV - And they shall dwell in the land that I have given unto Jacob my servant, wherein your fathers have dwelt; and they shall dwell therein, [even] they, and their children, and their children's children for ever: and MY SERVANT DAVID [SHALL BE] THEIR PRINCE FOR EVER.

CHAPTER 22

Eight Categories of Commandments of the Written Torah Will Absolutely Be Required to Enter into the New Jerusalem that Comes Down Out of Heaven!

FINALLY, AND ABOVE ALL, LET'S LOOK AT THE NEW JERUSALEM UNDER YEHOVAH ELOHIM'S RULE ON THE NEW EARTH!

Revelation 20 continues and lets us know that after the 1000 year reign of Yeshua ha Mashiach, satan will be loosed, just long enough for him to gather all the nations from the four quarters of the earth, the lands of Gog and Magog, to come against the beloved city (present Jerusalem) and the camp of the saints (I believe all of the land of Israel) one last time. **The Father Himself sends fire from heaven**, devouring these nations, and gets rid of satan for good in the Lake of Fire!!! As Yeshua turns over the Kingdom to the Father,**The Father will then judge everyone who was not resurrected in the first resurrection, small and great, ACCORDING TO THEIR WORKS**, as He judges from His Great White Throne. This is probably anyone who is not a Saint by Yehovah's standards, as they have already experienced resurrection. If by any chance there are any believers left who were not part of the first resurrection, if they are written in the Lamb's (Yeshua's) Book of Life, they will experience resurrection at that time. The Prophecy doesn't call it the second resurrection, but remember that the saints who came back with Yeshua (Revelation 20:4) and those who were still on earth but were changed instantly to immortal bodies, reigned with Him a thousand years and were part of the first resurrection. **Why would he call it the first resurrection if there were not to be another, a second resurrection? Most Christians believe that only the wicked will experience this second resurrection, which actually is never called that but is called the second death. As I stated earlier, all of this is , of course, totally in Yehovah's sovereignty – ALL of the people written in the Lamb's Book of Life may already have been resurrected!**

ALL THAT IS REALLY NECESSARY FOR US TO KNOW IS HOW TO AVOID THAT SECOND DEATH, THE LAKE OF FIRE!! DO NOT COMMIT THOSE EIGHT

CATEGORIES OF SINS AND MAKE SURE YOUR NAME IS WRITTEN IN THE LAMB'S BOOK OF LIFE!! BELIEF IN YESHUA IS A MAJOR PART OF THE LITMUS TEST!!!!

Rev 20:7 KJV - And when the thousand years are expired, Satan shall be loosed out of his prison,

Rev 20:8 KJV - And shall go out to deceive the nations which are in the four quarters of the earth, Gog and Magog, to gather them together to battle: the number of whom [is] as the sand of the sea.

Rev 20:9 KJV - And **THEY WENT UP ON THE BREADTH OF THE EARTH**, and **COMPASSED THE CAMP OF THE SAINTS** about, and **THE BELOVED CITY: AND FIRE CAME DOWN FROM GOD OUT OF HEAVEN, AND DEVOURED THEM.!!!!!**

Rev 20:10 KJV - **AND THE DEVIL THAT DECEIVED THEM WAS CAST INTO THE LAKE OF FIRE AND BRIMSTONE, WHERE THE BEAST AND THE FALSE PROPHET [ARE], AND SHALL BE TORMENTED DAY AND NIGHT FOR EVER AND EVER.**

Rev 20:11 KJV - **AND I SAW A GREAT WHITE THRONE, AND HIM THAT SAT ON IT, FROM WHOSE FACE THE EARTH AND THE HEAVEN FLED AWAY; AND THERE WAS FOUND NO PLACE FOR THEM.**

Rev 20:12 KJV - **AND I SAW THE DEAD, SMALL AND GREAT, STAND BEFORE GOD; AND THE BOOKS WERE OPENED: AND ANOTHER BOOK WAS OPENED, WHICH IS [THE BOOK] OF LIFE: AND THE DEAD WERE JUDGED OUT OF THOSE THINGS WHICH WERE WRITTEN IN THE BOOKS, ACCORDING TO THEIR WORKS.**

Rev 20:13 KJV - And the sea gave up the dead which were in it; and death and hell delivered up the dead which were in them: and **THEY WERE JUDGED EVERY MAN ACCORDING TO THEIR WORKS**.

Rev 20:14 KJV - **And death and hell were cast into THE LAKE OF FIRE. This is THE SECOND DEATH.** Rev 20:15 KJV - AND **WHOSOEVER WAS NOT FOUND WRITTEN IN THE BOOK OF LIFE WAS CAST INTO THE LAKE OF FIRE.**!!!

THE FATHER HIMSELF DESCRIBES WHO HE WILL ALLOW TO ENTER INTO

THE **NEW JERUSALEM** THAT WILL COME DOWN OUT OF HEAVEN TO THE NEW EARTH, after the Millenial Kingdom - AND WHO HE WILL NOT!!!

Rev 21:1 KJV – And **I saw a new heaven and a new earth**: for the first heaven and the first earth were passed away; and there was no more sea.

Rev 21:2 KJV - And I John saw **THE HOLY CITY, THE NEW JERUSALEM, COMING DOWN FROM GOD OUT OF HEAVEN**, prepared as a bride adorned for her husband.

Rev 21:3 KJV - **AND I HEARD A GREAT VOICE OUT OF HEAVEN SAYING, BEHOLD, THE TABERNACLE OF GOD [IS] WITH MEN, AND HE WILL DWELL WITH THEM, AND THEY SHALL BE HIS PEOPLE, AND GOD HIMSELF SHALL BE WITH THEM, [AND BE] THEIR GOD.**

REV 21:4 KJV - AND GOD SHALL WIPE AWAY ALL TEARS FROM THEIR EYES; AND THERE SHALL BE NO MORE DEATH, NEITHER SORROW, NOR CRYING, NEITHER SHALL THERE BE ANY MORE PAIN: FOR THE FORMER THINGS ARE PASSED AWAY.

Rev 21:5 KJV - **And HE THAT SAT UPON THE THRONE SAID, Behold, I make all things new. And he said unto me, Write: for these words are true and faithful.**

Rev 21:6 KJV - And He said unto me, IT IS DONE. I am Alpha and Omega, the beginning and the end. I will give unto him that is athirst of the fountain of the water of life freely.

Rev 21:7 KJV - He that OVERCOMETH shall INHERIT ALL THINGS; and I WILL BE HIS GOD, AND HE SHALL BE MY SON.

Rev 21:8 KJV – BUT, the FEARFUL, and UNBELIEVING, and THE ABOMINABLE, and MURDERERS, and WHOREMONGERS, and SORCERERS, and IDOLATERS, and ALL LIARS, shall have THEIR PART IN THE LAKE WHICH BURNETH WITH FIRE AND BRIMSTONE: which is THE SECOND DEATH!!!

THE FATHER IS THE ONE SITTING ON THE THRONE! THIS IS THE FATHER HIMSELF SPEAKING!! (WE WILL BE HIS SONS AND DAUGHTERS IF WE OVERCOME!!!)

Remember Revelation 20:13 that we just reviewed said that **YEHOVAH, SITTING**

ON THE GREAT WHITE THRONE, WILL BE JUDGING PEOPLE ACCORDING TO THEIR WORKS. THE DEEDS LISTED ABOVE, THESE EIGHT SINS, APPEAR TO BE THE WORKS THAT HE JUDGES BY!

WHERE DO YOU FIND THE LAWS THAT ARE SPOKEN OF HERE BUT IN THE WRITTEN TORAH! TAKE FOR EXAMPLE, THE WORD ABOMINABLE. THE WRITTEN TORAH IS THE ONLY PLACE THAT EXPLAINS WHAT IS ABOMINABLE TO THE FATHER - THIS ABSOLUTELY PROVES THAT THE WRITTEN TORAH IS NOT ABOLISHED!! If the abominable, those who do abominable things, can't go into the New Jerusalem and instead go into the Lake of Fire, it would be worth finding out all the things that are counted as abominations to The Father! There are many of them!! Here is an example from The Father:

[Deu 17:2-7 KJV] 2 If there be found among you, within any of thy gates which the LORD thy God giveth thee, **MAN OR WOMAN, THAT HATH WROUGHT WICKEDNESS IN THE SIGHT OF THE LORD THY GOD, IN TRANSGRESSING HIS COVENANT, 3 AND HATH GONE AND SERVED OTHER GODS, AND WORSHIPPED THEM, EITHER THE SUN, OR MOON, OR ANY OF THE HOST OF HEAVEN, WHICH I HAVE NOT COMMANDED;** 4 And it be told thee, and thou hast heard [of it], and enquired diligently, and, behold, [it be] true, [and] the thing certain, [that] such **ABOMINATION** is wrought in Israel: 5 Then shalt thou bring forth that man or that woman, which have committed that wicked thing, unto thy gates, [even] that man or that woman, and shalt stone them with stones, till they die. 6 At the mouth of two witnesses, or three witnesses, shall he that is worthy of death be put to death; [but] at the mouth of one witness he shall not be put to death. 7 The hands of the witnesses shall be first upon him to put him to death, and afterward the hands of all the people. So thou shalt put the evil away from among you.

These are just a few verses. You can use a Strong's Concordance and look up **ALL** the words "**abomination, abominations, and abominable**"! **[SEE APPENDIX II FOR A DETAILED LIST OF ABOMINATIONS, AS WELL AS OTHER SINS THAT WILL SEND YOU TO THE LAKE OF FIRE - UNLESS YOU REPENT (TURN FROM THEM!) AND ASK FOR FORGIVENESS IN YESHUA'S NAME!!]**

We need to remember that the "saints," the holy ones, the believers in Yeshua that keep the commandments of God, the ones who have not defiled their white, linen garments, have already been resurrected and the second death has no power over them. **But I still do not think it would ever be wise to be presumptuous and**

say, "this does not apply to me – I'm saved." Why? Hear what The Father said to Israel:

[Jer 7:8-12 KJV] 8 Behold, **ye trust in lying words**, that cannot profit. 9 **Will ye STEAL, MURDER, and COMMIT ADULTERY, and SWEAR FALSELY, and BURN INCENSE UNTO BAAL, and WALK AFTER OTHER GODS WHOM YE KNOW NOT; 10 And come and stand before me in this house, which is called by my name, AND SAY, WE ARE DELIVERED TO DO ALL THESE ABOMINATIONS?** 11 Is this house, which is called by my name, become a den of robbers in your eyes? Behold, even I have seen [it], saith the LORD. 12 **BUT GO YE NOW UNTO MY PLACE WHICH [WAS] IN SHILOH, WHERE I SET MY NAME AT THE FIRST, AND SEE WHAT I DID TO IT FOR THE WICKEDNESS OF MY PEOPLE ISRAEL!!!**

THE FATHER DOES NOT STATE ANY DIFFERENCE BETWEEN UNBELIEVERS, JEWISH BELIEVERS, BELIEVERS FROM THE HOUSE OF ISRAEL, DEVOUT GENTILE BELIEVERS JOINED TO ISRAEL BY THE MOSAIC COVENANT, OR COMPLETELY GENTILE BELIEVERS AT THIS POINT AS TO WHETHER THEY WILL BE GRANTED ACCESS INTO THE NEW JERUSALEM OR NOT.

THE LAWS IN REVELATION 21:8 ARE FOR ALL IT SEEMS!!!

The Father also says of the New Jerusalem:

Rev 21:27 KJV - And THERE SHALL IN NO WISE enter into it ANY THING THAT DEFILETH, neither [whatsoever] WORKETH ABOMINATION, or [MAKETH] A LIE: but THEY WHICH ARE WRITTEN IN THE LAMB'S BOOK OF LIFE.

*******It is also important to note that the Father seems to equate believers in Yeshua that don't break these certain laws of His as being THOSE WHO ARE [OR STAY] WRITTEN in the Lamb's Book of Life.** *****

Revelation 17:8 says that the Father has written the names of His people in the Lamb's Book of Life before the foundation of the world!:

[Rev 17:8 KJV] 8 The beast that thou sawest was, and is not; and shall ascend out of the bottomless pit, and go into perdition: and **they that dwell on the earth** shall wonder, **whose names were not written in the book of life from the foundation of the world**, when they behold the beast that was, and is not, and yet is.

BUT, a very important point in Revelation 3 below shows us that YOUR

<u>NAME CAN BE BLOTTED OUT OF THE LAMB'S BOOK OF LIFE BY YOU "DEFILING YOUR GARMENTS"</u>!! Defilement is listed above in Revelation 21:27 in the same category as sinning by "working abomination" and lying!!

YESHUA SAID:

Rev 3:1 KJV - And unto the angel of the church in Sardis write; These things saith he that hath the seven Spirits of God, and the seven stars; I know thy works, that thou hast a name that thou livest, and art dead.

Rev 3:2 KJV - Be watchful, and strengthen the things which remain, that are ready to die: for I have not found thy works perfect before God.

Rev 3:3 KJV - Remember therefore how thou hast received and heard, and **<u>HOLD FAST, AND REPENT</u>**. If therefore thou shalt not watch, I will come on thee as a thief, and thou shalt not know what hour I will come upon thee.

<u>Rev 3:4 KJV - Thou hast a FEW NAMES even in Sardis which HAVE NOT DEFILED THEIR GARMENTS; and THEY shall WALK WITH ME IN WHITE: for THEY ARE WORTHY.</u>

<u>Rev 3:5 KJV - He that OVERCOMETH, the same shall be CLOTHED IN WHITE RAIMENT; and I WILL NOT BLOT OUT HIS NAME OUT OF THE BOOK OF LIFE, but I WILL CONFESS HIS NAME BEFORE MY FATHER, and before his angels.</u>

Rev 3:6 KJV - He that hath an ear, let him hear what the Spirit saith unto the churches.

IF HE WILL NOT BLOT OUT THE NAMES OF THOSE WHO HAVE NOT DEFILED THEIR GARMENTS, IT SEEMS TO ME THAT HE IS SAYING HE <u>WILL</u> BLOT OUT THE NAMES OF <u>THOSE WHO DO DEFILE THEIR GARMENTS</u>, IF THEY DON'T REPENT!

Think about the enormity of this.

You can only see this if you read the entire Bible from Genesis to Revelation and try to see the entire picture without any preconceived notions or taking a scripture here and a scripture there. I think Yehovah is working a wonderful plan of redemption for mankind because He is so loving and merciful , **BUT HE INTENDS TO HAVE A CLEAN, CLOTHED IN WHITE AND BEAUTIFUL BRIDE FOR HIS SON!**

(Yeshua also describes what defiles a person in Matthew 15:18-19:

[Mat 15:18-19 KJV] 18 But those things which proceed out of the mouth come forth from the heart; and they **DEFILE** the man. 19 For out of the heart proceed **EVIL THOUGHTS, MURDERS, ADULTERIES, FORNICATIONS, THEFTS, FALSE WITNESS, BLASPHEMIES.)**

IT IS EVEN CLEARER THAT YOUR NAME ALSO CAN BE BLOTTED OUT BY DENYING FAITH IN YESHUA!!:

Mat 10:32 KJV - Whosoever therefore shall confess me before men, him will I confess also before my Father which is in heaven.

Mat 10:33 KJV - BUT WHOSOEVER SHALL DENY ME BEFORE MEN, HIM WILL I ALSO DENY BEFORE MY FATHER WHICH IS IN HEAVEN.

THE BIBLE ALSO LISTS ONE MORE WAY THAT YOUR NAME CAN BE BLOTTED OUT OF THE LAMB'S BOOK OF LIFE.

CONCERNING THE BOOK OF THE REVELATION OF YESHUA HA MASHIACH GIVEN TO THE APOSTLE JOHN, YESHUA STATES:

[Rev 22:19 KJV] 19 AND IF ANY MAN SHALL TAKE AWAY FROM THE WORDS OF THE BOOK OF THIS PROPHECY, GOD SHALL TAKE AWAY HIS PART OUT OF THE BOOK OF LIFE, AND OUT OF THE HOLY CITY, AND [FROM] THE THINGS WHICH ARE WRITTEN IN THIS BOOK.

Yeshua also says , by his Angel:

Rev 22:12 KJV - And, behold, I COME QUICKLY; and MY REWARD [IS] WITH ME, TO GIVE EVERY MAN ACCORDING AS HIS WORK SHALL BE.

Rev 22:13 KJV - I am Alpha and Omega, the beginning and the end, the first and the last.

Rev 22:14 KJV - BLESSED [are] they that DO HIS COMMANDMENTS, that they may have RIGHT TO THE TREE OF LIFE, and MAY ENTER IN THROUGH THE GATES INTO THE CITY.

Rev 22:15 KJV - FOR WITHOUT [are] DOGS, and SORCERERS, and WHOREMONGERS, and MURDERERS, and IDOLATERS, and WHOSOEVER LOVETH AND MAKETH A LIE.

We have seen from Revelation 21:8 above that these will be in the Lake of Fire! The term "DOGS" here may be those people who are FEARFUL, UNBELIEVING, AND ABOMINABLE from Revelation 21:8 since all the rest of those who are denied entrance are duplicated here as well.

IT IS COMPLETELY OBVIOUS TO ME THAT THERE IS GREAT REWARD IN KEEPING YOUR FAITH IN YESHUA AND KEEPING ALL THE COMMANDMENTS OF YEHOVAH AND THERE IS GREAT DAMNATION IN NOT KEEPING AT LEAST THESE EIGHT CATEGORIES OF COMMANDMENTS!

Rev 22:16 KJV - I Jesus have sent mine angel to testify unto you these things in the churches. I am the root and the offspring of David, [and] the bright and morning star.

NOTE THAT YESHUA SAYS TO DO THE FATHER'S COMMANDMENTS TO HAVE A RIGHT TO THE TREE OF LIFE AND BE ABLE TO GO THROUGH THE GATES INTO THE NEW JERUSALEM!!!!

Unfortunately, some of the practices of the church (the congregation of believers in Yeshua) have their source in one of his most hated sins, IDOLATRY, as we have discussed. It would be wise to change these as soon as you learn of them! I actually believe the gravity of how much Yehovah hates idolatry is one of the reasons that He is bringing this understanding of the Written Torah to the churches now BECAUSE YESHUA IS COMING BACK SOON!!! There are many books, CDs, and DVDs dedicated to revealing these practices, one of the best being Too Long in the Sun by Richard Rives. (See Recommended Reading and Research).

CHAPTER 23

Will It Be Worth It? Absolutely! OVERCOMING Will Allow Us to Be Yehovah's Sons and Daughters Forever!!!

SO, WILL IT REALLY BE WORTH IT? WILL IT BE WORTH BELIEVING IN AND OBEYING YESHUA AS WELL AS GIVING UP OUR OWN WILL TO KEEP THE FATHER'S WRITTEN TORAH?

YES!!!!!

IF WE DO, WE WILL BE ABLE TO BE YESHUA'S UPRIGHT AMBASSADORS ON EARTH NOW, BRINGING HIM GLORY AND NOT SHAME, AS VESSELS OF HONOR! WE CAN BE FILLED WITH THE HOLY SPIRIT OF YEHOVAH; EMPOWERED TO DISPLAY THE TRUE POWER OF THE KINGDOM OF YEHOVAH ELOHIM LIKE YESHUA DID; ABLE TO LOVE THE FATHER, YESHUA, AND OTHERS WITH HIS OWN LOVE POURED OUT IN OUR HEARTS; GIVEN THE POWER OF ATTORNEY TO SPEAK AND PRAY IN YESHUA'S NAME AND KNOW THAT OUR FATHER WILL CAUSE IT TO COME TO PASS BY THE POWER OF THE HOLY SPIRIT (JOHN 16:23-27, JOHN 15:7-8, MARK 11:22-24) BECAUSE WE ARE KEEPING OUR CONSCIENCE CLEAR OF SIN, SO THAT OUR FAITH IS NOT HINDERED BY GUILT!

IF WE DO SIN, BREAKING THE WRITTEN TORAH OR THE WORDS OF YESHUA, WE CAN REPENT QUICKLY, ASKING THE FATHER TO CLEANSE US BY YESHUA'S BLOOD, TURNING FROM THAT SIN WITH EVEN STRONGER RESOLVE TO LIVE RIGHT SO THAT....

WE CAN PLEASE OUR FATHER!!!

1JO 1:9 KJV - IF WE CONFESS OUR SINS, HE IS FAITHFUL AND JUST TO FORGIVE US [OUR] SINS, AND TO CLEANSE US FROM ALL UNRIGHTEOUSNESS.

1Jo 1:10 KJV - If we say that we have not sinned, we make him a liar, and his word is not in us.

1JO 2:1 KJV - MY LITTLE CHILDREN, THESE THINGS WRITE I UNTO YOU, THAT YE SIN NOT. And if any man sin, we have an advocate with the Father, Jesus Christ the righteous:

1Jo 2:2 KJV - And he is the propitiation for our sins: and not for ours only, but also for [the sins of] the whole world.

1Jo 2:3 KJV - AND HEREBY WE DO KNOW THAT WE KNOW HIM, IF WE KEEP HIS COMMANDMENTS.

LASTLY, AND MOST IMPORTANTLY:

THE MOST IMPORTANT THING IN THIS LIFE IS OVERCOMING, NO MATTER HOW HARD, SO THAT WE WILL BELONG TO YEHOVAH ELOHIM, OUR FATHER, AND YESHUA, HIS SON, HIS LAMB, OUR SAVIOR AND SOON COMING KING FOREVER, AND THAT SOMEDAY WE WILL HAVE ETERNAL RESURRECTION LIFE!! WE WILL BE WITH THE FATHER, YESHUA, AND ALL OF OUR TRUE FAMILY FOREVER!!!

[REV 21:7 KJV] 7 HE THAT OVERCOMETH

SHALL INHERIT ALL THINGS;

AND I WILL BE HIS GOD, AND

HE SHALL BE MY SON!

APPENDIX I

AUTHORITY IN THE CHURCH

I am trying not to address this subject from a pre-conceived notion of how authority in the church should be handled. I have actually questioned this for the last 26 years during which I have been conscientiously trying to serve Yehovah Elohim and Yeshua, the Messiah. Instead, I am praying to understand the truth as I study it out. I do absolutely believe that this issue needs to be thoughtfully considered, as the church has always been very divided on who actually has authority within the church, the congregation of believers in Yeshua.

I think Yeshua made it clear that His Twelve Apostles would be His "witnesses" (those who had been with Him throughout his ministry from the baptism of John and actually witnessed his death, burial, and resurrection, and ascension to heaven – Acts 1:21-26 says this is the criteria for Judas to be replaced by Matthias as the 12th apostle). They were apostles, a Greek word which means "sent ones," to start His "church" (originally "kehilla" in Hebrew, "ecclesia" in Greek, which would be better translated as "congregation" in English) on earth, under His rule as the Resurrected, Living Good Shepherd who will not be on earth, but will be sitting at the right hand of The Father until He returns to rule the earth (in the Father's name-Isaiah 41:10) in the millennial kingdom. When He returns, He said those Twelve Apostles will be ruling the twelve tribes of Israel.

[Mat 19:23-30 KJV] 23 Then **SAID JESUS UNTO HIS DISCIPLES**, Verily I say unto you, That a rich man shall hardly enter into the kingdom of heaven. 24 And again I say unto you, It is easier for a camel to go through the eye of a needle, than for a rich man to enter into the kingdom of God. 25 When his disciples heard [it], they were exceedingly amazed, saying, Who then can be saved? 26 But Jesus beheld [them], and said unto them, With men this is impossible; but with God all things are possible. 27 THEN ANSWERED PETER AND SAID UNTO HIM, BEHOLD, WE HAVE FORSAKEN ALL, AND FOLLOWED THEE; WHAT SHALL WE HAVE THEREFORE? 28 AND **JESUS SAID UNTO THEM, VERILY I SAY UNTO YOU, THAT YE WHICH HAVE FOLLOWED ME, IN THE REGENERATION WHEN THE SON OF MAN SHALL SIT IN THE THRONE OF HIS GLORY, YE ALSO SHALL SIT UPON TWELVE THRONES, JUDGING THE TWELVE TRIBES OF ISRAEL**. 29 And every one that hath forsaken houses, or brethren, or sisters, or father, or mother, or wife, or children, or lands, for my name's sake, shall receive an hundredfold, and shall inherit everlasting life. 30 But many [that are] first shall be last; and the last [shall be] first.

[Luk 22:24-32 KJV] 24 **AND THERE WAS ALSO A STRIFE AMONG THEM, WHICH OF THEM SHOULD BE ACCOUNTED THE GREATEST. 25 AND HE SAID UNTO THEM, THE KINGS OF THE GENTILES EXERCISE LORDSHIP OVER THEM; AND THEY THAT EXERCISE AUTHORITY UPON THEM ARE CALLED BENEFACTORS. 26 BUT YE [SHALL] NOT [BE] SO: BUT HE THAT IS GREATEST AMONG YOU, LET HIM BE AS THE YOUNGER; AND HE THAT IS CHIEF, AS HE THAT DOTH SERVE.** 27 For whether [is] greater, he that sitteth at meat, or he that serveth? [is] not he that sitteth at meat? but **I AM AMONG YOU AS HE THAT SERVETH**. 28 **YE ARE THEY WHICH HAVE CONTINUED WITH ME IN MY TEMPTATIONS. 29 AND I APPOINT UNTO YOU A KINGDOM, AS MY FATHER HATH APPOINTED UNTO ME; 30 THAT YE MAY EAT AND DRINK AT MY TABLE IN MY KINGDOM, AND SIT ON THRONES JUDGING THE TWELVE TRIBES OF ISRAEL**. 31 And the Lord said, Simon, Simon, behold, Satan hath desired [to have] you, that he may sift [you] as wheat: 32 But I have prayed for thee, that thy faith fail not: and when thou art converted, strengthen thy brethren.

[Mat 20:20-28 KJV] 20 Then came to him the mother of Zebedee's children with her sons, worshipping [him], and desiring a certain thing of him. 21 And he said unto her, What wilt thou? She saith unto him, Grant that these my two sons may sit, the one on thy right hand, and the other on the left, in thy kingdom. 22 But Jesus answered and said, Ye know not what ye ask. Are ye able to drink of the cup that I shall drink of, and to be baptized with the baptism that I am baptized with? They say unto him, We are able. 23 And he saith unto them, Ye shall drink indeed of my cup, and be baptized with the baptism that I am baptized with: but to sit on my right hand, and on my left, is not mine to give, but [it shall be given to them] for whom it is prepared of my Father. 24 And when the ten heard [it], they were moved with indignation against the two brethren. 25 **BUT JESUS CALLED THEM [UNTO HIM], AND SAID, YE KNOW THAT THE PRINCES OF THE GENTILES EXERCISE DOMINION OVER THEM, AND THEY THAT ARE GREAT EXERCISE AUTHORITY UPON THEM. 26 BUT IT SHALL NOT BE SO AMONG YOU: BUT WHOSOEVER WILL BE GREAT AMONG YOU, LET HIM BE YOUR MINISTER; 27 AND WHOSOEVER WILL BE CHIEF AMONG YOU, LET HIM BE YOUR SERVANT: 28 EVEN AS THE SON OF MAN CAME NOT TO BE MINISTERED UNTO, BUT TO MINISTER, AND TO GIVE HIS LIFE A RANSOM FOR MANY.**

The Strong's Concordance Greek #1249 is the word translated as minister, which also could be translated as deacon or deaconess:

διάκονος diákonos, dee-ak'-on-os; probably from an obsolete διάκω diákō (to run on errands; compare G1377); **AN ATTENDANT**, i.e. (genitive case) a waiter (at table or in other menial duties); specially, a Christian teacher and pastor (technically, a deacon or deaconess):—deacon, minister, servant.

Servant, as used in this verse, is Strong's Greek #1401, which could be a stronger word like slave, or bondservant:

†δοῦλος doûlos, doo'-los; from G1210; **A SLAVE** (literal or figurative, involuntary or voluntary; frequently, therefore in a qualified sense of subjection or subserviency):—bond(-man), servant.

Also, as seen below, Yeshua continues to make it clear that even the Twelve Apostles were NOT to be called MASTERS now (those that would rule over others), much less those that would come after them, in my opinion.

HE ALSO MAKES IT CLEAR THAT HE IS NOT MAKING ONE OF THE APOSTLES TO BE ABOVE THE REST! NOT EVEN PETER! DEFINITELY, THEY WERE NOT TO BE CALLED "FATHER" (POPE MEANS PAPA)!

[Mat 23:8-12 KJV] 8 **BUT BE NOT YE CALLED RABBI**: **FOR ONE IS YOUR MASTER, [EVEN] CHRIST**; and **ALL YE ARE BRETHREN**. 9
And **CALL NO [MAN] YOUR FATHER UPON THE EARTH: FOR ONE IS YOUR FATHER, WHICH IS IN HEAVEN**. 10 **NEITHER BE YE CALLED MASTERS: FOR ONE IS YOUR MASTER, [EVEN] CHRIST.** 11 **BUT HE THAT IS GREATEST AMONG YOU SHALL BE YOUR SERVANT.** **12 AND WHOSOEVER SHALL EXALT HIMSELF SHALL BE ABASED; AND HE THAT SHALL HUMBLE HIMSELF SHALL BE EXALTED.**

The word "MASTER" that Yeshua used both times in the above verses are #2519 in the Strong's concordance in the Greek language:

καθηγητής kathēgētés, kath-ayg-ay-tace'; from a compound of G2596 and G2233; a guide, i.e. (figuratively) a teacher:—**MASTER**

Strongs #2596 in the Greek is:

κατά katá, kat-ah'; a primary particle; (prepositionally) down (in place or time), in varied relations (according to the case (genitive, dative or accusative) with which it is joined):—about, according as (to), after, against, (when they were) ✕ alone, among, and, ✕ apart, (even, like) as (concerning, pertaining to touching), ✕

aside, at, before, beyond, by, to the charge of, (charita-)bly, concerning, + covered, (dai-)ly, down, every, (+ far more) exceeding, ✕ more excellent, for, from ... to, godly, in(-asmuch, divers, every, -to, respect of), ... by, after the manner of, + by any means, beyond (out of) measure, X mightily, more, ✕ natural, of (up-)on (X part), out (of every), over against, (+ your) ✕ own, + particularly, so, through(-oughout, -oughout every), thus, (un-)to(-gether, -ward), ✕ uttermost, where(-by), with.

Strongs #2233, which is the root of the word, in the Greek language is:

ἡγέομαι hēgéomai, hayg-eh'-om-ahee; middle voice of a (presumed) strengthened form of G71; **TO LEAD, I.E. COMMAND (WITH OFFICIAL AUTHORITY);** figuratively, to deem, i.e. consider:—account, **(BE) CHIEF**, count, esteem, governor, judge, **HAVE THE RULE OVER**, suppose, think.

*****What can we deduct from this other than that **YESHUA IS SAYING THERE IS NOT TO BE A RULER** over the church **EXCEPT HIM, THE CHRIST, THE MASHIACH**!!!*****

However, that being made clear, Matthew does record these words of Yeshua:

[Mat 24:45-51 KJV] 45 Who then is a faithful and wise SERVANT, whom his lord hath made ruler over his household, to give them meat in due season? 46 Blessed [is] that servant, whom his lord when he cometh shall find so doing. 47 Verily I say unto you, That he shall make him ruler over all his goods. 48 BUT and if that evil servant shall say in his heart, My lord delayeth his coming; 49 And shall begin to smite [HIS] FELLOWSERVANTS, and to eat and drink with the drunken; 50 The lord of that servant shall come in a day when he looketh not for [him], and in an hour that he is not aware of, 51 And shall cut him asunder, and appoint [him] his portion with the hypocrites: there shall be weeping and gnashing of teeth.

Yeshua describes in detail again how he wants this church organization to work:

[Luk 12:41-44, 46-48 KJV] 41 Then Peter said unto him, Lord, speakest thou this parable unto us, or even to all? 42 And the Lord said, **WHO THEN IS THAT FAITHFUL AND WISE STEWARD, WHOM [HIS] LORD SHALL MAKE RULER OVER HIS HOUSEHOLD, TO GIVE [THEM THEIR] PORTION OF MEAT IN DUE SEASON?** 43 Blessed [is] that **SERVANT**, whom his lord when he cometh **shall find so doing.** 44 **Of a truth I say unto you, that he will make him ruler over all that he hath. ... 46 The lord of that servant will come in a day when he looketh not for [him], and at an hour when he is not aware, and will cut him in sunder, and will appoint him his portion with the unbelievers.** 47 And that servant, which knew his lord's will, and prepared not [himself], neither did according to his will, shall be beaten with many [stripes]. 48 But he that knew not, and did commit things worthy of stripes, shall be beaten with few [stripes]. For unto whomsoever much is given, of him shall be much required: and to whom men have committed much, of him they will ask the more.

So, let's take this apart. First, YESHUA DOES SAY THERE WILL BE THOSE HE APPOINTS AS STEWARDS, NOT TO RULE THE CHURCH, BUT SERVANTS THAT HE IS GOING TO HOLD VERY RESPONSIBLE FOR FEEDING THE OTHER SERVANTS.

THE FAITHFUL STEWARDS WILL BE REWARDED IN THE KINGDOM OF GOD, AND THE UNFAITHFUL STEWARDS GO TO HELL!!!

The Strong's Concordance Greek # 3623 tells us this about the word translated as steward:

οἰκονόμος oikonómos, oy-kon-om'-os; from G3624 and the base of G3551; **A HOUSE-DISTRIBUTOR** (i.e. **MANAGER**), or overseer, i.e. an employee in that capacity; by extension, a fiscal agent (treasurer); figuratively, a preacher (of the Gospel):—chamberlain, governor, **STEWARD**

Strong's Greek#3624 is defined as:

οἶκος oîkos, oy'-kos; of uncertain affinity; a dwelling (more or less extensive, literal or figurative); by implication, **A FAMILY** (more or less related, literally or figuratively):—home, **HOUSE(-HOLD)**, temple.

The base of the word, Strong's Greek#3551, is:

νόμος nómos, nom'-os; from a primary νέμω némō **(TO PARCEL OUT, ESPECIALLY FOOD OR GRAZING TO ANIMALS)**; **LAW** (through the idea of prescriptive usage), genitive case (regulation), **SPECIALLY, (OF MOSES** (INCLUDING THE VOLUME); ALSO OF THE GOSPEL), or figuratively (a principle):—**LAW**.

Now, the phrase "make ruler over" in verse 42 is from Strongs Greek# 2525 – it is not a very good translation into the KJV. This is the Greek word:

καθίστημι kathístēmi, kath-is'-tay-mee; from G2596 and G2476; **TO PLACE DOWN (PERMANENTLY)**, i.e. (figuratively**) TO DESIGNATE**, constitute, convoy:—**APPOINT**, be, conduct, make, **ORDAIN,** set.

Strong's Greek#2596 is defined Ibid, 146.

Strong's Greek#2476 is:

†ἵστημι hístēmi, his'-tay-mee; a prolonged form of a primary στάω stáō stah'-o (of the same meaning, and used for it in certain tenses); to stand (transitively or intransitively), used in various applications (literally or figuratively):—abide, appoint, bring, continue, covenant, establish, hold up, lay, present, set (up), stanch, stand (by, forth, still, up). Compare G5087.

IT SEEMS THAT WE COULD PUT ALL THIS TOGETHER TO SAY THAT YESHUA APPOINTS OR ORDAINS BELIEVERS (BY THE HOLY SPIRIT) TO BE STEWARDS, MANAGERS OF YESHUA'S HOUSEHOLD, THAT ARE TO PARCEL OUT (GIVE) FOOD TO THE FAMILY OF GOD, WHICH IS THE LAW: THE TORAH OF MOSES, AND THE WORDS OF YESHUA.

This leads one to the picture of a **SERVANT OF YESHUA** put in charge of **FEEDING TRUTH** to the household – **definitely NOT A RULER DOMINATING them!**

It seems that, just as Yeshua came the first time on a covert mission to become the sacrifice for our sins, believers in Yeshua are to be busy now bringing people all over the world into this spiritual Kingdom of God, simply as brethren, with as little structure as possible – not as people trying to build some hierarchical kingdom on this earth! When Yeshua returns, **that is when** the Kingdom of God will most certainly be manifested to the whole world for 1000 years!

Yeshua will reign as the King of kings and Lord of lords and the Twelve Apostles will be ruling over the Twelve Tribes of Israel. Also, those stewards (elders, shepherds) that are busy now feeding (teaching) the believers the Words of Yeshua and the Written Torah, when he returns will be rewarded and made rulers in His Kingdom as well. However, THAT IS THEN AND THIS IS NOW!:

[Luk 12:42-44 KJV] 42 And the Lord said, Who then is that faithful and wise steward, whom [his] lord shall make ruler over his household, to give [them their] portion of meat in due season? 43 Blessed [is] that servant, whom his lord when he cometh shall find so doing. 44 OF A TRUTH I SAY UNTO YOU, THAT HE WILL MAKE HIM RULER OVER ALL THAT HE HATH.

If we think about it, **IN THE BEGINNING**, THE FATHER NEVER INTENDED ISRAEL TO HAVE A KING (RULER) ON EARTH – **YEHOVAH WAS THEIR KING IN HEAVEN!** The judges and the officers that he commanded to be set up were to judge according to the Torah, in conjunction with the priesthood:

[Deu 16:18 KJV] 18 Judges and officers shalt thou make thee in all thy gates, which the LORD thy God giveth thee, throughout thy tribes: and they shall judge the people with just judgment. (Notice that in Israel, there was to be no "separation of church and state"! The Torah was to be their "Constitution.")

So, even when he speaks of judges, it was in the context of feeding his people.

The Father says: [1Ch 17:6 KJV] 6 Wheresoever I have walked with all Israel, spake I a word to any of the **JUDGES OF ISRAEL**, **WHOM I COMMANDED TO FEED MY PEOPLE**, saying, Why have ye not built me an house of cedars?

ALSO, FEEDING TRUTH WOULD ALSO MEAN THAT NO MAN-MADE LAWS WOULD BE TAUGHT!!! (Isaiah 29:13)

Yeshua said: [Mat 16:12 KJV] 12 Then understood they how that he bade [them] not beware of the leaven of bread, but of the doctrine of the Pharisees and of the Sadducees.

No Pharisee Doctrine, no Sadducee Doctrine, and no Doctrine of Herod, no Roman Catholic or other Denominational Doctrine! No MAN-MADE LAWS! Remember that Yeshua specifically told his disciples to beware of what the Pharisees, Sadducees, and Herod were **feeding people** **(leaven was equated with doctrine or teaching , in this case, false teaching.)**

Feeding the people the Written Torah and the words of Yeshua is allegorized many times as The Father, and even Yeshua, as a Shepherd feeding the sheep. David speaks in Psalm 23:

[Psa 23:1-6 KJV] 1 [A Psalm of David.] **THE LORD [IS] MY SHEPHERD**; I shall not want. 2 He maketh me to lie down in **GREEN PASTURES (FOOD)**: he leadeth me beside the still **WATERS (DRINK)**. 3 He restoreth my soul: **HE LEADETH ME IN THE PATHS OF RIGHTEOUSNESS FOR HIS NAME'S SAKE (LEADS TO KEEP THE**

TORAH OF MOSES AND THE WORDS OF YESHUA). 4 Yea, though I walk through the valley of the shadow of death, I will fear no evil: for thou [art] with me; thy rod and thy staff they comfort me. 5 **THOU PREPAREST A TABLE BEFORE ME** in the presence of mine enemies: thou anointest my head with oil; my cup runneth over. 6 Surely goodness and mercy shall follow me all the days of my life: and I will dwell in the house of the LORD forever.

Strong's #7462 is the Hebrew word for **Shepherd:**

רָעָה râ'âh, raw-aw'; a primitive root; **to tend a flock**; i.e. **pasture it**; intransitively, **to graze** (literally or figuratively); generally to rule; by extension, to associate with (as a friend):—✕ break, companion, keep company with, devour, eat up, evil entreat, **feed,** use as a friend, make friendship with, herdsman, **keep (sheep)** (-er), **pastor,** shearing house, **shepherd**, wander, waste.

Yeshua called himself the Good Shepherd (given by The Father):

[Jhn 10:11-16 KJV] 11 **I AM THE GOOD SHEPHERD: THE GOOD SHEPHERD GIVETH HIS LIFE FOR THE SHEEP**. 12 But he that is an hireling, and not the shepherd, whose own the sheep are not, seeth the wolf coming, and leaveth the sheep, and fleeth: and the wolf catcheth them, and scattereth the sheep. 13 The hireling fleeth, because he is an hireling, and careth not for the sheep. 14 I am the good shepherd, and know my [sheep], and am known of mine. 15 As the Father knoweth me, even so know I the Father: and I lay down my life for the sheep. 16 And other sheep I have, which are not of this fold: them also I must bring, and **THEY SHALL HEAR MY VOICE**; and there shall be **ONE FOLD, [and] ONE SHEPHERD.**

The Father speaks of how angry He was with the shepherds of Israel in Ezekiel 34 and Malachi 2. Read below and see what they did wrong, so you can discern what He had wanted the shepherds to do. **I believe he was speaking of THE PRIESTS who were the ones who were to feed the true word of the Written Torah to the people, which would have brought health, healing and wholeness in every area of their life.** In fact, **THE VERY SAME HEBREW WORD (רָעָה râ'âh)**that is translated as **SHEPHERD** is also translated as **FEED** here!!

[Eze 34:1-24 KJV] 1 And the word of the LORD came unto me, saying, 2 Son of man, prophesy against the shepherds of Israel, prophesy, and say unto them, Thus saith the Lord GOD unto the shepherds; Woe [be] to the shepherds of Israel that do feed themselves! **SHOULD NOT THE SHEPHERDS (Ra'ah) FEED (Ra'ah)THE FLOCKS?** 3 Ye eat the fat, and ye clothe you with the wool, ye kill them that are fed: [but] **YE FEED NOT THE FLOCK. 4 THE DISEASED HAVE YE NOT STRENGTHENED, NEITHER HAVE YE HEALED THAT WHICH WAS SICK, NEITHER HAVE YE BOUND UP [THAT WHICH WAS] BROKEN, NEITHER HAVE YE BROUGHT AGAIN THAT WHICH WAS DRIVEN AWAY, NEITHER HAVE YE SOUGHT THAT WHICH WAS LOST; BUT WITH FORCE AND WITH CRUELTY HAVE YE RULED THEM**. 5 And they were scattered, because [there is] no shepherd: and they became meat to all the beasts of the field, when they were scattered. 6 My sheep wandered through all the mountains, and upon every high hill: yea, my flock was scattered upon all the face of the earth, and none did search or seek [after them]. 7 Therefore, ye shepherds, hear the word of the LORD; 8 [As] I live, saith the Lord GOD, surely because my flock became a prey, and my flock became meat to every beast of the field, because [there was] no shepherd, neither did my shepherds search for my flock, but the shepherds fed themselves, and fed not my flock; 9 Therefore, O ye shepherds, hear the word of the LORD; 10 Thus saith the Lord GOD; Behold, I [am] against the shepherds; and I will require my flock at their hand, and cause them to cease from feeding the flock; neither shall the shepherds feed themselves anymore; for I will deliver my flock from their mouth, that they may not be meat for them. 11 For thus saith the Lord GOD; Behold, I, [even] I, will both search my sheep, and seek them out. 12 As a shepherd seeketh out his flock in the day that he is among his sheep [that are] scattered; so will I seek out my sheep, and will deliver them out of all places where they have been scattered in the cloudy and dark day. 13 And I will bring them out from the people, and gather them from the countries, and will bring them to their own land, and feed them upon the mountains of Israel by the rivers, and in all the inhabited places of the country. **14 I WILL FEED THEM IN A GOOD PASTURE**, and upon the high mountains of Israel shall their fold be: there shall they lie in a good fold, and [in] a fat pasture shall they feed upon the mountains of Israel. 15 I will feed my flock, and I will cause them to lie down, saith the Lord GOD. 16 I will seek that which was lost, and bring again that which was driven away, and will bind up [that which was] broken, and will strengthen that which was sick: but I will destroy the fat and the strong; I will feed them with judgment. 17 And [as for] you, O my flock, thus saith the Lord GOD; Behold, I judge between cattle and cattle, between the rams and the he goats. 18 [Seemeth it] a small thing unto you to have eaten up the good pasture, but ye must tread down with your feet the residue of your pastures? and to have drunk of the deep waters, but ye must foul the residue with your feet? 19 And [as for] my flock, they eat that which ye have trodden with your feet; and they drink that which ye have fouled with your feet. 20 Therefore thus saith the Lord GOD unto them; Behold, I, [even] I, will judge between the fat cattle and between the lean cattle. 21 Because ye have thrust with side and with shoulder, and pushed all the diseased with your horns, till ye have scattered them abroad; 22 Therefore will I save my flock, and they shall no more be a prey; and I will judge between cattle and cattle. 23 **AND I WILL SET UP ONE SHEPHERD OVER THEM, AND HE SHALL FEED THEM, [EVEN] MY SERVANT DAVID; HE SHALL FEED THEM, AND HE SHALL BE THEIR SHEPHERD. 24 AND I THE LORD WILL BE THEIR GOD, AND MY SERVANT DAVID A PRINCE AMONG THEM; I THE LORD HAVE SPOKEN [IT].**

(OF COURSE, I BELIEVE YESHUA IS THE SON OF DAVID, THE MESSIAH, THE KING OF KINGS, THAT THE FATHER IS SPEAKING OF!!)

[Eze 37:24 KJV] 24 And DAVID MY SERVANT [SHALL BE] KING OVER THEM; and they all shall have ONE SHEPHERD: they shall also WALK IN MY JUDGMENTS, and OBSERVE MY STATUTES, and DO THEM.

*****NOTICE HERE THAT THE END RESULT OF THE SHEPHERD'S FEEDING IS THAT THE FLOCK WILL KEEP YEHOVAH ELOHIM'S, THE FATHER'S, WRITTEN TORAH!!!*****

[Jer 23:1-6, 11, 21-22 KJV] 1 WOE BE UNTO THE PASTORS (Strong's #7462 râ'âh, raw-aw'- -SHEPHERDS); _THAT DESTROY AND SCATTER THE SHEEP OF MY PASTURE! SAITH THE LORD. 2 THEREFORE THUS SAITH THE LORD GOD OF ISRAEL AGAINST THE PASTORS (SHEPHERDS) THAT FEED MY PEOPLE; YE HAVE SCATTERED MY FLOCK, AND DRIVEN THEM AWAY, AND HAVE NOT VISITED THEM: BEHOLD, I WILL VISIT UPON YOU THE EVIL OF YOUR DOINGS, SAITH THE LORD. 3 AND I WILL GATHER THE REMNANT OF MY FLOCK OUT OF ALL COUNTRIES WHITHER I HAVE DRIVEN THEM, AND WILL BRING THEM AGAIN TO THEIR FOLDS; AND THEY SHALL BE FRUITFUL AND INCREASE. 4 AND I WILL SET UP SHEPHERDS OVER THEM WHICH SHALL FEED THEM: AND THEY SHALL FEAR NO MORE, NOR BE DISMAYED, NEITHER SHALL THEY BE LACKING, SAITH THE LORD. 5 Behold, the days come, saith the LORD, that I WILL RAISE UNTO DAVID A RIGHTEOUS BRANCH, AND A KING SHALL REIGN AND PROSPER, AND SHALL EXECUTE JUDGMENT AND JUSTICE IN THE EARTH. 6 In his days Judah shall be saved, and Israel shall dwell safely: and this [is] his name whereby he shall be called, THE LORD OUR RIGHTEOUSNESS. ... 11 For BOTH PROPHET AND PRIEST ARE PROFANE; yea, in my house have I found their wickedness, saith the LORD. ... 21 I have not sent these prophets, yet they ran: I have not spoken to them, yet they prophesied. 22 BUT IF THEY HAD STOOD IN MY COUNSEL, AND HAD CAUSED MY PEOPLE TO HEAR MY

WORDS, THEN THEY SHOULD HAVE TURNED THEM FROM THEIR EVIL WAY, AND FROM THE EVIL OF THEIR DOINGS.

(Notice in these scriptures that the PASTORS/SHEPHERDS , WHICH WERE THE PRIESTS, and the PROPHETS, were to lead people to the true Word of Yehovah, the Written Torah, which would turn them away from doing evil.)

(Note also that Levi was the tribe that Aaron, the High Priest, and his sons, which comprised the priesthood, came from.)

[Mal 2:1-9 KJV] 1 And now, O YE PRIESTS, THIS COMMANDMENT [IS] FOR YOU. 2 If ye will not hear, and if ye will not lay [it] to heart, to give glory unto my name, saith the LORD of hosts, I will even send a curse upon you, and I will curse your blessings: yea, I have cursed them already, because ye do not lay [it] to heart. 3 Behold, I will corrupt your seed, and spread dung upon your faces, [even] the dung of your solemn feasts; and [one] shall take you away with it. 4 And ye shall know that I have sent this commandment unto you, that my covenant might be with LEVI, saith the LORD of hosts. 5 My covenant was with him of life and peace; and I gave them to HIM [FOR] THE FEAR WHEREWITH HE FEARED ME, AND WAS AFRAID BEFORE MY NAME. 6 THE LAW OF TRUTH WAS IN HIS MOUTH, AND INIQUITY WAS NOT FOUND IN HIS LIPS: HE WALKED WITH ME IN PEACE AND EQUITY, AND DID TURN MANY AWAY FROM INIQUITY. 7 FOR THE PRIEST'S LIPS SHOULD KEEP KNOWLEDGE, AND THEY SHOULD SEEK THE LAW AT HIS MOUTH: FOR HE [IS] THE MESSENGER OF THE LORD OF HOSTS. 8 BUT ye are departed out of the way; YE HAVE CAUSED MANY TO STUMBLE AT THE LAW; ye have CORRUPTED THE COVENANT OF LEVI, saith the LORD of hosts. 9 Therefore have I also made you contemptible and base before all the people, according as YE HAVE NOT KEPT MY WAYS, BUT HAVE BEEN PARTIAL IN THE LAW.

THESE SCRIPTURES TELL US EXACTLY WHAT THE FATHER EXPECTED OUT OF THE SHEPHERDS OVER HIS PEOPLE, THE PRIESTS, AND WHAT HE DIDN'T!

So, after Yeshua was resurrected and had spoken to them of the kingdom of Yehovah, he was preparing to leave his twelve disciples for the last time. As he did, HE SPOKE TO PETER:

[Jhn 21:14-19 KJV] 14 This is now the third time that Jesus shewed himself to his disciples, after that he was risen from the dead. 15 So when they had dined, **JESUS SAITH TO SIMON PETER, SIMON, [SON] OF JONAS, LOVEST THOU ME MORE THAN THESE? He saith unto him, Yea, Lord; thou knowest that I love thee. He saith unto him, FEED MY LAMBS. 16 He saith to him again the second time, SIMON, [SON] OF JONAS, LOVEST THOU ME? He saith unto him, Yea, Lord; thou knowest that I love thee. He saith unto him, FEED MY SHEEP. 17 He saith unto him the third time, SIMON, [SON] OF JONAS, LOVEST THOU ME? Peter was grieved because he said unto him the third time, Lovest thou me? And he said unto him, Lord, thou knowest all things; thou knowest that I love thee. Jesus saith unto him, FEED MY SHEEP.** 18 Verily, verily, I say unto thee, When thou wast young, thou girdedst thyself, and walkedst whither thou wouldest: but when thou shalt be old, thou shalt stretch forth thy hands, and another shall gird thee, and carry [thee] whither thou wouldest not. 19 This spake he, signifying by what death he should glorify God. And when he had spoken this, he saith unto him, Follow me.

SUFFICE IT TO SAY THAT YESHUA WANTED PETER TO FEED HIS SHEEP!!! HIS SHEEP WOULD PROBABLY BE THOSE THAT WOULD COME TO FAITH IN HIM.

FEED THEM WHAT?

THE WORDS OF YESHUA AND THE WRITTEN TORAH!!!

I don't believe that He was setting up Peter above the rest of the Apostles to rule over them, as we have discussed in length already (Matthew 23:8-12.) (Neither was he to be called "Father", the title given to him by the Roman Catholic Church, calling him the first Pope [Papa]).

I believe that Peter understood what Yeshua was saying, as reflected in his first letter:

[1Pe 2:19-25 KJV] 19 For this [is] thankworthy, if a man for conscience toward God endure grief, suffering wrongfully. 20 For what glory [is it], if, when ye be buffeted for your faults, ye shall take it patiently? but if, when ye do well, and suffer [for it], ye take it patiently, this [is] acceptable with God. 21 For even hereunto were ye called: because **CHRIST** also suffered for us, **LEAVING US AN EXAMPLE**, that **YE SHOULD FOLLOW HIS STEPS: 22 WHO DID NO SIN, NEITHER WAS GUILE FOUND IN HIS MOUTH:** 23 Who, when he was reviled, reviled not again; when he suffered, he threatened not; but committed [himself] to him that judgeth righteously: 24 Who his own self bare our sins in his own body on the tree, that **we, being dead to sins, should live unto righteousness**: by whose stripes ye were healed. 25 **FOR YE WERE AS SHEEP GOING ASTRAY**; BUT ARE NOW **RETURNED UNTO THE SHEPHERD** AND BISHOP **OF YOUR SOULS**. (Bishop will be dealt with below.)

[1Pe 5:1-4 KJV] 1 The **ELDERS** which are among you I exhort, who am **ALSO AN ELDER**, and a witness of the sufferings of Christ, and also a partaker of the glory that shall be revealed: 2 **FEED THE FLOCK OF GOD WHICH IS AMONG YOU**, taking the oversight [thereof], not by constraint, but willingly; not for filthy lucre, but of a ready mind; **3 NEITHER AS BEING LORDS OVER [GOD'S] HERITAGE, BUT BEING ENSAMPLES (EXAMPLES) TO THE FLOCK**. **4 AND WHEN THE CHIEF SHEPHERD SHALL APPEAR, YE SHALL RECEIVE A CROWN OF GLORY THAT FADETH NOT AWAY.**

The word that is translated as **ELDERS** is Strong's Greek# 4245:

πρεσβύτερος PRESBÝTEROS, pres-boo'-ter-os; comparative of πρέσβυς présbys (elderly); **older;** as noun, a senior; specially, an Israelite Sanhedrist (also figuratively, member of the celestial council) or Christian "presbyter":—elder(-est), old.

The Epistle of Paul to Titus is one book that deals with how Paul explained to Titus that "elders" should behave. Paul seemed to push the idea of setting up Bishops as well as Elders (again, we will discuss Bishops later.) It is worthy of notice here that chapter 2 speaks of elders, in the plural, and they are men and women! The King James version uses the masculine and the feminine use of the same word with its root as Strong's #4245 (presbyteros) for them when it refers to "aged men" (presbytes- Strong's #4246) and "aged women" presbytis – Strong's #4247). The contrasting words, "young women" and "young men" that they are to teach are both from a completely different Greek word - Strong's #3501 (neos – new, or newly born). **A synopsis of his instructions is that women elders and men elders are to live holy lives, so that no one could say anything evil about them, and show a pattern of "good works."** Exactly what good works are is not defined. Titus 2:3 does continue on to say that in their doctrine (**TEACHING**), there should be uncorruptness, gravity, and sincerity – sound speech that cannot be condemned. **Titus 1:10 -14 gives us a clue that there were some Jewish believers there in Crete that were still pushing the Oral Torah (possibly out of ignorance), and Paul, thankfully, condemns this, saying that Titus should not give heed to Jewish fables or "Commandments of Men." Hopefully, then, when he refers to sound teaching, holy living, and good works, he was upholding the teaching of the Words of Yeshua and the teaching of the**

Written Torah! (Remember Paul <u>SAID</u> that he had done nothing against the laws of the Jews –[Act 25:8 KJV] 8 While he answered for himself, <u>Neither against the law of the Jews</u>, neither against the temple, nor yet against Caesar, <u>have I offended anything at all</u>.)

<u>Continuing on however, the word Peter uses about himself that is translated as "**ALSO AN ELDER**" is Strong's Greek # 4850</u>:

συμπρεσβύτερος SYMPRESBÝTEROS, soom-pres-boo'-ter-os; from <u>G4862</u> and <u>G4245</u>; **<u>A CO-PRESBYTER</u>:**—presbyter, **also an elder**.

He says that he is a fellow elder, a co-presbyter. **IT SEEMS TO ME THAT HE MUST BE SPEAKING OF THOSE WHO ARE <u>OLDER IN THE FAITH</u> THAT <u>CAN FEED THE WORDS OF YESHUA AND THE WRITTEN TORAH TO OTHERS</u>**. He does mention that he is a "witness of the sufferings of Christ." – obviously referring to the fact that he is one of the Twelve Apostles. **BUT, HE DEFINITELY DOES NOT SAY, "I AM THE HEAD APOSTLE!"**

The **<u>APOSTLE JOHN</u> DOES <u>NOT</u> USE THE WORD "<u>BISHOP</u>" (STRONG'S #1985) AT ALL**, but **<u>ONLY CALLS HIMSELF AN ELDER (#4245) OR PRESBYTER</u>, <u>just as Peter does</u>.**

AS JUST STATED, AN ELDER IS BASICALLY SOMEONE WHO IS OLDER IN THE FAITH AND CAN BE TRUSTED AS <u>A TEACHER</u> WHO FEEDS THE WORDS OF YESHUA AND THE WRITTEN TORAH TO THE PEOPLE.

[2Jo 1:1 KJV] 1 **THE ELDER** unto the elect lady and her children, whom I love in the truth; and not I only, but also all they that have known the truth;

[3Jo 1:1 KJV] 1 **THE ELDER** unto the well beloved Gaius, whom I love in the truth.

SO, IF PETER AND JOHN DO NOT EVEN REFER TO THEMSELVES AS BISHOPS, WHERE DOES THIS TITLE COME FROM IN THE CHURCH?

The word translated as "bishop" almost always in the New Testament is from the Greek language Strong's # 1985:

ἐπίσκοπος epískopos, ep-is'-kop-os; from <u>G1909</u> and <u>G4649</u> (in the sense of <u>G1983); a superintendent,</u> i.e. Christian officer in genitive case charge of a (or the) church (literally or figuratively):—<u>bishop, overseer</u>.

<u>Strong's Greek #1909 is</u>:

ἐπί epí, ep-ee'; a primary preposition; properly, meaning superimposition (of time, place, order, etc.), as a relation of distribution (with the genitive case), i.e. over, upon, etc.; of rest (with the dative case) at, on, etc.; of direction (with the accusative case) towards, upon, etc.:—about (the times), above, after, against, among, as long as (touching), at, beside, ✕ have charge of, (be-, (where-))fore, in (a place, as much as, the time of, -to), (because) of, (up-)on (behalf of), over, (by, for) the space of, through(-out), (un-)to(-ward), with.

Strong's Greek # 4649 is:

σκοπός SKOPÓS, skop-os'; from σκέπτομαι sképtomai (to peer about ("skeptic"); perhaps akin to G4626 through the idea of concealment; compare G4629); a watch (sentry or scout), i.e. (by implication) a goal:—mark

This is the word (episcopos #1985) that gets translated basically as "**EPISCOPAL**" also, as well as its translation as **"BISHOP." It has a tendency to make us think this person who is called a "BISHOP" would actually have some AUTHORITY over the sheep....**

THIS IS A GOOD PLACE TO REMEMBER THAT YESHUA NEVER USED THE WORD BISHOP AT ALL - ABOUT THE APOSTLES OR OTHERS!!! HE ONLY SAYS "FEED MY SHEEP"!

Looking at anything Yeshua has to say about the church government is, of course, the best place to look for direction. Some of his instructions came to my mind, as he tells us how to deal with another believer when they have harmed us in some way.

[Mat 18:15-17, 21-22 KJV] 15 Moreover **if thy brother shall trespass against thee**, go and tell him his fault between thee and him alone: if he shall hear thee, thou hast gained thy brother. 16 But if he will not hear [thee, then] take with thee one or two more, that in the mouth of two or three witnesses every word may be established. 17 And if he shall neglect to hear them, **tell [it] unto the church: but if he neglect to hear the church, let him be unto thee as an heathen man and a publican**. ... 21 Then came Peter to him, and said, Lord, how oft shall my brother sin against me, and I forgive him? till seven times? 22 Jesus saith unto him, I say not unto thee, Until seven times: but, Until seventy times seven.

I believe Yeshua clarifies that the offending party is to repent and ask for your forgiveness in order for you to be **obligated** to forgive him. Otherwise Matthew 18:15-17 would not ever need to be applied. Yeshua says:

[Luk 17:3-4 KJV] 3 Take heed to yourselves: If thy brother trespass against thee, rebuke him; and **if he repent, forgive him**. 4 And **if he trespass against thee seven times in a day, and seven times in a day turn again to thee, saying, I repent; thou shalt forgive him**.

What I think is evident, however, is that **THE HIGHEST LEVEL OF CONFRONTATION** is the offending party's being brought before the **WHOLE CONGREGATION**, resembling an" intervention." **YESHUA DOES NOT MENTION ANY RULING AUTHORITY (ELDER, BISHOP OR COUNCIL) THAT WOULD BE SET UP TO MAKE JUDGMENTS.** In fact, it seems that if the offending party does not listen to the congregation and repent, then Yeshua says that you, individually, can stop treating him as a part of the family.

Maybe if we actually followed Yeshua's instructions within our congregations, we would eliminate almost all of the strife.

CONTINUING IN OUR STUDY , HOWEVER, DOES IT MATTER WHETHER SOMEONE IS CLASSIFIED AS A BISHOP OR AS AN ELDER? I THINK SO, BASED ON HISTORY!!

I am not qualified to be a true historian, but I will make some observations.

"POWER CONCENTRATED IS POWER ABUSED" - author unknown

"POWER TENDS TO CORRUPT AND ABSOLUTE POWER CORRUPTS ABSOLUTELY" - Lord Acton

IN MY OPINION, THE HISTORY OF THE HIERARCHY OF BISHOPS AND COUNCILS IN THE CHURCH HAS PROVEN THIS TRUE.

The first council recorded (Acts 15) was in Jerusalem and the record says that there were Apostles and Elders (not Bishops) there, but it was obviously **HEADED** by James, who **was established** as **THE FIRST BISHOP OF JERUSALEM. As you will see, because he was the Bishop, he supposedly could make the ultimate judgment concerning the gentile believers' obligation to keep the Written Torah...2000 YEARS LATER WE ARE STILL FEELING THE EFFECT OF THIS DECISION... (But what did Yeshua say about keeping the Written Torah in Matthew 5:19?....)**

The following is one synopsis of that council:

> **THE COUNCIL OF JERUSALEM** (OR **APOSTOLIC CONFERENCE**) is a name applied by historians and theologians to a Christian Apostolic Age council

that was held in Jerusalem and dated to around the year 50 AD. It is unique among the ancient pre-ecumenical councils in that it is considered by Catholics and Orthodox to be a prototype and forerunner of the later Ecumenical Councils and a key part of Christian ethics. **THE COUNCIL DECIDED THAT GENTILE CONVERTS TO CHRISTIANITY WERE NOT OBLIGATED TO KEEP MOST OF THE LAW OF MOSES, INCLUDING THE RULES CONCERNING CIRCUMCISION OF MALES**. The Council did, however, retain the prohibitions on eating blood, meat containing blood, and meat of animals not properly slain, and on fornication and idolatry, sometimes referred to as the **Apostolic Decree** or **Jerusalem Quadrilateral**. Accounts of the council are found in Acts of the Apostles chapter 15 (in two different forms, the Alexandrian and Western versions) and also possibly in Paul's letter to the Galatians chapter 2. Some scholars dispute that Galatians 2 is about the Council of Jerusalem (notably because Galatians 2 describes a private meeting) while other scholars dispute the historical reliability of the Acts of the Apostles.

The Council of Jerusalem is generally dated to around the year 50 AD, roughly twenty years after the crucifixion of Jesus, which is dated between 26 and 36 AD. Acts 15 and Galatians 2 both suggest that the meeting was called to debate whether or not male Gentiles who were converting to become followers of Jesus were required to become circumcised. Circumcision was considered repulsive during the period of Hellenization of the Eastern Mediterranean.

At the time, most followers of Jesus (which historians refer to as Jewish Christians) were Jewish by birth and even converts would have considered the early Christians as a part of Judaism. According to Alister McGrath, the Jewish Christians affirmed every aspect of then contemporary Second Temple Judaism with the addition of the belief that Jesus was the Messiah. Unless males were circumcised, they could not be God's People. The meeting was called to decide whether circumcision for gentile converts was requisite for community membership since certain individuals were teaching that "[u]nless you are circumcised according to the custom of Moses, you cannot be saved".

Circumcision as a mandate was associated with Abraham (see also Abrahamic covenant), but it is cited as 'the custom of Moses' because Moses is considered the traditional giver of the Law as a whole. The circumcision mandate was made more official and binding in the Mosaic Law Covenant. In John 7:22 the words of Jesus are reported to be that Moses gave the people circumcision.

The purpose of the meeting, according to Acts, was to resolve a disagreement in Antioch, which had wider implications than just circumcision, since circumcision is the "everlasting" sign of the Abrahamic Covenant (Genesis 17:9–14). Some of the Pharisees who had become believers insisted that it was "needful to circumcise them, and to command [them] to keep the law of Moses" (KJV).

The primary issue which was addressed related to the requirement of circumcision, as the author of Acts relates, but other important matters arose as well, as the Apostolic Decree indicates. **The dispute was between those, such as the followers of the "Pillars of the Church," led by James, who believed, following his interpretation of the Great Commission, that the church must observe the Torah, i.e. the rules of traditional Judaism, and Paul the Apostle, who believed there was no such necessity**.

At the Council, following advice offered by Simon Peter (Acts 15:7–11 and Acts 15:14), Barnabas and Paul gave an account of their ministry among the gentiles (Acts 15:12), and the apostle James quoted from the words of the prophet Amos (Acts 15:16–17, quoting Amos 9:11–12). James added his own words to the quotation: 'Known to God from eternity are all His works' and then submitted a proposal, which was accepted by the Church and became known as the Apostolic Decree:

IT IS MY JUDGMENT, THEREFORE, THAT WE SHOULD NOT MAKE IT DIFFICULT FOR THE GENTILES WHO ARE TURNING TO GOD. Instead we should write to them, telling them to abstain from food polluted by idols, from sexual immorality, from the meat of strangled animals and from blood. **FOR THE LAW OF MOSES HAS BEEN PREACHED IN EVERY CITY FROM THE EARLIEST TIMES AND IS READ IN THE SYNAGOGUES ON EVERY SABBATH. (ACTS 15:19–21)**

Acts 15:23–29 sets out the content of the letter written in accordance with James' proposal.

The Western version of Acts (see Acts of the Apostles: Manuscripts) adds the negative form of the Golden Rule ("and whatever things ye would not have done to yourselves, do not do to another").

This determined questions wider than that of circumcision, particularly dietary questions, but also fornication and idolatry and blood, and also the application of Biblical law to non-Jews. It was stated by the Apostles and Elders in the Council: "**THE HOLY SPIRIT AND WE OURSELVES** have favored adding no further burden to you, except these necessary things, to abstain from things sacrificed to idols, and from blood, and from things strangled, and from fornication. If you carefully keep yourselves from these things, you will prosper." (Acts 15:27–28) **AND THIS APOSTOLIC DECREE WAS CONSIDERED BINDING ON ALL THE OTHER LOCAL CHRISTIAN CONGREGATIONS IN OTHER REGIONS.**

The writer of Acts gives an account of a restatement by James and the elders in Jerusalem of the contents of the letter on the occasion of Paul's final Jerusalem visit, immediately prior to Paul's arrest at the temple, recounting: 'When we had come to Jerusalem, the brothers received us gladly. On the following day Paul went in with us to James, and all the elders were present.' (Acts 21:17–18, ESV) The elders then proceed to notify Paul of what seems to have been a common concern among Jewish believers, that he was teaching Diaspora Jewish converts to Christianity 'to forsake Moses, telling them not to circumcise their children or walk according to our customs.' They remind the assembly that, '...as for the Gentiles who have believed, we have sent a letter with our judgment that they should abstain from what has been sacrificed to idols, and from blood, and from what has been strangled, and from sexual immorality.' **In the view of some scholars, the reminder of James and the elders here is an expression of concern that Paul was not fully teaching the decision of the Jerusalem Council's letter to Gentiles, particularly in regard to non-strangled *kosher* meat, which contrasts with Paul's advice to Gentiles in Corinth, to 'eat whatever is sold in the meat markets.'**(I Corinthians 10:25)

Jewish Encyclopedia: New Testament — Spirit of Jewish Proselytism in Christianity states:

For great as was the success of Barnabas and Paul in the heathen world, the authorities in Jerusalem insisted upon circumcision as the condition of admission of members into the church, until, on the initiative of Peter, and of James, the head of the Jerusalem church, it was agreed that acceptance of the Noachian Laws — namely, regarding avoidance of idolatry, fornication, and the eating of flesh cut from a living animal — should be demanded of the heathen desirous of entering the Church.

According to Hebrew Roots: **'The main question of the so-called Jerusalem Council was not 'How Should Gentiles BEHAVE?' The question was 'What Do Gentiles Need To Do In Order To Be Saved". AT THE TIME OF THE JERUSALEM COUNCIL, THE NEW TESTAMENT WAS NOT YET WRITTEN. PAUL INSTRUCTS TIMOTHY (II TIM 2:15 AND 3:15–16) TO STUDY THE WORD OF SCRIPTURE. THE ONLY SCRIPTURE AVAILABLE AT THAT TIME WAS THE OLD TESTAMENT. ARE WE TO CONCLUDE THAT IT IS PERMISSIBLE FOR GENTILE BELIEVERS TO COVET, STEAL, DISHONOR THEIR PARENTS, AND**

DABBLE IN THE OCCULT, FOR NONE OF THE COMMANDMENTS FORBIDDING THESE THINGS ARE SPECIFIED HERE [IN ACTS 15].

AND TO SAY THAT COMMANDMENTS AGAINST COVETING, STEALING, ETC. APPEAR ON OTHER PAGES OF THE NEW TESTAMENT IS JUST EVADING THE ISSUE, FOR THERE WAS NO 'NEW TESTAMENT' BOOK YET IN EXISTENCE TO INSTRUCT THESE BELIEVERS ... OBVIOUSLY JAMES' WORDS CANNOT MEAN THAT NONE OF THE TORAH'S COMMANDS ARE VALID EXCEPT FOR THESE FOUR THINGS, FOR THE WRITERS OF THE NEW TESTAMENT EPISTLES, WHEN WRITING YEARS LATER, CONSTANTLY QUOTED FROM THE TORAH TO INSTRUCT GENTILE BELIEVERS. THE CONFUSION BEGINS TO CLEAR UP WHEN THE REST OF JAMES' STATEMENT IS READ: 'FOR MOSES OF OLD TIME HAS IN EVERY CITY THEM THAT PREACH HIM, BEING READ IN THE SYNAGOGUE EVERY SABBATH DAY.' (ACTS 15:21). IN OTHER WORDS, THIS IS SIMILAR TO WHAT ONE HEARS FROM TV EVANGELISTS TODAY (PARAPHRASED): 'GO TO A BIBLE BELIEVING CHURCH TO HEAR THE WORD OF GOD AFTER ONE ACCEPTS JESUS CHRIST AS SAVIOR.' (Wikipedia contributors, "Council of Jerusalem")

The real question to me is WHETHER THIS COUNCIL, made up of the Apostles and some Elders, under the direction of this James REALLY HAD THE AUTHORITY TO MAKE A RULING AT ALL, especially one that would CAUSE THE FLOCK TO BE DIVIDED IN TWO FOLDS—THOSE THAT WERE TO KEEP THE TORAH AND THOSE WHO DID NOT HAVE TO!! YEHOVAH, THROUGH THE PROPHETS, AND YESHUA HIMSELF (THE SON OF DAVID THAT WILL BE KING OF KINGS) CONTINUALLY SAY THERE WILL BE ONE FOLD AND ONE SHEPHERD WHEN YESHUA RETURNS. IF THE JEWISH PART OF THE FOLD IS TO KEEP THE WRITTEN TORAH, THE OTHER PART SHOULD TOO, IN ORDER FOR THEM TO BE "ONE." IT IS CLEAR FROM THE FOLLOWING VERSE THAT THEY ALL WILL WHEN YESHUA RETURNS!!!

[Eze 37:24 KJV] 24 And DAVID MY SERVANT [SHALL BE] KING OVER THEM; and THEY ALL shall have ONE SHEPHERD: they shall also WALK IN MY JUDGMENTS, and OBSERVE MY STATUTES, and DO THEM.

SO, SINCE THIS SAME COUNCIL SAYS THAT THE JEWISH CHRISTIANS ARE DEFINITELY TO CONTINUE TO KEEP THE TORAH (ACTS 21: 17-24), WHY

SHOULD THE CHRISTIANS THAT HAVE COME OUT OF THE GENTILE NATIONS NOT START LEARNING AND KEEPING IT TOO, AFTER THEY BECOME BELIEVERS IN YESHUA? EVERYTHING IN THE TORAH AND THE PROPHETS SAYS THAT THEY WILL IN THE MILLENIAL KINGDOM , AS STATED ABOVE!! REMEMBER, THE SHEPHERDS WERE AND ARE TO FEED THE WORDS OF YESHUA AND THE WRITTEN TORAH TO THE SHEEP!

There is debate as to which James this was that made this judgment. One of the Apostles named James, James the brother of John, the son of Zebedee, had already been martyred by Herod (Acts 12: 1-2.) There was another Apostle named James, however, James of Alphaeus, so this could have been one of the twelve Apostles. There are others who believe that the James mentioned here was the brother of Yeshua. Whichever one he was, he became **THE FIRST BISHOP OF JERUSALEM** according to my research (**which is why HE is the one making the judgment**.) Although it may be important, I don't think there is a way to know for sure which James it was.

However, this is some information on him:

> **James** (Hebrew: יעקב *Ya'akov*; Greek Ἰάκωβος *Iákōbos*, can also be Anglicized as Jacob), who died in martyrdom in 62 or 69 AD, was an important figure of the Apostolic Age. Other epithets used to refer to James include **James the Just**, or a variation of **James, brother of the Lord**. Roman Catholic tradition generally holds that this James is to be identified with James, son of Alphaeus, and James the Less. It is agreed by most that he should not be confused with James, son of Zebedee.
>
> Interpretations of the phrase "brother of the Lord" vary. Some scholars and Christians believe that James was a true half-brother of Jesus (a son of Mary, begotten by a human father); other Christians such as Catholics, Eastern Christians, and some Protestants (such as the Anglicans and some Lutherans) who hold the belief of the perpetual virginity of Mary, teach that James along with others named as "brothers" of Jesus were not the biological children of Mary, but were either Jesus' adoptive brothers, stepbrothers (through Saint Joseph), or according to one popular theory, cousins of Jesus.
>
> **As a bishop of Jerusalem:**
>
> In a 4th-century letter pseudographically ascribed to the 1st century Clement of Rome, **JAMES WAS CALLED THE 'BISHOP OF BISHOPS, WHO RULES JERUSALEM, THE HOLY ASSEMBLY OF HEBREWS, AND ALL ASSEMBLIES EVERYWHERE'.** Hegesippus, in his fifth book of his Commentaries, mentions that James was made a bishop of Jerusalem **but he does not mention by whom**: 'After the apostles, James the brother of

the Lord surnamed the Just was made head of the Church at Jerusalem.' But, like the rest of the early Christians, information about his life is scarce and ambiguous. CLEMENT OF ALEXANDRIA **wrote in the sixth book of his Hypotyposes that James the Just was chosen as a bishop of Jerusalem by** Peter, James (the Greater) **and** John: **'For they say that Peter and James and John after the ascension of our Saviour, as if also preferred by our Lord, strove not after honor, but chose James the Just bishop of Jerusalem.' But the same writer, in the seventh book of the same work, relates also the following concerning him: 'The Lord after his resurrection imparted** knowledge (gnōsin) **to James the Just and to John and Peter, and they imparted it to the rest of the apostles, and the rest of the apostles to the seventy, of whom Barnabas was one.'**

According to Eusebius James was named a bishop of Jerusalem by the apostles: 'James, the brother of the Lord, to whom the **episcopal seat at Jerusalem** had been entrusted by the apostles' Jerome wrote the same: 'James... after our Lord's passion.. ordained by the apostles bishop of Jerusalem...' and that James 'ruled the church of Jerusalem thirty years'.

The *Oxford Dictionary of the Christian Church* claims that James the Just was 'from an early date with Peter a leader of the Church at Jerusalem and from the time when Peter left Jerusalem after Herod's attempt to kill him, James appears as the principal authority who presided at Council of Jerusalem. (Wikipedia contributors, "James (brother of Jesus)")

I FEEL THIS IS A GOOD TIME TO RE-ITERATE THE POINT THAT YESHUA SAID HE WAS NOT PUTTING ONE OF THE APOSTLES AS HEAD OVER ANOTHER AS A RULER!!! But that seems to be exactly what they did !!!

SO, MAYBE ONE OF THE OTHER APOSTLES (OR ELDERS-SHEPHERDS) SHOULD HAVE REMEMBERED THESE VERSES FROM ISAIAH 56 DURING THIS COUNCIL!!!:

[Isa 56:6-8 KJV] 6 Also THE SONS OF THE STRANGER, that JOIN THEMSELVES TO THE LORD, to serve him, and to love the name of the LORD, to be his servants, EVERY ONE THAT KEEPETH THE SABBATH FROM POLLUTING IT,

AND TAKETH HOLD OF MY COVENANT; 7 Even them will I bring to my holy mountain, and make them joyful in my house of prayer: their burnt offerings and their sacrifices [shall be] accepted upon mine altar; for mine house shall be called an house of prayer for all people. 8 THE LORD GOD WHICH GATHERETH THE OUTCASTS OF ISRAEL SAITH, YET WILL I GATHER [OTHERS] TO HIM, BESIDE THOSE THAT ARE GATHERED UNTO HIM.

THIS SCRIPTURE WOULD HAVE CLARIFIED THAT THE GENTILES, THE SONS OF THE STRANGER, THAT CAME INTO COVENANT WITH YEHOVAH (TO LOVE HIM, SERVE HIM, KEEP HIS SABBATHS, AND KEEP HIS COMMANDMENTS, WHICH IS WHAT TAKING HOLD OF THE COVENANT MEANT) WERE LITERALLY BEING JOINED TO THE ONE ISRAEL!

Before someone thinks that this scripture may have been only referring to strangers joining Yehovah in the Old Covenant, note that this scripture sounds very much like the MILLENNIAL KINGDOM described in Isaiah 2:

[Isa 2:1-3 KJV] 1 The word that Isaiah the son of Amoz saw concerning Judah and Jerusalem. 2 And it shall come to pass IN THE LAST DAYS, [that] THE MOUNTAIN OF THE LORD'S HOUSE shall be established in the top of the mountains, and shall be exalted above the hills; and ALL NATIONS shall flow unto it. 3 And MANY PEOPLE shall go and say, Come ye, and let us go up to the mountain of the LORD, to the house of the God of Jacob; and HE WILL TEACH US OF HIS WAYS, AND WE WILL WALK IN HIS PATHS: FOR OUT OF ZION SHALL GO FORTH THE LAW, AND THE WORD OF THE LORD FROM JERUSALEM.

Since the judgment made by this council was made first by James **HIMSELF**(Acts 15:13-21), and then in Acts 15:28 it is ascribed to all of the council and the Holy Spirit, it is also necessary to remember that Isaiah 56:6-8 above was **PROPHECY ALSO GIVEN BY INSPIRATION OF THE HOLY SPIRIT** and **WAS EVEN QUOTED BY YESHUA (so it definitely was inspired by the Holy Spirit!)** as he was overthrowing the tables of the moneychangers in the temple!!:

[Mar 11:17 KJV] 17 And he taught, saying unto them, **IS IT NOT WRITTEN, MY HOUSE SHALL BE CALLED OF ALL NATIONS THE HOUSE OF PRAYER?** but ye have made it a den of thieves. (Yeshua is quoting Isaiah 56:7).

IF ACTS 15:28-29 AND ISAIAH 56:6-8 SEEM CONTRADICTORY, AND IF WE WERE TO TRY TO DECIDE WHICH ONE WAS BY THE HOLY SPIRIT, WE NEED TO REMEMBER THAT THE ISAIAH SCRIPTURE WAS FIRST AND WAS NOT NEGATED BY YESHUA, WHILE HE WAS ON THE EARTH, BUT INSTEAD

CONFIRMED BY HIM!!!

HONESTLY, THE POINT I AM MAKING IS THAT THIS JUDGMENT OF THIS COUNCIL HAS CAUSED TREMENDOUS PROBLEMS AND UNTOLD DIVISION IN THE CHURCH FOR TWO MILLENNIA.... WHEN ALL THAT THE SHEPHERDS OF ISRAEL WERE TO BE DOING WAS TEACHING THE WORDS OF YESHUA AND THE WRITTEN TORAH....

SO, DID THIS COUNCIL AND SUBSEQUENT COUNCILS HAVE "TRUE AUTHORITY" OVER THE CHURCH (THE SHEEP)??

Let's continue looking at history to decide....

As stated earlier, these councils are referred to as pre-ecumenical councils by the Catholic Church, from which many other councils followed. The first ecumenical council is that of Nicaea, called by the Emperor Constantine in 325 A. D. Although I have researched them, I don't have room to even synopsize this extensive church history. However, **MANY "JUDGMENTS" ALONG WITH SEVERE PUNISHMENTS** have been decreed by these Councils upon the church through the years that are **ABSOLUTELY ABOVE AND BEYOND THE WORDS OF YESHUA AND THE WRITTEN TORAH**. I would highly encourage everyone to research for themselves.

However, there is a book that I have reviewed, **Ecclesiastical and Civil History Philosophically Considered with Reference to the Future Re-union of Christians, the First Three Books, Comprising the Period from the Ascension of Our Lord to the Death of Wycliffe, Vol. II, Book 3** written in 1847. I have only briefly reviewed it, though, as the table of contents itself is over twenty pages and the book is 761 pages! **(It is available in downloadable pdf form from Google for free!) ALL THE POPES AND COUNCILS ARE DISCUSSED.** In the book, I discovered, in reviewing **POPE GREGORY** (died 604 AD) that it states :

> He committed, at his accession, when he presented his confession of faith, according to the custom of the day, to the bishops and patriarchs of the Church, **the fatal error**, of **EQUALIZING THE FIRST FOUR GENERAL COUNCILS WITH THE FOUR GOSPELS, BY AFFIRMING THAT HE HELD THEM IN EQUAL REVERENCE WITH THE INSPIRED WRITINGS. (Townsend, 7)**

HOW LUDICROUS!! Let me reiterate this. This Pope, in his authority, declared that the first four "Councils" were equal to the four Gospel

accounts of Yeshua!!

THIS IS THE ADDING OF MAN-MADE LAWS TO YESHUA'S WORDS, WHICH HE HAD CONSTANTLY RAILED AGAINST IN HIS DAY WHEN THE JEWS IN POWER HAD DONE THE SAME THING TO THE WRITTEN TORAH!

> **ANOTHER EVIL WAS INFLICTED ON THE CHURCHES BY THIS BISHOP. GREGORY PERMITTED THE CEREMONIES OF THE PAGAN WORSHIP TO BE INTERWOVEN WITH THE CHRISTIAN SERVICE OF THE TRUE GOD. HE ONLY CHANGED THE NAMES OF THE OBJECTS OF THEIR WORSHIP. (Townsend, 11)**

Now, I am going to fast forward to the **SUPPOSED PRIMACY or HEADSHIP OF THE "BISHOP OF ROME" – THE POPE over the entire church:**

> The **Pope** (Latin: *papa* from Greek: πάππας *pappas*,[1] a child's word for "father") is the Bishop of Rome and the leader of the worldwide Catholic Church. The primacy of the Roman bishop is largely derived from his role as the traditional successor to Saint Peter, to whom Jesus is supposed to have given the keys of Heaven and the powers of 'binding and loosing', naming him as the 'rock' upon which the church would be built. The current pope is Francis, who was elected on 13 March 2013, succeeding Benedict XVI. (Wikipedia contributors, "Pope")

I HAVE TO INSERT HERE THE SCRIPTURE WHERE THIS WAS GIVEN: [Mat
16:15-19, 21-23 KJV] 15 **He saith unto them, But whom say ye that I am?**
16 And Simon Peter answered and said, Thou art the Christ, the Son of
the living God. 17 And Jesus answered and said unto him, Blessed art
thou, Simon Barjona: for flesh and blood hath not revealed [it] unto
thee, but my Father which is in heaven. 18 And I say also unto thee,
That thou art Peter, and upon this rock I will build my church; and the
gates of hell shall not prevail against it. 19 **And I will give unto thee the**
keys of the kingdom of heaven: and whatsoever thou shalt bind on
earth shall be bound in heaven: and whatsoever thou shalt loose on
earth shall be loosed in heaven.

HOWEVER, WHAT THE ROMAN CATHOLIC CHURCH DOES NOT RECOGNIZE, I ASSUME, IS THAT JUST TWO VERSES DOWN, THIS HAPPENS!:

[Mat 16:21-23 KJV] 21 From that time forth began Jesus to shew unto his disciples, how that he must go unto Jerusalem, and suffer many things of the elders and chief priests and scribes, and be killed, and be raised again the third day. 22 Then Peter took him, and began to rebuke him, saying, Be it far from thee, Lord: this shall not be unto thee. 23 **BUT HE TURNED, AND SAID UNTO PETER, GET THEE BEHIND ME, SATAN: thou art an offence unto me: for thou savourest not the things that be of God, but those that be of men.**

Peter had the profound revelation given to him by The Father that Yeshua was the Mashiach, the Son of the Living God, and Yeshua said on this rock of revelation He would build his church. But, when Peter listened to the devil, Yeshua pointed that out too. Peter was not perfect- he could choose to listen to The Father or listen to Satan.

******ALSO, ANOTHER FACT THAT THE ROMAN CATHOLIC CHURCH SKIPS OVER IS THAT, A FEW CHAPTERS LATER, <u>THESE SAME KEYS OF THE KINGDOM OF BINDING AND LOOSING WERE ALSO GIVEN BY YESHUA TO THE REST OF THE DISCIPLES TOO!!! (see below Matthew 18:18-20.)</u>******

ALSO, <u>EVEN AMONG ONLY TWO OR THREE BELIEVERS</u>, YESHUA PROMISED TO BE THERE - <u>WITHOUT AN ELDER</u> OR <u>A BISHOP</u> OR <u>A POPE !!!</u>

******In speaking to <u>ALL HIS DISCIPLES</u>, <u>Yeshua said</u>: [Mat 18:18-20 KJV] 18 <u>VERILY I SAY UNTO YOU, WHATSOEVER YE SHALL BIND ON EARTH SHALL BE BOUND IN HEAVEN: AND WHATSOEVER YE SHALL LOOSE ON EARTH SHALL BE LOOSED IN HEAVEN</u>. 19 Again I say unto you, That if two of you shall agree on earth as touching any thing that they shall ask, it shall be done for them of my Father which is in heaven. 20 <u>FOR WHERE TWO OR THREE ARE GATHERED TOGETHER IN MY NAME, THERE AM I IN THE MIDST OF THEM.</u>**

<u>This scripture obviously is never taught by the Roman Catholic Church, as the authority of the Pope would be negated!</u>

Now let's continue seeing how this truth derailed into **<u>A POPE RULING</u>** over the church!:

> The office of the Pope is the **papacy**. His <u>ecclesiastical jurisdiction</u>, the <u>Diocese of Rome</u>, is often called 'the <u>Holy See</u>' or 'the <u>Apostolic See</u>', the latter name being based upon **THE BELIEF** that the Bishop of Rome is the successor of <u>Peter the Apostle</u>. **THE POPE IS CONSIDERED ONE OF THE WORLD'S MOST POWERFUL PEOPLE BECAUSE OF ITS DIPLOMATIC AND CULTURAL INFLUENCE.** He is also <u>HEAD OF STATE</u> **OF** <u>VATICAN</u>

CITY, a sovereign city-state entirely enclaved within the Italian capital city of Rome.

The papacy is one of the most enduring institutions in the world and has had a prominent part in world history. The popes in ancient times helped in the spread of Christianity and **THE RESOLUTION OF VARIOUS DOCTRINAL DISPUTES**. In the Middle Ages, they played a role of secular importance in Western Europe, often acting as arbitrators between Christian monarchs. Currently, in addition to the expansion of the Christian faith and doctrine, the popes are involved in ecumenism and interfaith dialog, charitable work, and the defense of human rights.

Popes, who originally had no temporal powers, in some periods of history **ACCRUED WIDE POWERS SIMILAR TO THOSE OF TEMPORAL RULERS**. In recent centuries, popes were gradually forced to give up temporal power, and papal authority is now once again almost exclusively restricted to matters of religion. **OVER THE CENTURIES, PAPAL CLAIMS OF SPIRITUAL AUTHORITY HAVE BEEN EVER MORE FIRMLY EXPRESSED, CULMINATING IN 1870 WITH THE PROCLAMATION OF THE** DOGMA **OF** PAPAL INFALLIBILITY **FOR RARE OCCASIONS WHEN THE POPE SPEAKS** *EX CATHEDRA*—**LITERALLY "FROM THE CHAIR (OF SAINT PETER)"—TO ISSUE A FORMAL DEFINITION OF** FAITH **OR** MORALS.

The word *pope* derives from Greek πάππας meaning 'father'. In the early centuries of Christianity, this title was applied, especially in the east, to all bishops and other senior clergy, and later became reserved in the west to the Bishop of Rome, a reservation made official only in the 11th century. The earliest record of the use of this title was in regard to the by then deceased Patriarch of Alexandria, Pope Heraclas of Alexandria (232–248). The earliest recorded use of the title 'pope' in English dates to the mid-10th century, when it was used in reference to Pope Vitalian in an Old English translation of Bede's *Historia ecclesiastica gentis Anglorum*.

The Catholic Church teaches that the pastoral office, the office of shepherding the Church, that was held by the apostles, as a group or 'college' **WITH** SAINT PETER **AT THEIR HEAD**, is now held by their successors, the bishops, with **THE BISHOP OF ROME (THE POPE) AT THEIR HEAD**.

The Catholic Church teaches that Jesus personally appointed Peter as leader of the Church and in its dogmatic constitution *Lumen gentium* makes a clear distinction between apostles and bishops, presenting the latter as the successors of the former, with the pope as successor of Peter in that he is head of the bishops as Peter was head of the apostles. **SOME**

HISTORIANS HAVE ARGUED THAT THE NOTION THAT PETER WAS THE FIRST BISHOP OF ROME AND FOUNDED THE EPISCOPAL SEE THERE CAN BE TRACED BACK NO EARLIER THAN THE 3RD CENTURY. The writings of the Church Father Irenaeus who wrote around AD 180 reflect a belief that Peter 'founded and organised' the Church at Rome. Moreover, Irenaeus was not the first to write of Peter's presence in the early Roman Church. Clement of Rome wrote in a letter to the Corinthians, *c.* 96, about the persecution of Christians in Rome as the 'struggles in our time' and presented to the Corinthians its heroes, 'first, the greatest and most just columns', the 'good apostles' Peter and Paul. St. Ignatius of Antioch wrote shortly after Clement and in his letter from the city of Smyrna to the Romans he said he would not command them as Peter and Paul did. Given this and other evidence, many scholars agree that Peter was martyred in Rome under Nero, **ALTHOUGH SOME SCHOLARS ARGUE THAT HE MAY HAVE BEEN MARTYRED IN PALESTINE.**

PROTESTANTS CONTEND THAT THE NEW TESTAMENT OFFERS NO PROOF THAT JESUS ESTABLISHED THE PAPACY NOR EVEN THAT HE ESTABLISHED PETER AS THE FIRST BISHOP OF ROME. Others, using Peter's own words, argue that Christ intended himself as the foundation of the church and not Peter. Others have argued that the church is indeed built upon Jesus and faith, but also on the disciples as the roots and foundations of the church on the basis of Paul's teaching in Romans and Ephesians, though not primarily Peter.

FIRST-CENTURY CHRISTIAN COMMUNITIES WOULD HAVE HAD A GROUP OF PRESBYTER-BISHOPS FUNCTIONING AS LEADERS OF THEIR LOCAL CHURCHES. Gradually, episcopacies were established in metropolitan areas. Antioch may have developed such a structure before Rome. In Rome there were many who claimed to be the rightful bishop though again Irenaeus stressed the validity of one line of bishops from the time of St. Peter up to his contemporary Pope Victor I and listed them. Some writers claim that the emergence of a single bishop in Rome probably did not occur until the middle of the 2nd century. In their view, Linus, Cletus and Clement were possibly prominent presbyter-bishops but not necessarily monarchical bishops.

Documents of the 1st century and early 2nd century indicate that the Holy See had some kind of pre-eminence and prominence in the Church as a whole, though the detail of what this meant is very unclear at this period.

Early Christianity (*c.* 30–325)

It seems that at first the terms '**episcopos'** and '**presbyter'** were used interchangeably. The consensus among scholars has been that, at the turn of the 1st and 2nd centuries, local congregations were led by bishops and presbyters whose offices were overlapping or indistinguishable. Some say that there was probably **'NO SINGLE 'MONARCHICAL'**bishop in Rome before the middle of the 2nd century...and likely later.' Other scholars and historians disagree, citing the historical records of St. Ignatius of Antioch (d 107) and St. Irenaeus who recorded the linear succession of Bishops of Rome (the popes) up until their own times. They also cite **the importance accorded to the Bishops of Rome in the** ecumenical councils, **including the early ones.**

In the early Christian era, Rome and a few other cities had claims on the leadership of worldwide Church. James the Just, known as 'the brother of the Lord', served as head of the Jerusalem church, which is still honored as the 'Mother Church' in Orthodox tradition. Alexandria had been a center of Jewish learning and became a center of Christian learning. Rome had a large congregation early in the apostolic period whom Paul the Apostle addressed in his Epistle to the Romans, and according to tradition Paul was martyred there.

During the 1st century of the Church (*ca.* 30–130), the Roman capital became recognized as a Christian center of exceptional importance. Clement I, at the end of the 1st century, wrote an epistle to the Church in Corinth intervening in a major dispute, and apologizing for not having taken action earlier. However, there are only a few other references of that time to recognition of the authoritative primacy of the Roman See outside of Rome. In the Ravenna Document of 13 October 2007, theologians chosen by the Roman Catholic and the Eastern Orthodox Churches stated: '41. Both sides agree...that Rome, as the Church that 'presides in love' according to the phrase of St Ignatius of Antioch, occupied the first place in the *taxis*, and that the bishop of Rome was therefore the *protos* among the patriarchs. They disagree, however, on the interpretation of the historical evidence from this era regarding the prerogatives of the Bishop of Rome as *protos*, a matter that was already understood in different ways in the first millennium.'

IN THE LATE 2ND CENTURY AD, THERE WERE MORE MANIFESTATIONS OF ROMAN AUTHORITY OVER OTHER CHURCHES. In 189, assertion of the primacy of the Church of Rome may be indicated in Irenaeus's *Against Heresies* (3:3:2): **'With [the Church of Rome], because of its superior origin, all the churches MUST AGREE...and it is in her that the faithful everywhere have maintained the apostolic tradition.' IN AD 195,** POPE VICTOR I, **IN WHAT IS SEEN AS AN EXERCISE OF ROMAN AUTHORITY OVER OTHER CHURCHES, EXCOMMUNICATED THE QUARTODECIMANS FOR OBSERVING EASTER ON THE 14TH OF NISAN, THE DATE OF THE JEWISH PASSOVER, A TRADITION HANDED**

DOWN BY JOHN THE EVANGELIST (SEE EASTER CONTROVERSY). Celebration of Easter on a Sunday, **AS INSISTED ON BY THE POPE**, is **THE SYSTEM THAT HAS PREVAILED** (see computus).' (Wikipedia contributors, "Pope")

It seems obvious to me that the APPOINTMENT OF "BISHOPS" AND THE REST OF THE HIERARCHICAL RULING STRUCTURE that started even in the very beginning of the church, INSTEAD OF JUST SHEPHERDS TEACHING THE SHEEP, has caused more problems than it has ever helped! The protestant reformation in the 1500's, that rejected the authority of the papacy, proves the enormity of the problem, or else the whole church would still be Roman Catholic. Of course, that is what they would like....

THE PROBLEM WITH POWER IS THAT IT IS EASILY ABUSED. IN THIS CASE, DOCTRINES DEVELOPED THAT WERE NOT BIBLICAL AND WERE FORCED UPON THE CHURCH EVEN TO THE POINT OF DEATH IF THEY WERE NOT ACCEPTED.

An example of this abuse is the **UNBIBLICAL IMMACULATE CONCEPTION OF MARY DOCTRINE**:

> The **Immaculate Conception**, according to the teaching of the Catholic Church, was the conception of the Blessed Virgin Mary in the womb of her mother, Saint Anne, free from original sin by virtue of the foreseen merits of her son Jesus Christ. The Catholic Church teaches that Mary was conceived by normal biological means, but God acted upon her soul (keeping her "immaculate") at the time of her conception.
>
> The Immaculate Conception is commonly and mistakenly taken to mean the conception of Mary's son Jesus Christ in her own womb, and the Virgin Birth of Jesus. These are covered by the Doctrine of Incarnation, while the Immaculate Conception deals with the conception of Mary *herself*, not that of her son.
>
> Although the belief that Mary was sinless and conceived immaculate has been widely held since Late Antiquity, the doctrine was not DOGMATICALLY defined until 1854, by Pope Pius IX in his PAPAL BULL *Ineffabilis Deus*. The Catholic Church celebrates the Feast of the Immaculate Conception on December 8; in many Catholic countries, it is a holy day of obligation or patronal feast, and in some a national public holiday. (Wikipedia contributors, "Immaculate Conception")

Another false teaching that is forced on the church (if you are Roman Catholic) is the Assumption of Mary:

> The **Assumption of the Virgin Mary into Heaven**, often shortened to **the Assumption**, and also known as the **Falling Asleep of the Blessed Virgin Mary**, according to the beliefs of the Catholic Church, Eastern Orthodoxy, Oriental Orthodoxy, and parts of Anglicanism, was the bodily taking up of the Virgin Mary into Heaven at the end of her earthly life.
>
> The Catholic Church teaches as dogma that the Virgin Mary 'having completed the course of her earthly life, was assumed body and soul into heavenly glory'. This doctrine was DOGMATICALLY DEFINED **BY** POPE PIUS XII on November 1, 1950, in the apostolic constitution *Munificentissimus Deus* by **EXERCISING** PAPAL INFALLIBILITY. While the Catholic Church and Eastern Orthodox Church believe in the Dormition of the Theotokos, which is the same as the Assumption, the alleged physical death of Mary has not been dogmatically defined.
>
> In *Munificentissimus Deus* (item 39) Pope Pius XII pointed to the Book of Genesis (3:15) as scriptural support for the dogma in terms of Mary's victory over sin and death as also reflected in 1 Corinthians 15:54: "then shall come to pass the saying that is written, Death is swallowed up in victory".
>
> In the churches that observe it, the Assumption is a major feast day, commonly celebrated on August 15. In many countries the feast is also marked as a HOLY DAY OF OBLIGATION in the Roman Catholic Church and as a Festival in the Anglican Communion.
>
> On November 1, 1950, in the Apostolic Constitution *Munificentissimus Deus* Pope Pius XII declared the Assumption of Mary as a dogma:
>
> **'By the authority of our Lord Jesus Christ, of the Blessed Apostles Peter and Paul, and BY OUR OWN AUTHORITY**, we pronounce, **DECLARE**, and define it to be a **DIVINELY REVEALED DOGMA**: that the **IMMACULATE MOTHER OF GOD, THE EVER VIRGIN MARY, HAVING COMPLETED THE COURSE OF HER EARTHLY LIFE, WAS ASSUMED BODY AND SOUL INTO HEAVENLY GLORY.'**
>
> Pope Pius XII deliberately left open the question of whether Mary died before her Assumption. (Wikipedia contributors, "Assumption of Mary")

(Notice that Paul is put in the same category as Peter – as one of the Twelve Apostles – which he was not. Also, the word dogma means something laid down as incontrovertibly true!! Think about that! I suppose if you were a Roman Catholic, you would be termed a heretic, then, if you voiced that you did not believe this.... **The POWER of the church could, and probably would, BE USED AGAINST YOU...**)

EVEN WORSE IS THE CATHOLIC CHURCH'S CHANGE OF THE MEANING OF TWO OF THE TEN COMMANDMENTS!:

Both the Roman Catholics and the Eastern Orthodox church have icons and idols that are part of their worship and service.

'FROM THE VERY EARLIEST DAYS OF THE CHURCH THERE HAS BEEN A TRADITION WHEREBY <u>IMAGES</u> OF <u>OUR LORD, HIS HOLY MOTHER, AND OF THE SAINTS</u> ARE DISPLAYED IN CHURCHES FOR THE VENERATION OF THE FAITHFUL...THIS PRACTICE OF PLACING SACRED IMAGES IN CHURCHES SO THAT THEY CAN BE <u>VENERATED</u> BY THE FAITHFUL <u>IS TO BE MAINTAINED</u>.' (VATICAN II)

'THE <u>IMAGES</u> OF CHRIST AND THE VIRGIN MOTHER OF GOD, AND OF THE OTHER SAINTS, ARE TO BE HAD AND TO BE KEPT, ESPECIALLY IN CHURCHES, AND DUE HONOR AND VENERATION <u>ARE</u> TO BE GIVEN THEM.' COUNCIL OF TRENT, 25TH SESS. (1563).

The Roman Catholic church divides the first two commandments and combines them into one in Ex.20. In doing this they end up dividing another commandment into two so they can still have ten. The commandment of idols and images is intentionally ignored and even protested. 'The Christian veneration of images <u>is not contrary</u> to the first commandment which proscribes idols. Indeed, 'the honor rendered to an image passes to its prototype.' And whoever venerates an image venerates the person behind it'. (Catechism of the Catholic church)

If one has an image of Mary then it is Mary who is venerated, just as much as an image of Jesus. Nowhere do we see this practice in the New Testament, but we do have many warnings about it. Nowhere does God approve of any type of worship toward objects that are **<u>even of Himself</u>**, neither the tabernacle which housed His presence, nor the ark which had the tablets, were to be worshipped. Yet these were some of the most sacred objects used toward God.

Remember when Moses lifted up the Brazen altar in the wilderness for people to be healed by the bite of the serpents. Later when the Israelites entered the land of Canaan, they brought the bronze serpent with them and turned it into an idol. It was used until King Hezekiah finally destroyed it (2 Kings 18:4). <u>We see that something that was used even by God can be turned into a superstitious idol</u>.

<u>In Ex.20:4-5 God forbids anyone who follows Him to make images for use in their worship. Within this context they are also not to bow down to them or do any reverence to them. The Hebrew word for worship is to kiss toward or bow down.</u>

Idolatry is described by God as an abomination (Ezek.16:36), no matter who makes them or is worshipping them . 'Cursed is any man who makes any graven image or molten image it is an abomination to the Lord' (Lev. 26:1, Deut.27:15). **WHILE CATHOLICS ACCEPT THIS PRACTICE OF BOWING IN FRONT OF STATUES OF MARY OR SAINTS GOD DOES NOT ACCEPT IT, HE FORBIDS IT!**

Deut. 4:16... 'that you do not become corrupt and make for yourselves an idol, an image of any shape, whether formed like a man or a woman' (NIV).

Deut. 12:3-4: 'And you shall destroy their altars, break their sacred pillars, and burn their wooden images with fire; you shall cut down the carved images of their gods and destroy their names from that place.' '<u>You shall not worship the LORD your God with such things</u>.'

The biblical prohibition against having images for religious purposes and bowing down before them (and God's abhorrence of this pagan practice) is clearly set forth in the second of the Ten Commandments and in numerous other passages of Scripture. For example: 'Ye shall make you no idols nor graven image.. **to bow down unto it**.... Cursed be the man that maketh any graven or molten image, an abomination unto the Lord' (Leviticus 26:1; Deuteronomy 27:15).

In Hebrew the word for Idols is *Elim* , *avodot zerah* means foreign worship. The Hebrew word for <u>idolatry means to bow down or genuflect is to worship</u> *Tishtacheweh*. To bow down or genuflect as an act of worship. (7812 shachah (shaw-khaw');a primitive root; to depress, i.e. prostrate (especially reflexive, in homage to royalty or God): bow (self) down, crouch, fall down (flat), humbly beseech, do (make) obeisance, do reverence, make to stoop, worship. ("'Statues of Saints' God Ordained or Idolatry?")

HOW SAD TO THINK THAT THE HIERARCHY OF THE CATHOLIC CHURCH WOULD TWIST THE SIMPLE, EASILY UNDERSTOOD, SECOND COMMANDMENT TO NOT WORSHIP GRAVEN IMAGES INTO A WAY TO DO JUST THAT – SAYING THAT THEY ARE NOT DOING IT – <u>TEACHING THE PEOPLE (SHEEP) TO SIN!</u> THIS IS A <u>COMPLETE ABUSE OF AUTHORITY AND POWER!</u>

PEOPLE WERE SEVERELY PUNISHED IF THEY SPOKE AGAINST THIS, AND COULD BE EXCOMMUNICATED.

BUT ONE OF THE ULTIMATE ABUSES OF POWER IS THE ROMAN CATHOLIC CHURCH'S BLATANT AUDACITY TO ACTUALLY CHANGE YEHOVAH'S FOURTH COMMANDMENT TO KEEP THE SABBATH DAY HOLY - AND SAY THEY HAVE THE AUTHORITY TO CHANGE IT TO SUNDAY!!!

The following is from Roman Catholic Church teaching:

> **Concerning the Authority of the Church. - The Scripture teaches: Remember that you keep the Saturday; six days shalt thou labor and do all thy work, but the seventh day is the Sabbath of the Lord thy God, etc. However, THE CHURCH HAS TRANSFERRED THE OBSERVANCE FROM SATURDAY TO SUNDAY BY VIRTUE OF HER OWN POWER, WITHOUT SCRIPTURE, without doubt UNDER THE INSPIRATION OF THE HOLY SPIRIT.**
>
> 'Concerning Holidays and Fast-Days. - The Sabbath is commanded in various places in the Scriptures. But there is no mention of the cessation of the Sabbath and the institution of Sunday in the Gospels, or in Paul's writings, or in all the Bible; therefore this has taken place by the apostolic church instituting it without Scripture.
>
> 'If, however, the church has had power to change the Sabbath of the Bible into Sunday and to command Sunday - keeping, why should it not have also this power concerning other days, many of which are based on the Scriptures - such as Christmas, circumcision of the heart, three kings, etc. **IF YOU OMIT THE LATTER, AND TURN FROM THE CHURCH TO THE SCRIPTURES ALONE, THEN YOU MUST KEEP THE SABBATH WITH THE JEWS, WHICH HAS BEEN KEPT FROM THE BEGINNING OF THE WORLD.'12**

12 Dr. Eck's Enchiridion, 1533, pp. 78, 79. [Johann Eck was the principle adversary of Andreas Carlstadtt and Martin Luther at the disputation at Leipzig in 1519]

Source: *History Of The Sabbath And First Day Of The Week* by John Nevins Andrews and L. R. Conradi, Review and Herald Publishing, pg. 587. (Schieffler 10)

OBVIOUSLY, THEN, THE PROTESTANT REFORMATION DID NOT COMPLETE ITS WORK, AS IT KEPT SUNDAY AS THE SABBATH, CHRISTMAS, AND EASTER AS COMMANDED BY CATHOLIC CHURCH! There were some, even at that time, such as the Waldensians, who tried to have these changed back to be scriptural, but Martin Luther wouldn't go that far, and THEIR VOICE WAS SILENCED. So, the Protestant denominations of the church still keep these Catholic mandates!!

ALSO, note that **THIS CHANGE OF THE THE IMMUTABLE WORD OF YEHOVAH ELOHIM, this change of Sabbath to Sunday**, is **ATTRIBUTED by the Roman Catholic Church to the HOLY SPIRIT'S INSPIRATION!!!**

This cannot be true, of course! It is ludicrous!

I BELIEVE, MORE AND MORE, THAT WE EACH BETTER JUDGE EVERYTHING BY THE WRITTEN TORAH AND YESHUA'S WORDS!! EVEN WORDS ATTRIBUTED TO THE HOLY SPIRIT!!

MAN-MADE COMMANDMENTS CAN DECEIVE US INTO ACTUALLY BREAKING THE FATHER'S COMMANDMENTS!!!

In conclusion, my opinion is that history has proven that the setting up of 'Popes,""Bishops," "Councils," and other hierarchical offices (even in the later Protestant denominations and non-denominational congregations) that make RULINGS over Yeshua's sheep that are not based ONLY on YESHUA'S WORDS OR THE WRITTEN TORAH is UNSCRIPTURAL! Prophets are scriptural and may speak directions by the Holy Spirit. HOWEVER, IF A PROPHET SPEAKS, CLAIMING IT IS BY THE HOLY SPIRIT, BUT HIS WORDS NEGATE YESHUA'S WORDS OR THE WRITTEN TORAH, THEN I BELIEVE HE IS A FALSE PROPHET!!!

[Deu 13:1-5 KJV] 1 If there arise among you a prophet, or a dreamer of dreams, and giveth thee a sign or a wonder, 2 And the sign or the wonder come to pass, whereof he spake unto thee, saying, Let us go after other gods, which thou hast not known, and let us serve them; 3 Thou shalt not hearken unto the words of that prophet, or that dreamer of dreams: for the LORD your God proveth you, to know whether ye love the LORD your God with all your heart and with all your soul. 4 Ye shall walk after the LORD your God, and fear him, and keep his commandments, and obey his voice, and ye shall serve him, and cleave unto him. 5 And that prophet, or that dreamer of dreams, shall be put to death; because he hath spoken to turn [you] away

from the LORD your God, which brought you out of the land of Egypt, and redeemed you out of the house of bondage, to thrust thee out of the way which the LORD thy God commanded thee to walk in. So shalt thou put the evil away from the midst of thee.

AS STATED PREVIOUSLY, YESHUA SAID: [Mat 18:20 KJV] 20 FOR WHERE <u>TWO OR THREE</u> ARE <u>GATHERED TOGETHER IN MY NAME</u>, <u>THERE AM I IN THE MIDST OF THEM.</u>

What better promise is there than to have HIM in our midst!

This realization of the believers in Yeshua not being under the authority of "Bishops" and "Councils" is not a new one. Consider this information about the groups of Christians who started the founding of America from the online Encyclopedia Britannica (also consider it from the point of view of how Yehovah blessed America....):

> **Separatist,** also called Independent, any of the English Protestants in the 16th and 17th centuries who wished to separate from the perceived corruption of the Church of England and form independent local churches. Separatists were most influential politically in England during the time of the Commonwealth (1649–60) under Oliver Cromwell, the lord protector, who was himself a Separatist. Subsequently, they survived repression and gradually became an important religious minority in England.
>
> **A fundamental belief of the Separatists was the idea of the "gathered church" founded by the Holy Spirit, not man or the state. <u>Believing that true Christian believers should seek out other Christians and together form their churches, Separatists emphasized the right and responsibility of each congregation to determine its own affairs, without having to submit those decisions to the judgment of any higher human authority</u>. That notion stood in contrast to the territorial basis of the Church of England, in which everyone in a certain area was assigned to the parish church, and each local parish submitted to the oversight of the larger church hierarchy.**
>
> The Separatist movement was initially illegal in England, and many of its adherents were persecuted by the state and its church. Often labeled as traitors, many Separatists fled England for more tolerant lands. One such group left England for Holland in 1608, and in 1620 some of them, the Pilgrims, famously settled at Plymouth, Massachusetts. The Plymouth Separatists cooperated with the Puritans who settled the Massachusetts Bay Colony in 1630. Although the Puritans had originally hoped to purify and reform the Church of England, in New England they accepted the congregational form of church government established by the Pilgrims. Thus, the churches of the Separatists and the Puritans became the

Congregationalists of the United States. ("Separatist")

IN SUMMARY, I BELIEVE WE CAN GATHER TOGETHER IN YESHUA'S NAME TO WORSHIP, PRAY, AND STUDY THE WORD OF YEHOVAH, EVEN IN VERY SMALL GROUPS IF NECESSARY, WHERE WE ALL ARE JUST BROTHERS AND SISTERS (AS YESHUA SAID), EVERYONE HAVING A VOICE, AND BE PLEASING TO YESHUA! There may be some Shepherds/Elders (older in the faith) that teach the words of Yeshua and the Written Torah and prophets that prophesy, but they are not authorities over us that cannot be questioned, especially if you see that their teaching or prophecy deviates from the pure Words of Yeshua and the Written Torah! WE MUST THINK FOR OURSELVES AND OBEY GOD RATHER THAN MEN!!

BE VERY CAREFUL ABOUT SUBMITTING YOURSELF TO ANY PRESUMED CHURCH "AUTHORITY"!

APPENDIX II

LIST OF SINS THAT WILL SEND YOU TO THE LAKE OF FIRE!!!

[UNLESS YOU REPENT (TURN FROM THEM!) AND ASK FOR FORGIVENESS IN YESHUA'S NAME!]

DISCLAIMER: ONLY YEHOVAH ELOHIM, WHO IS THE CREATOR OF THE HEAVENS AND THE EARTH, THE SEA, AND ALL THAT IS IN THEM; THE ANCIENT OF DAYS; THE GOD OF ABRAHAM, ISAAC, AND JACOB; THE HOLY ONE OF ISRAEL; THE FATHER IN HEAVEN IS THE ULTIMATE JUDGE! THIS LIST MAY BE INCOMPLETE AND/OR MY CONCLUSIONS MAY BE INCORRECT.

HOWEVER, HE SAYS:

.[Rev 21:8 KJV] 8 But the FEARFUL, and UNBELIEVING, and THE ABOMINABLE, and MURDERERS, and WHOREMONGERS, and SORCERERS, and IDOLATERS, and ALL LIARS, shall have their part IN THE LAKE WHICH BURNETH WITH FIRE AND BRIMSTONE: WHICH IS THE SECOND DEATH.

FEARFUL:

Fear is the opposite of faith, or belief, so being fearful may be related to the next word: unbelieving. (Also, see "Fearful and Unbelieving, Continued" below.)

UNBELIEVING:

YEHOVAH ELOHIM SAID ABOUT HIMSELF BEING THE ONLY GOD: [Isa 43:10 KJV] 10 Ye [are] my witnesses, saith the LORD, and my servant whom I have chosen: that ye may know and BELIEVE ME, and UNDERSTAND THAT I [AM] HE: BEFORE ME THERE WAS NO GOD FORMED, NEITHER SHALL THERE BE

AFTER ME.

[EXODUS 20: 2-3 KJV] I AM THE LORD THY GOD, WHICH HAVE BROUGHT THEE OUT OF THE LAND OF EGYPT, OUT OF THE HOUSE OF BONDAGE. THOU SHALT NO OTHER GODS BEFORE ME.

YESHUA SAID ABOUT HIMSELF BEING THE LAMB OF GOD WHO CAME AND TOOK AWAY THE SIN OF THE WORLD, THE SON OF MAN (THE MESSIAH), AND THE SON OF GOD: [Jhn 8:23-24 KJV] 23 And he said unto them, Ye are from beneath; I am from above: ye are of this world; I am not of this world. 24 I said therefore unto you, that ye shall die in your sins: for IF YE BELIEVE NOT THAT I AM [HE], YE SHALL DIE IN YOUR SINS.!!!

[JHN 3:14-18 KJV] 14 AND AS MOSES LIFTED UP THE SERPENT IN THE WILDERNESS, EVEN SO MUST THE SON OF MAN BE LIFTED UP: 15 THAT WHOSOEVER BELIEVETH IN HIM SHOULD NOT PERISH, BUT HAVE ETERNAL LIFE. 16 For God so loved the world, that he gave HIS ONLY BEGOTTEN SON, that whosoever BELIEVETH IN HIM should not perish, but have everlasting life. 17 For God sent not his Son into the world to condemn the world; but that the world through him might be saved. 18 HE THAT BELIEVETH ON HIM IS NOT CONDEMNED: but HE THAT BELIEVETH NOT IS CONDEMNED ALREADY, BECAUSE HE HATH NOT BELIEVED IN THE NAME OF THE ONLY BEGOTTEN SON OF GOD.

(FEARFUL AND UNBELIEVING, CONTINUED):

Ultimately, fear of death is people's greatest fear!

Yeshua said concerning the end of this age before He returns: [Luk 21:12-19 KJV] 12 But before all these, THEY SHALL LAY THEIR HANDS ON YOU, AND PERSECUTE [YOU], DELIVERING [YOU] UP TO THE SYNAGOGUES, AND INTO PRISONS, BEING BROUGHT BEFORE KINGS AND RULERS FOR MY NAME'S SAKE. 13 And it shall turn to you for a testimony. 14 Settle [it] therefore in your hearts, not to meditate before what ye shall answer: 15 For I will give you a mouth and wisdom, which all your adversaries shall not be able to gainsay nor resist. 16 AND YE SHALL BE BETRAYED BOTH BY PARENTS, AND BRETHREN, AND KINSFOLKS, AND FRIENDS; AND [SOME] OF YOU SHALL THEY CAUSE TO BE PUT TO DEATH. 17 AND YE SHALL BE HATED OF ALL [MEN] FOR MY NAME'S SAKE. 18 BUT THERE SHALL NOT AN HAIR OF YOUR HEAD PERISH. 19 IN YOUR PATIENCE POSSESS YE YOUR SOULS.

The Greek word in vs. 19 translated as "patience," can also be translated as "endurance. " This goes along with the many other verses where Yeshua said, "He who endures to the end shall be saved." IN OTHER WORDS, THOSE WHO OVERCOME THEIR FEAR OF BETRAYAL, PERSECUTION, AND DEATH FOR THEIR BELIEF IN YESHUA AND ARE COURAGEOUS AND STAY IN FAITH WILL BE SAVED. BUT, THOSE THAT BECOME FEARFUL AND UNBELIEVING WILL DO SO AT THE EXPENSE OF BEING CAST IN THE LAKE OF FIRE!

Yeshua said : [Mar 4:17 KJV] 17 And have no root in themselves, and so ENDURE BUT FOR A TIME: afterward, when affliction or persecution ariseth for the word's sake, immediately they are offended.

[Mat 24:13 KJV] 13 But he that shall **ENDURE UNTO THE END**, the same shall be saved.

BELIEF IN THE COMMANDMENTS OF GOD, WHICH IS THE WORD OF GOD, ALONG WITH YOUR BELIEF IN YESHUA, IS ALSO NECESSARY AS THE APOSTLE JOHN SHOWS US IN VERSES FROM THE BOOK OF THE REVELATION BELOW, AS WELL AS IN THE FUNDAMENTAL VERSE OF THIS DOCUMENT, REVELATION 21:8:

[Rev 1:2 KJV] 2 WHO BARE RECORD OF THE WORD OF GOD, **AND** OF THE TESTIMONY OF JESUS CHRIST, and of all things that he saw.

[Rev 1:9 KJV] 9 I John, who also am your brother, and companion in tribulation, and in the kingdom and patience of Jesus Christ, was in the isle that is called Patmos, for THE WORD OF GOD, **AND** FOR THE TESTIMONY OF JESUS CHRIST.

[Rev 6:9 KJV] 9 And when he had opened the fifth seal, I SAW UNDER THE ALTAR THE SOULS OF THEM THAT WERE SLAIN FOR THE WORD OF GOD, **AND** FOR THE TESTIMONY WHICH THEY HELD:

[Rev 20:4 KJV] 4 And I saw thrones, and they sat upon them, and judgment was given unto them: and [I SAW] THE SOULS OF THEM THAT WERE BEHEADED FOR THE WITNESS OF JESUS, **AND** FOR THE WORD OF GOD, and which had not worshipped the beast, neither his image, neither had received [his] mark upon their foreheads, or in their hands; and they lived and reigned with Christ a thousand years.

[Rev 21:8 KJV] 8 But the fearful, and unbelieving (THOSE WITHOUT THE

TESTIMONY OF JESUS), AND the <u>abominable, and murderers, and whoremongers, and sorcerers, and idolaters, and all liars</u> (THOSE NOT KEEPING THE WORD OF GOD), shall have their part in the lake which burneth with fire and brimstone: which is the second death.

<u>LYING:</u>

<u>[Lev 19:11 KJV] 11 Ye shall not steal, neither deal falsely, NEITHER LIE ONE TO ANOTHER.</u>

[Pro 12:22 KJV] 22 <u>LYING LIPS</u> [ARE] ABOMINATION TO THE LORD: but they that deal truly [are] his delight.

[Isa 59:1-4 KJV] 1 Behold, the LORD'S hand is not shortened, that it cannot save; neither his ear heavy, that it cannot hear: 2 But your iniquities have separated between you and your God, and your sins have hid [his] face from you, that he will not hear. 3 For your hands are defiled with blood, and your fingers with iniquity; <u>YOUR LIPS HAVE SPOKEN LIES, YOUR TONGUE HATH MUTTERED PERVERSENESS. 4 NONE CALLETH FOR JUSTICE, NOR [ANY] PLEADETH FOR TRUTH: THEY TRUST IN VANITY, AND SPEAK LIES; THEY CONCEIVE MISCHIEF, AND BRING FORTH INIQUITY.</u>

<u>SORCERY:</u>

[Mal 3:5 KJV] 5 And I will come near to you to judgment; <u>and I WILL BE A SWIFT WITNESS AGAINST THE SORCERERS</u>, and against the adulterers, and against false swearers, and against those that oppress the hireling in [his] wages, the widow, and the fatherless, and that turn aside the stranger [from his right], and fear not me, saith the LORD of hosts.

WITCHCRAFT (OR SORCERY) IS A DEATH PENALTY SIN LISTED IN THE WRITTEN TORAH:

[Exo 22:18 KJV] 18 <u>Thou shalt not suffer a **WITCH**[H3784] to live.</u>[H2421]

Strong's #H3784 shows that the Hebrew word can be translated either as witch or sorcerer:

כָּשַׁף **kâshaph,** kaw-shaf'; a primitive root; properly, **<u>to whisper a spell, i.e. to</u>**

inchant or practise magic:—SORCERER, (USE) WITCH(-CRAFT).

FASCINATION WITH MAGIC, WITCHCRAFT, AND SORCERY IS BECOMING MORE AND MORE RAMPANT IN THE WORLD AND EVEN AMONG BELIEVERS IN YESHUA! YOUR ETERNAL SOUL COULD BE AT STAKE!!!

MURDER:

[Exo 20:13 KJV] 13 THOU SHALT NOT KILL.[H7523]

This particular word, kill, would be better translated as "murder". Yehovah says there are times to kill according to the Written Torah and there are other words for kill, such as for the sacrifices, and to carry out the death penalty on certain sins. The KJV translates Strongs H7523 in the following manner: slayer (16x), murderer (14x), kill (5x), MURDER (3x), slain (3x), manslayer (2x), killing (1x), slayer (with H310) (1x), slayeth (1x), death (1x).

[Jer 7:9-12 KJV] 9 Will ye STEAL, MURDER, AND COMMIT ADULTERY, AND SWEAR FALSELY, and burn incense unto Baal, and walk after other gods whom ye know not; 10 And come and stand before me in this house, which is called by my name, and say, We are delivered to do all these abominations? 11 Is this house, which is called by my name, become a den of robbers in your eyes? Behold, even I have seen [it], saith the LORD. 12 But go ye now unto my place which [was] in Shiloh, where I set my name at the first, and see what I did to it for the wickedness of my people Israel.

Notice what Yeshua says!

[Mat 19:16-19 KJV] 16 And, behold, one came and said unto him, Good Master, what good thing shall I do, that I may have eternal life? 17 And he said unto him, Why callest thou me good? [there is] none good but one, [that is], God: BUT IF THOU WILT ENTER INTO LIFE, KEEP THE COMMANDMENTS. 18 He saith unto him, Which? Jesus said, THOU SHALT DO NO MURDER, THOU SHALT NOT COMMIT ADULTERY, THOU SHALT NOT STEAL, THOU SHALT NOT BEAR FALSE WITNESS, 19 HONOUR THY FATHER AND [THY] MOTHER: AND, THOU SHALT LOVE THY NEIGHBOUR AS THYSELF.

WHOREMONGERS:

There are no verses in the Written Torah that use this specific word, so I cannot find the Hebrew meaning. But, it obviously has to do with sexual sin. Also, there are plenty of scriptures that lead us to believe this could be talking about adultery, as adultery is one of the 10 commandments; The Father lists it in many of the scriptures below as something he hates along with murder, stealing, swearing and lying; and it is punishable by death:

[Exo 20:14 KJV] 14 THOU SHALT NOT COMMIT ADULTERY.

[Lev 20:10 KJV] 10 And the man that committeth adultery with [another] man's wife, [even he] that committeth adultery with his neighbour's wife, the adulterer and the adulteress shall surely be put to death.

[Pro 6:32 KJV] 32 [But] whoso committeth adultery with a woman lacketh understanding: HE [THAT] DOETH IT DESTROYETH HIS OWN SOUL.

[Jer 5:7 KJV] 7 How shall I pardon thee for this? thy children have forsaken me, and sworn by [them that are] no gods: when I had fed them to the full, they then COMMITTED ADULTERY, and ASSEMBLED THEMSELVES BY TROOPS IN THE HARLOTS' HOUSES.

[Eze 23:37 KJV] 37 That they have committed adultery, and blood [is] in their hands, and with their idols have they committed adultery, and have also caused their sons, whom they bare unto me, to pass for them through [the fire], to devour [them].

[Hos 4:2 KJV] 2 By swearing, and lying, and killing, and stealing, and committing adultery, they break out, and blood toucheth blood.

HOWEVER, the Greek word, Strong's #4205, that is translated as "whoremongers" is:

πόρνος pórnos, por'-nos; from πέρνημι pérnēmi (to sell; akin to the base of G4097): **a (male) prostitute (as venal)**, i.e. (by analogy) a debauchee (libertine):—**fornicator, whoremonger**

It is translated as FORNICATOR 5 times in the New Testament and 5 times as WHOREMONGER.

In this case, it seems that it could be related to the **Hebrew word "dog", Strong's H #3611**, which is translated sometimes as an actual dog (animal) and sometimes as a male prostitute:

כֶּלֶב **keleb,** keh'-leb; from an unused root means. to yelp, or else <u>to attack</u>; a dog; hence (by euphemism) **<u>a male prostitute:—dog</u>**.

It is also used in the same verses as Sodomite in Deuteronomy 23:

[Deu 23:17-18 KJV] 17 There shall be no whore of the daughters of Israel, nor a sodomite of the sons of Israel. 18 Thou shalt not bring the hire of a whore, or the price of a dog, into the house of the LORD thy God for any vow: for even both these [are] abomination unto the LORD thy God.

Remember there is a Torah Commandment concerning male sexual intercourse : [Lev 20:13 KJV] 13 IF A MAN ALSO LIE WITH MANKIND, AS HE LIETH WITH A WOMAN, BOTH OF THEM HAVE COMMITTED AN ABOMINATION: they shall surely be PUT TO DEATH; their blood [shall be] upon them.

MY CONCLUSION IS THAT <u>YEHOVAH HATES SEXUAL SIN IN ANY FORM</u>!!!

I DON'T THINK A WISE PERSON WILL TRY TO "SPLIT HAIRS" OVER THE MEANING OF "WHOREMONGERS" .... AND JUST LIVE A CLEAN SEXUAL LIFE!!

<u>IDOLATRY:</u>

[Exo 20:3-6 KJV] 3 <u>THOU SHALT HAVE NO OTHER GODS BEFORE ME. 4 THOU SHALT NOT MAKE UNTO THEE ANY GRAVEN IMAGE, OR ANY LIKENESS [OF ANY THING] THAT [IS] IN HEAVEN ABOVE, OR THAT [IS] IN THE EARTH BENEATH, OR THAT [IS] IN THE WATER UNDER THE EARTH: 5 THOU SHALT NOT BOW DOWN THYSELF TO THEM, NOR SERVE THEM</u>: for I the LORD thy God [am] a jealous God, visiting the iniquity of the fathers upon the children unto the third and fourth [generation] of them that hate me; 6 And shewing mercy unto thousands of them that love me, and keep my commandments.

[Deu 17:2-7 KJV] 2 If there be found among you, within any of thy gates which the LORD thy God giveth thee, <u>MAN OR WOMAN, THAT HATH WROUGHT WICKEDNESS IN THE SIGHT OF THE LORD THY GOD, IN TRANSGRESSING HIS COVENANT</u>, 3 AND <u>HATH GONE AND SERVED OTHER GODS, AND WORSHIPPED THEM</u>, EITHER <u>THE SUN, OR MOON, OR ANY OF THE HOST OF HEAVEN, WHICH I HAVE NOT COMMANDED</u>; 4 And it be told thee, and thou hast heard [of it], and enquired diligently, and, behold, [it be] true, [and] the thing certain, [that] such abomination is wrought in Israel: 5 Then shalt thou bring forth that man or that woman, which have committed

that wicked thing, unto thy gates, [even] that man or that woman, and shalt stone them with stones, till they die. 6 At the mouth of two witnesses, or three witnesses, shall he that is worthy of death be put to death; [but] at the mouth of one witness he shall not be put to death. 7 The hands of the witnesses shall be first upon him to put him to death, and afterward the hands of all the people. So thou shalt put the evil away from among you.

[Deu 7:25 KJV] 25 <u>THE GRAVEN IMAGES OF THEIR GODS SHALL YE BURN WITH FIRE: thou shalt not desire the silver or gold [that is] on them, nor take [it] unto thee, lest thou be snared therein</u>: for it [is] an abomination to the Lord thy God.

ABOMINATIONS :

<u>*PLEASE NOTE THAT MANY EVEN OF THE ABOVE SINS ARE ALSO CALLED ABOMINATIONS! WHATEVER YEHOVAH HATES INTENSLY, MANY TIMES HE CALLS THEM ABOMINATIONS!***</u>**

[Deu 17:2-7 KJV] 2 If there be found among you, within any of thy gates which the LORD thy God giveth thee, <u>MAN OR WOMAN, THAT HATH WROUGHT WICKEDNESS IN THE SIGHT OF THE LORD THY GOD, IN TRANSGRESSING HIS COVENANT</u>, 3 AND <u>HATH GONE AND SERVED OTHER GODS, AND WORSHIPPED THEM</u>, EITHER <u>THE SUN, OR MOON, OR ANY OF THE HOST OF HEAVEN, WHICH I HAVE NOT COMMANDED</u>; 4 And it be told thee, and thou hast heard [of it], and enquired diligently, and, behold, [it be] true, [and] the thing certain, <u>[THAT] SUCH ABOMINATION IS WROUGHT IN ISRAEL</u>: 5 Then shalt thou bring forth that man or that woman, which have committed that wicked thing, unto thy gates, [even] that man or that woman, and shalt stone them with stones, till they die. 6 At the mouth of two witnesses, or three witnesses, shall he that is worthy of death be put to death; [but] at the mouth of one witness he shall not be put to death. 7 The hands of the witnesses shall be first upon him to put him to death, and afterward the hands of all the people. So thou shalt put the evil away from among you.

[Deu 7:25 KJV] 25 THE GRAVEN IMAGES OF THEIR GODS SHALL YE BURN WITH FIRE: thou shalt not desire the silver or gold [that is] on them, nor take [it] unto thee, lest thou be snared therein: FOR IT [IS] AN ABOMINATION TO THE LORD THY GOD.

[Pro 11:1, 20 KJV] 1 A FALSE BALANCE [IS] ABOMINATION TO THE LORD: but

a just weight [is] his delight. ... 20 THEY THAT ARE OF A FROWARD HEART [ARE] ABOMINATION TO THE LORD: but [such as are] upright in [their] way [are] his delight.

[Pro 12:22 KJV] 22 LYING LIPS [ARE] ABOMINATION TO THE LORD: but they that deal truly [are] his delight.

[Pro 17:15 KJV] 15 HE THAT JUSTIFIETH THE WICKED, AND HE THAT CONDEMNETH THE JUST, EVEN THEY BOTH [ARE] ABOMINATION TO THE LORD.

[Lev 18:22 KJV] 22 THOU SHALT NOT LIE WITH MANKIND, AS WITH WOMANKIND: IT [IS] ABOMINATION.

*****READ ALL OF LEVITICUS 18 AS IT LISTS SINS THAT YEHOVAH, AT THE END OF THE CHAPTER, DECLARES ALL TO BE ABOMINATIONS THAT DEFILE MEN:**

[Lev 18:1-30 KJV] 1 And the LORD spake unto Moses, saying, 2 Speak unto the children of Israel, and say unto them, I am the LORD your God. 3 After the doings of the land of Egypt, wherein ye dwelt, shall ye not do: and after the doings of the land of Canaan, whither I bring you, shall ye not do: neither shall ye walk in their ordinances. 4 Ye shall do my judgments, and keep mine ordinances, to walk therein: I [am] the LORD your God. 5 Ye shall therefore keep my statutes, and my judgments: which if a man do, he shall live in them: I [am] the LORD. 6 None of you shall approach to any that is near of kin to him, to uncover [their] nakedness: I [am] the LORD. 7 The nakedness of thy father, or the nakedness of thy mother, shalt thou not uncover: she [is] thy mother; thou shalt not uncover her nakedness. 8 The nakedness of thy father's wife shalt thou not uncover: it [is] thy father's nakedness. 9 The nakedness of thy sister, the daughter of thy father, or daughter of thy mother, [whether she be] born at home, or born abroad, [even] their nakedness thou shalt not uncover. 10 The nakedness of thy son's daughter, or of thy daughter's daughter, [even] their nakedness thou shalt not uncover: for theirs [is] thine own nakedness. 11 The nakedness of thy father's wife's daughter, begotten of thy father, she [is] thy sister, thou shalt not uncover her nakedness. 12 Thou shalt not uncover the nakedness of thy father's sister: she [is] thy father's near kinswoman. 13 Thou shalt not uncover the nakedness of thy mother's sister: for she [is] thy mother's near kinswoman. 14 Thou shalt not uncover the nakedness of thy father's brother, thou shalt not approach to his wife: she [is] thine aunt. 15 Thou

shalt not uncover the nakedness of thy daughter in law: she [is] thy son's wife; thou shalt not uncover her nakedness. 16 Thou shalt not uncover the nakedness of thy brother's wife: it [is] thy brother's nakedness. 17 Thou shalt not uncover the nakedness of a woman and her daughter, neither shalt thou take her son's daughter, or her daughter's daughter, to uncover her nakedness; [for] they [are] her near kinswomen: it [is] wickedness. 18 Neither shalt thou take a wife to her sister, to vex [her], to uncover her nakedness, beside the other in her life [time]. 19 Also thou shalt not approach unto a woman to uncover her nakedness, as long as she is put apart for her uncleanness. 20 Moreover thou shalt not lie carnally with thy neighbour's wife, to defile thyself with her. 21 And thou shalt not let any of thy seed pass through [the fire] to Molech, neither shalt thou profane the name of thy God: I [am] the LORD. 22 Thou shalt not lie with mankind, as with womankind: it [is] ABOMINATION. 23 Neither shalt thou lie with any beast to defile thyself therewith: neither shall any woman stand before a beast to lie down thereto: it [is] confusion. 24 DEFILE NOT YE YOURSELVES IN ANY OF THESE THINGS: FOR IN ALL THESE THE NATIONS ARE DEFILED WHICH I CAST OUT BEFORE YOU: 25 AND THE LAND IS DEFILED: THEREFORE I DO VISIT THE INIQUITY THEREOF UPON IT, AND THE LAND ITSELF VOMITETH OUT HER INHABITANTS. 26 Ye shall therefore keep my statutes and my judgments, and shall not commit [any] of THESE ABOMINATIONS; <u>[NEITHER] ANY OF YOUR OWN NATION, NOR ANY STRANGER THAT SOJOURNETH AMONG YOU</u>: 27 (For ALL THESE ABOMINATIONS have the men of the land done, which [were] before you, and the land is defiled;) 28 That the land spue not you out also, when ye defile it, as it spued out the nations that [were] before you. 29 FOR WHOSOEVER SHALL COMMIT ANY OF THESE ABOMINATIONS, EVEN THE SOULS THAT COMMIT [THEM] SHALL BE CUT OFF FROM AMONG THEIR PEOPLE. 30 Therefore shall ye keep mine ordinance, that [ye] commit not [any one] of these ABOMINABLE CUSTOMS, which were committed before you, and that ye defile not yourselves therein: I [am] the LORD your God.

****** AGAIN, NOTE, ALL OF LEVITICUS 18 IS DEALING WITH WHAT YEHOVAH ELOHIM, OUR CREATOR AND FATHER, CALLS <u>ABOMINATIONS</u> THAT HE HATES AND <u>WILL NOT</u>**

<u>ALLOW IN HEAVEN – THE NEW JERUSALEM</u> – <u>BUT WILL CAST THOSE WHO PRACTICE THEM IN THE LAKE OF FIRE</u>!!!

[Lev 20:13 KJV] 13 IF A MAN ALSO LIE WITH MANKIND, AS HE LIETH WITH A WOMAN, BOTH OF THEM HAVE COMMITTED AN ABOMINATION: they shall surely be PUT TO DEATH; their blood [shall be] upon them.

[Isa 66:17 KJV] 17 They that sanctify themselves, and purify themselves in the gardens behind one [tree] in the midst, EATING SWINE'S FLESH, AND THE ABOMINATION, AND THE MOUSE, SHALL BE CONSUMED TOGETHER, SAITH THE LORD.

[Eze 22:11 KJV] 11 And ONE HATH COMMITTED ABOMINATION WITH HIS NEIGHBOUR'S WIFE; and another hath lewdly defiled his daughter in law; and another in thee hath humbled his sister, his father's daughter.

[Lev 7:21 KJV] 21 Moreover the soul that shall touch any unclean [thing, as] the uncleanness of man, or [any] unclean beast, or ANY ABOMINABLE UNCLEAN [THING], and eat of the flesh of the sacrifice of peace offerings, which [pertain] unto the LORD, even that soul shall be cut off from his people.

[Lev 11:10-12 KJV] 10 And all that have not fins and scales in the seas, and in the rivers, of all that move in the waters, and of any living thing which [is] in the waters, they [shall be] an ABOMINATION unto you: 11 They shall be even an ABOMINATION unto you; ye shall not eat of their flesh, but ye shall have their carcases in ABOMINATION. 12 WHATSOEVER HATH NO FINS NOR SCALES IN THE WATERS, THAT [SHALL BE] AN ABOMINATION UNTO YOU.

[Lev 20:25 KJV] 25 Ye shall therefore put difference between clean beasts and unclean, and between unclean fowls and clean: and YE SHALL NOT MAKE YOUR SOULS ABOMINABLE BY BEAST, OR BY FOWL, OR BY ANY MANNER OF LIVING THING THAT CREEPETH ON THE GROUND, WHICH I HAVE SEPARATED FROM YOU AS UNCLEAN.

[Deu 14:3 KJV] 3 THOU SHALT NOT EAT ANY ABOMINABLE THING.

[Mic 6:10 KJV] 10 Are there yet the TREASURES OF WICKEDNESS in the house of the wicked, and THE SCANT MEASURE [THAT IS] ABOMINABLE?

[Deu 18:9 KJV] 9 WHEN THOU ART COME INTO THE LAND WHICH THE LORD THY GOD GIVETH THEE, <u>THOU SHALT NOT LEARN TO DO AFTER THE</u>

ABOMINATIONS OF THOSE NATIONS.

[Deu 24:1-4 KJV] 1 When a man hath taken a wife, and married her, and it come to pass that she find no favour in his eyes, because he hath found some uncleanness in her: then let him write her a bill of divorcement, and give [it] in her hand, and send her out of his house. 2 And when she is departed out of his house, she may go and be another man's [wife]. 3 And [if] the latter husband hate her, and write her a bill of divorcement, and giveth [it] in her hand, and sendeth her out of his house; or if the latter husband die, which took her [to be] his wife; 4 Her former husband, which sent her away, may not take her again to be his wife, after that she is defiled; for that [is] ABOMINATION before the LORD: and thou shalt not cause the land to sin, which the LORD thy God giveth thee [for] an inheritance.

[Deu 29:17 KJV] 17 And ye have seen their ABOMINATIONS, and their idols, wood and stone, silver and gold, which [were] among them:)

[1Ki 14:24 KJV] 24 And there were also SODOMITES in the land: [and] they did according to all THE ABOMINATIONS OF THE NATIONS which the LORD cast out before the children of Israel.

[2Ki 16:3 KJV] 3 But he walked in the way of the kings of Israel, yea, AND MADE HIS SON TO PASS THROUGH THE FIRE, ACCORDING TO THE ABOMINATIONS OF THE HEATHEN, whom the LORD cast out from before the children of Israel.

[2Ch 28:3 KJV] 3 Moreover he BURNT INCENSE IN THE VALLEY OF THE SON OF HINNOM, and BURNT HIS CHILDREN IN THE FIRE, after THE ABOMINATIONS OF THE HEATHEN whom the LORD had cast out before the children of Israel.

[Eze 14:6 KJV] 6 Therefore say unto the house of Israel, Thus saith the Lord GOD; REPENT, and TURN [YOURSELVES] FROM YOUR IDOLS; and TURN AWAY YOUR FACES FROM ALL YOUR ABOMINATIONS.

THIS ONE SUMS IT UP AND IS VERY SERIOUS:

[Pro 28:9 KJV] 9 HE THAT TURNETH AWAY HIS EAR FROM HEARING THE LAW, EVEN HIS PRAYER [SHALL BE] ABOMINATION.

He even states where all these abominations started:

[Rev 17:5 KJV] 5 And upon her forehead [was] a name written, **MYSTERY, BABYLON THE GREAT, THE MOTHER OF HARLOTS AND ABOMINATIONS OF THE EARTH.**

(We know that Yehovah will destroy Babylon in the end of days for this – Isaiah, Jeremiah, and Revelation all prophesy her destruction!!!)

IN CONCLUSION:

[Rev 22:14-15 KJV] 14 BLESSED [ARE] THEY THAT DO HIS COMMANDMENTS, THAT THEY MAY HAVE RIGHT TO THE TREE OF LIFE, AND MAY ENTER IN THROUGH THE GATES INTO THE CITY. 15 FOR WITHOUT [ARE] DOGS, AND SORCERERS, AND WHOREMONGERS, AND MURDERERS, AND IDOLATERS, AND WHOSOEVER LOVETH AND MAKETH A LIE.!!!!

APPENDIX III

CONSTANTINE THE GREAT AND SUN-GOD WORSHIP

The following are quotes from articles about Constantine the Great from two encyclopedias and one very informative book . I also would encourage you to study more on your own to get a fuller understanding of the history of Constantine the Great and how his policies inserted parts of sun-god worship into Christianity.

REFERENCES:

White, Lew. *Fossilized Customs: The Pagan Sources of Popular Customs*. Special Edition. Louisville: Strawberry Islands Publishers, 2002. Print.

Wikipedia contributors. "Constantine the Great." *Wikipedia, The Free Encyclopedia*. Wikipedia, The Free Encyclopedia. 18 Aug. 2014. Web. 21 Aug. 2014. <http://en.wikipedia.org/wiki/Constantine_the_Great>

"Constantine the Great (C.ad 285--337)." *The Hutchinson Unabridged Encyclopedia with Atlas and Weather Guide*, edited by Helicon, 2016. *Credo Reference*. Web. Accessed 08 Nov 2016. <http://search.credoreference.com/content/entry/heliconhe/constantine_the_great_c_ad_285_337/0>

The first source succinctly describes sun-god worship through the ages:

> **SUN-DAY** (day #1)
>
> From Latin, *dies Solis*, the *Day-of-the-Sun*. Since Babylon was established, Pagans have worshipped the **Sun**. Here's a few of the names they've used:
>
> Baal, Shamash, Moloch, Ahura-Mazda, Dagon, Sol, Marduk, Mithras, Krishna, Amon-Ra, Aton, Woden (Odin), Zeus, Deus, and the Druid / Teutonic 'God'. You may recall that the Pharaoh and the Caesar (Khazar/Czar) were worshipped as the sun. This began with the first king, **Nimrod**, discussed later. This pattern of worshipping the sun, moon, planets, and stars permeated the Babylonians, Persians, Chaldeans, Egyptians, Greeks, Romans, Celts, Mayans, Aztecs, and Indians. The governments were the religion. If they were 'good' pagans, at death they would be transported to the skies (Heaven) to live with their deities. This

was called *Nirvana, Shambala*, or *Elysian Fields*. The Roman Consul/Emperor **Constantine I** gave us the term *Sun-Day*, which he also called *Sol Invictus Mithras* (the day of the unconquerable sun, Mithras). In 321 CE he decreed under the penalty of death that all artisans, merchants, and people of his Empire cease to work on the Venerable Day of the Sun, to honor Mithras. This was a Universal Edict and is still enforced in our western culture with our 'blue laws'. (Interestingly, the government phone numbers are printed on blue pages in our US phone books). It was a weekly ritual of sun-worshippers to assemble at dawn on this day to greet the sun at its rising. A great pillar, or sun-ray obelisk was the solar religion's primitive high place, condemned by Scripture as a 'pillar of jealousy' ~ secretly interpreted as a male fertility symbol. Various tower designs such as steeples, pagodas, turrets, ziggurats, minarets, spires, obelisks, and pyramids have served Pagans well. The Temple did not have a high place, nor do synagogues! These high places would receive the first hallowed rays of dawn. At this point, bells were rung by hand, as in a shaker-grid, and large ones were struck with oak logs swung horizontally. Gongs struck with hammers were especially fun for the Oriental Pagan, but they also used the familiar bell shape too. In the book, *The Conquest of Peru*, Prescott is an eye-witness to blatant sun-worship:

'The Inca would assemble at dawn eagerly. They watched the coming of **the deity**, and no sooner did his first yellow rays strike the turrets, than a shout of gratulation broke forth from the assembled multitude, the wild tunes from barbaric instruments swelled louder and louder as his bright orb shone in full splendor on his votaries.'

The Romans considered anyone who did not worship the sun to be an atheist and a traitor, **SINCE CAESAR WAS THE SUN ENTHRONED IN A MAN**. Religion, politics, and sports were all in different facets of the same thing. Sun-Day will be discussed later too. (White, 7-8)

The next source describes Constantine as the first Christian Roman Emperor, although it does allude to the fact that sun worship was retained at least symbolically:

Religious policy

Constantine is perhaps best known for being the first Christian Roman emperor.

In February 313, Constantine met with Licinius in Milan, where they developed the Edict of Milan. The edict stated that Christians should be allowed to follow the faith without oppression. This removed penalties for professing Christianity, under which many had been martyred previously, and returned confiscated Church property. The edict protected from religious persecution not only Christians but all religions, allowing anyone to worship whichever deity they chose. A similar edict had been issued in 311 by Galerius, then senior emperor of the Tetrarchy; Galerius' edict granted Christians the right to practice their religion but did not restore any property to them. The Edict of Milan included several clauses which stated that all confiscated churches would be returned as well as other provisions for previously persecuted Christians.

Scholars debate whether Constantine adopted his mother St. Helena's Christianity in his youth, or whether he adopted it gradually over the course of his life. Constantine would retain the title of *pontifex maximus* until his death, a title emperors bore as heads of the pagan priesthood, as would his Christian successors on to Gratian (*r.* 375–83). According to Christian writers, Constantine was over 40 when he finally declared himself a Christian, writing to Christians to make clear that he believed he owed his successes to the protection of the Christian High God alone. Throughout his rule, Constantine supported the Church financially, built basilicas, granted privileges to clergy (e.g. exemption from certain taxes), promoted Christians to high office, and returned property confiscated during the Diocletianic persecution. His most famous building projects include the Church of the Holy Sepulchre, and Old Saint Peter's Basilica.

However, Constantine certainly did not patronize Christianity alone. After gaining victory in the Battle of the Milvian Bridge (312), a triumphal arch—the Arch of Constantine—was built (315) to celebrate his triumph. The arch is decorated with images of the goddess Victoria. At the time of its dedication, sacrifices to gods like Apollo, Diana, and Hercules were made. Absent from the Arch are any depictions of Christian symbolism. However, as the Arch was commissioned by the Senate, the absence of Christian symbols may reflect the role of the Curia at the time as a pagan redoubt.

Later in 321, Constantine instructed that Christians and non-Christians should be united in observing the **venerable day of the sun**, referring to the sun-worship that Aurelian had established as an official cult. Furthermore, and long after his oft alleged conversion to Christianity, Constantine's coinage continued to carry the symbols of the sun. Even after the pagan gods had disappeared from the coinage, Christian symbols appeared only as Constantine's *personal* attributes: the chi rho between his hands or on his labarum, but never on the coin itself. Even when Constantine dedicated the new capital of Constantinople, which became the seat of Byzantine Christianity for a millennium, he did so wearing the Apollonian sun-rayed Diadem; no Christian symbols were present at this dedication.

The reign of Constantine established a precedent for the position of the emperor as having great influence and ultimate regulatory authority within the religious discussions involving the early Christian councils of that time, e.g., most notably the dispute over Arianism, and the nature of God. Constantine himself disliked the risks to societal stability that religious disputes and controversies brought with them, preferring where possible to establish an orthodoxy. One way in which Constantine used his influence over the early Church councils was to seek to establish a consensus over the oft debated and argued issue over the nature of God.

Most notably, from 313–316 bishops in North Africa struggled with other Christian bishops who had been ordained by Donatus in opposition to Caecilian. The African bishops could not come to terms and the Donatists asked Constantine to act as a judge in the dispute. Three regional Church councils and another trial before Constantine all ruled against Donatus and the Donatism movement in North Africa. In 317 Constantine issued an edict to confiscate Donatist church property and to send Donatist clergy into exile. More significantly, in 325 he summoned the Council of Nicaea, effectively the first Ecumenical Council (unless the Council of Jerusalem is so classified). The Council of Nicaea is most known for its dealing with Arianism and for instituting the Nicene Creed.

Constantine enforced the prohibition of the First Council of Nicaea against celebrating the Lord's Supper on the day before the Jewish Passover (14 *Nisan*) (see Quartodecimanism and Easter controversy). This marked a definite break of Christianity from the Judaic tradition. From then on the Roman Julian Calendar, a solar calendar, was given precedence over the lunar Hebrew Calendar among the Christian churches of the Roman Empire.

Constantine made new laws regarding the Jews. They were forbidden to own Christian slaves or to circumcise their slaves. (Wikipedia contributors, "Constantine, the Great")

Notice that this next source says that the sign of the cross was "superimposed upon the sun." It makes one wonder if this could have contributed to Constantine's continuation of sun-god worship symbols and placing them in Christian worship, even to the extent of **transferring the commanded rest and worship on Sabbath to Sunday... :**

Constantine the Great (c.AD 285–337)

from The Hutchinson Unabridged Encyclopedia with Atlas and Weather Guide:

First Christian emperor of Rome and founder of Constantinople. He defeated Maxentius, joint emperor of Rome in AD 312, and in 313 formally recognized Christianity. As sole emperor of the west of the empire, he defeated Licinius, emperor of the east, to become ruler of the Roman world in 324. He presided over the church's first council at Nicaea in 325. Constantine moved his capital to Byzantium on the Bosporus in 330, renaming it Constantinople (now Istanbul).

Constantine was born at Naissus (Niš, Serbia), the son of Constantius. He was already well known as a soldier when his father died in York in 306 and he was acclaimed by the troops there as joint emperor in his father's place. A few years later Maxentius, the joint emperor in Rome (whose sister had married Constantine), challenged his authority and mobilized his armies to invade Gaul. Constantine won a crushing victory outside Rome in 312. **DURING THIS CAMPAIGN HE WAS SAID TO HAVE SEEN A VISION OF THE CROSS OF JESUS SUPERIMPOSED UPON THE SUN, ACCOMPANIED BY THE WORDS: 'IN THIS SIGN, CONQUER'**. By the Edict of Milan 313 he formally recognized Christianity as one of the religions legally permitted within the Roman empire and in 314 he summoned the bishops of the Western world to the Council of Arles. However, there has never been agreement on whether Constantine adopted Christianity for reasons of faith or as an act of imperial absolutism to further his power. Constantine increased the autocratic power of the emperor, issued legislation to tie the farmers and workers to their crafts in a sort of caste system, and enlisted the support of the Christian church. He summoned, and presided over, the first general council of the church in Nicaea 325. In 337 he set out to defend the Euphrates frontier against the Persians, but he died before reaching it, at Nicomedia in Asia Minor. ("Constantine the Great [C.ad 285—337]")

APPENDIX IV

ORAL TORAH

The following is text quoted from an article on the Oral Torah from Wikipedia (see GNU Free Documentation License):

REFERENCE:
Wikipedia contributors. "Oral Torah." *Wikipedia, The Free Encyclopedia*. Wikipedia, The Free Encyclopedia, 11 Jul. 2016. Web. 18 Sep. 2016.

Oral Torah
From Wikipedia, the free encyclopedia

According to Rabbinic Judaism, the **Oral Torah** or **Oral Law** (Hebrew: תורה שבעל פה, *Torah she-be-`al peh*, lit "Torah that is spoken") represents those laws, statutes, and legal interpretations that were not recorded in the Five Books of Moses, the "Written Torah" (Hebrew: תורה שבכתב, *Torah she-bi-khtav*, lit. "Torah that is written"), but nonetheless are regarded by Orthodox Jews as prescriptive and co-given. This holistic Jewish code of conduct encompass a wide swath of ritual, worship, God-man and interpersonal relationships, from dietary laws to Sabbath and festival observance to marital relations, agricultural practices, and civil claims and damages.

According to Jewish tradition, the Oral Torah was passed down orally in an unbroken chain from generation to generation until its contents were finally committed to writing following the destruction of the Second Temple in 70 CE, when Jewish civilization was faced with an existential threat.[1]

The major repositories of the Oral Torah are the *Mishnah*, compiled between 200–220 CE by Rabbi Yehudah haNasi, and the *Gemara*, a series of running commentaries and debates concerning the Mishnah, which together are the *Talmud*, the preeminent text of Rabbinic Judaism. In fact, two "versions" of the Talmud exist: one produced in Jerusalem c. 300–350 CE (the Jerusalem Talmud), and second, more extensive Talmud compiled in Babylonia and published c. 450–500 CE (the Babylonian Talmud).

Belief that the Oral Torah was transmitted orally from God to Moses on Mount Sinai during the Exodus from Egypt is a fundamental tenet of faith of Orthodox Judaism, and was recognized as one of the Thirteen Principles of Faith by Maimonides. However, not all branches of Rabbinic Judaism accept the divine provenance of the Oral Torah, such that Conservative and (to a greater extent) Reform Jews give deference to the Talmudic sages while empowering themselves to formulate and adopt their own rulings and interpretations.

There have also been historical dissenters to the Oral Torah in its entirety, including adherents to Karaite Judaism, who attempt to derive their religious practice strictly from the Written Torah, using Scripture's most natural meaning to form their basis of Jewish law.

Components

Halakha #Sources and process

Components of the Oral Law

1. Explanations of certain statutes of the written law, which are not altogether intelligible without them, and which statutes therefore presuppose an oral interpretation. Such explanations admit of being connected in some artificial way with Scripture.
2. Ancient halakot which have no connection whatever with Scripture and can not be connected with it, thus deriving their authority only from the tradition which ascribes them to Moses on Sinai ("Halakha LeMoshe MiSinai"). In the case of these two groups it is impossible to ascertain which elucidations and rules were really given to Moses on Sinai, and which were added later.
3. Halakot found in the prophetic books. Some of these originated at the time of the Prophets; but others are much older, perhaps having been transmitted orally, and committed to writing by the Prophets. They are called also *"Dibre Ḳabbalah"* (Words of Tradition).
4. Interpretations and regulations defining many written laws, as well as new halakhot, which the first scribes, beginning with the time of Ezra, formulated. These are called also *"Dibre Soferim"* (Words of the Scribes).

5. Interpretations and regulations covering the written law, as well as new halakhot, which the Tannaim deduced from Scripture by means of hermeneutic rules or by logical conclusions. There are differences of opinion among the scholars in regard to most of these explanations and definitions; but they are of equal weight with the written law, and are called also *"Debar Torah"* (Regulation of the Torah).
6. Customs and observances (*"takkanot"*) which were introduced at various times by different scholars. They are ascribed partly to Moses, partly to Joshua, but chiefly to the members of the Great Synagogue or the *Soferim* ("Scribes"), and are called also *"Dibre Soferim"* ("Words of the Scribes").
7. Statutes and decisions (*"gezerot"*) decreed by the Sanhedrin or court, and generally accepted, thus becoming laws which could be abrogated only by another court superior to the first one in numbers and scholarship.
8. Statutes and regulations for which the scholars had no tradition or allusion in Scripture, but which they accepted as standards after deriving them from the customs and laws of the country in which they were living. These are called *"Hilkot Medinah"* (Statutes of the Country).

The term "Oral Torah" should not be understood as a monolith. The *Jewish Encyclopedia* divides the Oral Torah into eight categories, ranked according to the relative level of authoritativeness, which are found within the Talmud, the Tosefta and the halakhic Midrashim, as aside.[2] The regulations, observances, and statutes included in the last three groups were not considered equal in validity to the written law (*"De'oraita"*), but were regarded merely as rabbinical regulations (*"de-rabbanan"*).[2]

Historical development

Source and transmission

According to modern scholarship, the traditions embodied in what later became known as the "Oral Torah" developed over generations among the inhabitants of Judea and were passed down through various modes of cultural transmission, including but not restricted to oral transmission. It is hypothesized that, sometime prior to the Babylonian exile of 586-530 BCE, in applying the Mosaic code to daily life and Temple worship, "a multitude of usages arising out of practical necessity or convenience or experience became part of the routine of observance of the code, and, in the course of time, shared the sanctity and authority which were inherent in the divinely inspired code itself."[3]

Such practices experienced exponential growth from the time of Ezra to the Romans' destruction of the Second Temple due to the changing social and religious conditions experienced by inhabitants of Judea.[3] Many of these practices were advocated by the Pharisees, a sect of largely lower- and middle-class Jews who stood in opposition to the Sadducees, the priestly caste who dominated the Temple cult.[4] The Sadducees rejected the legitimacy of any extra-biblical law or tradition, as well as increasingly popular notions such as the immortality of the soul and divine intervention.[4][5] Danby notes the following:

It is a reasonable hypothesis that a result of this controversy—a controversy which continued for two centuries—was a deliberate compilation and justification of the unwritten tradition by the Pharisean party, perhaps unsystematic and on a small scale in the earlier stages, but stimulated and fostered from time to time both by opposition from the Sadducees and by internal controversy (such as, e.g., the disputes between the Schools of Hillel and Shammai) within the ranks of the Pharisees, culminating in the collections of traditional laws (*Halakoth*) from which the present Mishnah draws its material.[3]

With the destruction of the Second Temple around 70 CE, the Sadducees were divested of their main source of authority, without which their theology could not survive. On the other hand, the Pharisees became the progenitor of the rabbinic class, who formalized the traditions of their predecessors. Following the fall of the Temple, it appears that the Pharisaic leader Johanan ben Zakkai (30-90 CE) established himself in Yavneh (a town south of Jaffa known to the Greeks as *Jamnia*), where he established a school that came to be regarded by fellow Jews as the successors of the Jerusalem Sanhedrin.[3] Upon this Council of Jabneh fell the duty of administering and interpreting religious law, conserving tradition, and solving problems that arose by the past dependence of numerous observances on the existence of the Temple and priesthood.[3] Thus, from 70 to 130 CE, when the Bar Kochba revolt further decimated the Jewish community, the Oral Law experienced a significant period of development and an unprecedented level of legal and religious authority among the populace.

Codification

The Mishnah

The destruction of the Second Temple and the fall of Jerusalem in the 1st and early 2nd Centuries CE devastated the Jewish community. The First Jewish–Roman War of 66–73 CE and the Bar Kokhba revolt cost more than a million Jewish lives, the destruction of leading yeshivot, and thousands of scholars and students.[6] At that point, it became apparent that the Hebrew community and its learning were threatened, and that publication was the only way to ensure that the law could be preserved.[6][7] Thus, around 200 CE, a redaction of oral law in writing was completed. Both Rabbinic tradition and scholarship ascribe this effort to Rabbi Judah HaNasi (or "Judah the Prince"). The product of this effort, the Mishnah, is generally considered the first work of Rabbinic literature.

"Mishnah" is the name given to the sixty-three tractates that HaNasi systematically codified, which in turn are divided into six "orders." Unlike the Torah, in which, for example, laws of the Sabbath are scattered throughout the books of Exodus, Leviticus, and Numbers, all the Mishnaic laws of the Sabbath are located in a single tractate called *Shabbat* (Hebrew for "Sabbath").[6] Moreover, the laws contained in the twenty-four chapters that make up that tractate are far more extensive than those contained in the Torah, reflecting the extensiveness of the Oral Law.[6] Some authority suggests HaNasi made use of as many as 13 separate collections of Halakhot from different schools and time periods, and reassembled that material into a coherent whole, arranged it systematically, summarized discussions, and in some cases rendered his own rulings where alternative traditions existed.[3]

However, Jacob Neusner argues that the Mishnah does far more than expound upon and organize the Biblical commandments. Rather, important topics covered by the Mishnah "rest on no scriptural foundations whatsoever," such as portions of the civil law tractates of *Bava Kamma*, *Bava Metzia* and *Bava Batra*.[8] In other words, "To perfect the [Written] Torah, the Oral tradition had to provide for a variety of transactions left without any law at all in Scripture."[8] Just as portions of the Torah reflect (according to the documentary hypothesis) the agenda of the Levite priesthood in centralizing worship in the Temple in Jerusalem and legitimizing their exclusive authority over the sacrificial cult, so too can the Mishnah be seen as reflecting the unique "program" of the Tannaim and their successors to develop an egalitarian form of Judaism with an emphasis on social justice and an applicability throughout the Jewish diaspora.[8][9] As a result, the Talmud often finds the rabbis combing scripture for textual support to justify existing religious practice, rather than deriving the practice organically from the language of scripture.[8]

The Gemara

HaNasi's method of codification, in which he often included minority viewpoints and citation by name to rabbis who championed different viewpoints, became a template for the Gemara, a compendium of discussions and commentaries on the Mishnah's laws by generations of leading rabbis during the next four centuries in the two centers of Jewish life, Judea and Babylonia.[6] The Gemara with the Mishnah came to be edited together into compilations known as the Talmud. Both the Babylonian Talmud and the Jerusalem Talmud (or "Yerushalmi Talmud") have been transmitted in written form to the present day, although the more extensive Babylonian Talmud is widely considered to be more authoritative.[6]

The Talmud's discussions follow the order of the Mishnah, although not all tractates are discussed. Generally, a law from the Mishnah is cited, which is followed by a rabbinic deliberation on its meaning. The discussion often, but not always, results in a decision regarding the more persuasive or authoritative position based on available sources or anecdotal evidence.[6]

Archaeology

Archaeologists have uncovered evidence relating to religious rituals and practices current, prior to the codification of the Mishnah, from which it can be inferred that Judah HaNasi and his contemporaries recorded, rather than innovated, normative Judaism as authentically practiced during the 1st century CE and prior. For example, excavations at Qumran have yielded specimens of *tefillin* and parchment scrolls.[10] Likewise, the structure and placement of Mikvah ritual baths at the Judean fortress of Masada (see Map) appears to be consistent with the rabbinic requirements per the Mishnaic tractate *Mikvaot*, but was constructed approximately 120 years before the Mishnah was compiled.[11] A clay seal discovered in Jerusalem in 2011 is consistent with the tradition recorded in tractate *Shekalim* chapter 5.[12] The Elephantine papyri 419 BCE include a "Passover letter" which already included many of the pesach observances of today;[13] Among the papyri is the first known text of a Ketubah (Jewish marriage contract) from about 440 BCE. The *Halachic Letter* (*Miqsat Ma'ase Ha-Torah*/ Qumran Cave 4), which records approximately a dozen disputes regarding the application of halachah, also testifies to the evolutionary process of the oral law.

Similarly, the Targum Onkelos (1st century CE) is largely consistent with the oral tradition as recorded in the midrash, redacted into writing only in the 3rd or 4th century.[14]

In Jewish tradition

Orthodox Judaism

Rabbinic Judaism has long held the Oral Law to be of divine origin. The divinity and authoritativeness of the Oral Law as transmitted from God to Moses on Mount Sinai, continues to be universally accepted by Orthodox and Haredi Judaism as a fundamental precept of Judaism.[15] The oral law was the basis for nearly all subsequent Rabbinic literature. It is therefore intricately related to the development of Halacha. As such, despite codification, interpretation of the "oral law" is likewise required.

Divine source and transmission

Rabbis of the Talmudic era conceived of the Oral Torah in two distinct ways.[16] First, Rabbinic tradition conceived of the Oral Torah as an unbroken chain of transmission. The distinctive feature of this view was that Oral Torah was "conveyed by word of mouth and memorized."[17] Second, the Rabbis also conceived of the Oral Torah as an interpretive tradition, and not merely as memorized traditions. In this view, the written Torah was seen as containing many levels of interpretation. It was left to later generations, who were steeped in the *oral tradition* of interpretation to discover those ("hidden") interpretations not revealed by Moses.[18] Instead, Moses was obligated to impart the explanations orally to students, children, and fellow adults. It was thus forbidden to write and publish the Oral Torah.[19]

Jewish tradition identifies the individuals, starting from Moses, who were entrusted with the Oral Law and passed it down to subsequent generations. The unbroken historical chain from Sinai to the present day is attested to in the opening passage of the Mishnaic tractate Pirkei Avot ("Sayings of the Fathers"): "Moses received the Torah and handed it down to Joshua; Joshua to the Elders; the Elders to the prophets; and the prophets handed it down to the men of the Great Assembly."[20] Similarly, in his introduction to Mishneh Torah Maimonides provides a generation by generation account of the names of all those in the direct line that transmitted this tradition, beginning with Moses up until Ravina and Rav Ashi, the rabbis who compiled the Babylonian Talmud.

The interplay of the Oral and Written Law

According to traditional Judaism, the Oral Law must have been disseminated at the same time as the Written Torah because certain Torah commandments would be indecipherable without a separate explanatory codex and, presumably, God would not demand adherence to commandments that could not be understood. Many terms used in the Torah are left undefined, such as the word *totafot*, usually translated as "frontlets," which is used three times in the Pentateuch (in Exodus 13:9 and Deuteronomy 6:8 and 11:18) but only identified with tefillin in the Mishnah (see Menachot 3:7). Similarly, many procedures are mentioned without explanation or instructions, or assume familiarity on the part of the reader.[21][22][23] For example, the discussion of *shechita* (kosher slaughter) in Deuteronomy 12 states "you shall kill of your herd and of your flock which God

Lord has given you, as I have commanded you," without any clear indication of what had been "commanded"; only in the Oral Torah are the various requirements of ritual slaughter explicated. Similarly, Deuteronomy 24 discusses the laws of divorce in passing; these laws are set forth with great specificity in the Mishnah and Gemara. Also, the blue string of tekhelet on the tzitzit is to be dyed with a dye extracted from what some scholars believe to be a snail is a detail only spoken of in the oral Torah.[24] For other examples and further discussion here see *Kuzari* 3:35.

Moreover, according to the traditional view, without an Oral Law, blind adherence to the plain text of certain Torah commandments would lead to unethical acts, or would cause the practitioner to violate a commandment elsewhere in the Torah. Neither of these results could have been intended by God; thus, *a priori*, a set of supplementary "instructions" must have been provided. A classic example involves the phrase "An eye for an eye, a tooth for a tooth, a hand for a hand, a foot for a foot" Ex 21:22–27 is held in the oral tradition to imply monetary compensation – as opposed to a literal *Lex talionis*.[25]

Finally, the Oral Torah is needed to explain seemingly discordant actions of biblical actors. For example, the marriage of Boaz, a member of the tribe of Judah to Ruth, a Moabitess, as described in the Book of Ruth, appears on its face to contradict the prohibition of Deuteronomy 23:3–4 against marrying Moabites; however, the Oral Torah explains that this prohibition is limited to Moabite *men*. Similarly, the rabbinic practice for the Counting of the Omer (Leviticus 23:15–16) is at odds with the Karaite practice, which appears to accord with a more literal reading of these verses, but is in fact borne out by Joshua 5:10–12.[26]

In Rabbinic literature and commentary

As above, the Oral Law is recorded in the Midrash and Talmud, while later Rabbinic literature builds on these works. This section, then, discusses the treatment of the Written Law in light of the Oral Law, and the consequent overlap of the oral and written (and is not a general discussion of Rabbinic Literature, *per se*). Here, it is important to note that these source, "oral", documents, are nevertheless intimately connected to the written. Thus, the midrash provides a verse by verse discussion of the entire (written) Tanakh, per the oral Torah. similarly, the Talmud, although applying a different framework, discusses and analyses the written Torah—both from an aggadic and halakhic perspective—drawing from (and recording) the oral tradition; here the discussion is organized around the Mishnah, and the discussion does not proceed verse-wise as with the Midrash.

The era of the *Rishonim* sees the oral law incorporated into the first formal Torah commentaries, where the biblical text is discussed and / or analysed based on the various Midrashic and Talmudic traditions. The chief of these is perhaps Rashi's commentary on Tanakh. This work clarifies the "simple" meaning of the text, by addressing questions implied[27] by the wording or verse or paragraph structure, by drawing on the Midrashic, Talmudic and Aggadic literature. It has given rise to numerous counter- (e.g., Ramban) and super-commentaries (e.g., Mizrachi), all similarly drawing on the Oral Torah, and widely studied to this day (see *Mikraot Gedolot*).

In more recent times, *Acharonic* times, several (Orthodox) commentaries have been produced, which, to some extent, *reverse* the direction of the analysis. These originated in response to the (erstwhile) challenges of *haskalah* and Biblical criticism, and were intended "to demonstrate the indivisibility of the written Torah and its counterpart, the oral Torah",[28] and in so doing, "showing the organic relationship between the Written Law and the Oral Law",[29] often in the light of the above. Given this purpose, these provide a further detailed and explicit analysis here. The main of these:

- *Ha'emek Davar* ("The Depth [of the] Word") on Torah, and *Davar Ha'emek* on *Nevi'im* and *Ketuvim*, by Naftali Zvi Yehuda Berlin, the "Netziv"
- *Haketav VehaKabbalah* ("The Written [Torah] and the [Oral] Tradition") on Torah, by Yaakov Tzvi Mecklenburg
- *HaTorah vehaMitzva* ("The Torah and the Commandment") by Meïr Leibush, the "Malbim", covers all of *Tanakh* except *Kohelet* and *Eicha*.
- *Uebersetzung und Erklärung des Pentateuchs* ("Translation and Commentary of the Pentateuch") by Samson Raphael Hirsch.
- *Torah Temimah* ("The Perfect Torah") on Torah, by Baruch Epstein.

Contemporaneous with, and complementary to these commentaries, were specific, monograph-like works discussing the Oral Torah in concept and historically. These included:

- *Dor Dor v'Dor'shav* ("Each generation and its Scholars"), by Rabbi Isaac Hirsch Weiss, a five volume history of the oral law, Halakha and Aggada, from Biblical times until the composition of the *Shulchan Aruch*.
- *Mevo Hatalmud* ("Introduction to the Talmud") and *Torat Neviim* ("Teachings of the Prophets"), by Rabbi Zvi Hirsch Chajes. The first, a detailed history and classification of the Talmud and its underlying oral tradition, formulating the nature, extent, and authority of tradition. The second, treatises on the authority of Talmudic tradition, and on the organic structure and methodology of the Talmud. Other well known works here, if perhaps less modern in orientation, include Maimonides' (Rambam's) *Introduction to the Mishnah*—dealing with the nature of the oral law, the distinction between the prophet and the sage, and the organizational structure of the Mishnah—as well as Isaiah Horowitz, "The Shelah"'s, *Introduction to the Oral Torah* in part 2 of his *Shenei Luchot HaBerit* ("Two Tablets of the Covenant").

- *Matteh Dan* (or *Kuzari Hasheini*; London 1714) written by Rabbi David Nieto demonstrates the authority of the Oral Law, and defends the tradition against attacks by Karaites and skeptics.

Several works by Rabbi Immanuel Aboab, especially his *Nomologia*, defend the traditional law and discuss its chronology.

Finally, other major works discussing the Bible as based on the Oral Torah include the following.

- *El Conciliador* ("The Conciliator"), by Rabbi Menasseh Ben Israel, a work written to reconcile the apparent contradictions in numerous passages throughout the Bible by utilizing "an astounding range of sources", primarily the Talmud and the classic Jewish commentaries. It was written in Spanish, in Amsterdam, 1632, primarily to strengthen the faith of the Marranos.
- Weiss' *Dor Dor v'Dor'shav* similarly discusses apparent divergencies in the Pentateuch and the various books of the Prophets.
- *Me'am Lo'ez*, begun by Rabbi Yaakov Culi in 1730, a detailed explanation of each chapter of the Torah, explaining it from "countless approaches", especially according to the Midrash and Talmud; also discusses the relevant *Halacha* as based on the *Shulchan Aruch* and *Mishneh Torah*. The work was intended as a "compendium" of the major fields of Torah study, for the Ladino-speaking community.

Dissenting viewpoints

From Pharisaic times, there has always been some level of opposition to the concept of a "Dual Torah" within the umbrella of Judaism, although today only the Karaite sect formally opposes the incorporation of any extra-biblical law into their practice. Rather, the branches of modern Judaism differ more in their views regarding the divinity and immutability of the Oral Torah than they do in their belief in the importance of an interpretive tradition as exemplified in the Talmud.[30]

Sadducees

Sadducees rejected the Pharisaic oral traditions. They based their interpretations on their own traditions emphasizing a more literal understanding of the verses. In many respects, this led to a more severe observance than that of the Pharisees especially as regards purity laws and temple practice. Most aspects of Sadduceean law and methods of interpretation are not known.[31]

Essenes

Essenes, a monastic group of people, had a "monastic organization". Though they had non-biblical rules and customs, they rejected much of the oral traditions.[32]

Samaritans

The Samaritans, an ancient sect that has survived in small numbers to the present day, have their own rich interpretative tradition, as reflected in the Medieval Samaritan legal collection called the *Hilukh*, which shares etymological roots with the term *Halakhah*. However, the concept of a divinely ordained Oral Law having equal value with the written one is foreign to Samaritan theology.[33]

Karaites

Main article: Karaite Judaism

Karaite Judaism or Karaism is a Jewish denomination that began in eighth century Baghdad to form a separate sect that rejected of the "Oral Torah" and Talmud, and placed sole reliance on the Tanakh as scripture.[6] Thus, for example, Karaite understood Exodus 35:3 ("Do not light a fire in any of your dwellings on the Sabbath day") as forbidding the use of any kind of fire on the Sabbath, including fires lit before the start of the Sabbath, which are permitted by the Oral Law.[6] Karaites also do not adhere to widespread customs such as the donning of *tefillin* and the prohibition against eating milk and meat together on the grounds that such practices are grounded in the Oral Law.[6]

Some Karaites strive to adhere only to the *peshat'* (plain meaning) of the text. This is in contrast to Rabbinic Judaism, which relies on the Oral Torah and employs several interpretive methods which, at times, stray from the literal meaning.

Modern perspectives

Reform Judaism

Reform Judaism generally considers the Oral Law to reflect interpretations or perspectives on the Torah authored by groups of Rabbis in Babylonia and Palestine over a period of time, which are not inherently more legitimate or authoritative than the opinions of Jewish scholars, philosophers, or religious leaders at any other time, including the present.[15]

Conservative Judaism

Conservative Judaism (also known as "Masorti" outside North America) takes an intermediate perspective, claiming that the Oral tradition is entitled to authority, but regarding its rulings as flexible guidelines rather than immutable precepts, that may be viewed through the lens of modernity.[34] Jewish scholar and philosopher Ismar Schorsch has postulated that Conservative Judaism is tied to "sensing divinity both in the Torah and in the Oral Law," but not in a literalist manner.[35] Rabbi Zecharias Frankel, considered intellectual founder of Conservative Judaism, was respected by many Orthodox until writing in 1859 that the Talmudic term "Law given to Moses at Sinai" always meant ancient customs accepted as such. His opponents demanded that he issue an unequivocal statement of belief in the total divinity of Oral Law, yet he refrained from doing so. He was consequently ostracized and declared a heretic by several authorities.

References

1. **Jump up ^** Howard Schwartz, *Tree of Souls: The Mythology of Judaism*, Oxford University Press, 2004. p lv
2. ^ Jump up to: *a b* *"Oral Law". Jewish Encyclopedia. 1906. Retrieved 3 January 2014.*
3. ^ Jump up to: *a b c d e f* *Danby, Herbert (2012). The Mishnah: Translated from the Hebrew with Introduction and Brief Explanatory Notes. Hendrickson Publishers. pp. xvii–xix. ISBN 978-1-59856-902-5.*
4. ^ Jump up to: *a b* *Magness, Jodi (2003). Archaeology of Qumran and the Dead Sea Scrolls. Wm. B. Eerdmans Publishing. pp. 41–43. ISBN 978-0-8028-2687-9.*
5. **Jump up ^** According to Josephus, *Antiquities* XIII. x. 6, "The Pharisees have delivered to the people a great many observances by succession from their fathers which are not written in the law of Moses; and for that reason it is that the Sadducees reject them, and say that we are to esteem those observances to be obligatory which are in the Written Word, but are not to observe what are derived from the tradition of our forefathers."
6. ^ Jump up to: *a b c d e f g h i j* *Telushkin, Joseph (2001). Jewish Literacy: Revised Edition. New York, USA: William Morrow and Company, Inc. pp. 146–152. ISBN 0-688-08506-7.*
7. **Jump up ^** Tosefta Eduyot 1:1 "*When the Sages went to Yavneh they said: The time will come that a man will seek a matter in the Torah but will not find it. He will seek a matter from the Scribes but will not find it. ... They said: Let us begin [to record] with Hillel and Shammai.*" See generally Timeline of Jewish history.
8. ^ Jump up to: *a b c d* *Neusner, Jacob (2003). The Perfect Torah: Volume 13 of The Brill Reference Library of Ancient Judaism. BRILL. pp. 2–4. ISBN 9789004130333.*
9. **Jump up ^** *Ska, Jean-Louis (2006). Introduction to reading the Pentateuch. Eisenbrauns. ISBN 978-1-57506-122-1.*
10. **Jump up ^** See for example, Yigal Yadin: Tefilin from Qumran.
11. **Jump up ^** Rabbi Yosef Back: "Southern mikveh on Masada".
12. **Jump up ^** See references under "Clay Seal Confirms Ancient Temple Service: Archaeologists".

13. **Jump up ^** Schiffman, Lawrence. Texts and Traditions: A Source Reader for the Study of Second Temple and Rabbinic Judaism. Hoboken: Ktav Publishing House, 1998.
14. **Jump up ^** See: prof. A Segal Targum "Onkelos" to the Torah; Rabbi G. Student: Onkelos and the Oral Torah.
15. ^ Jump up to: *a b* *Gaventa, William (2012). Jewish Perspectives on Theology and the Human Experience of Disability. Routledge. pp. 109–112. ISBN 978-1-136-45351-9.*
16. **Jump up ^** *Dane, Perry (Winter 1991). "The Oral Law and the Jurisprudence of a Textless Text". S'vara: A Journal of Philosophy, Law, and Judaism.* ***2****: 11.*
17. **Jump up ^** Elizabeth Shanks Alexander, *The Orality of Rabbinic Writing*, in The Cambridge Companion to the Talmud, ed. Martin Jaffee, 2007. p. 39. This is attested to in numerous sources, such as Mishnah Avot 1:1. The manner of teaching and memorization is described in B. Eruvin 54b.
18. **Jump up ^** In Rabbinic literature this view is exemplified by the story of Rabbi Akiva who expounded heaps and heaps of laws from the scriptural crowns of the letters in the written Torah. According to traditional Judaism, the laws transmitted to Moses contained in the Written Torah (or Chumash) were written down on scrolls, but God enjoined Moses from writing down the explanation of these laws. Indeed, the Talmud relays that Moses himself would not understand all of these interpretations, nevertheless, these are also called Mosaic traditions (*Halakha leMoshe miSinai*). B Menahot 29b. See, Elizabeth Shanks Alexander, op cit.
19. **Jump up ^** See BT Temurah 14b, and, BT Gittin 60b. Also, Y Meggila 4:1
20. **Jump up ^** *Fackenheim, Emil L. (1999). What is Judaism?: An Interpretation for the Present Age. Syracuse University Press. pp. 68–71. ISBN 978-0-8156-0623-9.*
21. **Jump up ^** David Charles Kraemer, *The Mind of the Talmud*, Oxford University Press, 1990. pp 157–159
22. **Jump up ^** *Oral Law*, Jewish Encyclopedia
23. **Jump up ^** Rabbi Gil Student: Proofs for the Oral Torah
24. **Jump up ^** See http://www.tekhelet.com Ptil Tekhelet
25. **Jump up ^** The Talmud explains this concept entails monetary compensation in tort cases. The Torah's first mention of the phrase "an eye for an eye, a tooth for a tooth, a hand for a hand, a foot for a foot" appears in Ex 21:22–27. The Talmud (in *Bava Kamma*, 84a), based upon a critical interpretation of the original Hebrew text, explains that this biblical concept entails monetary compensation in tort cases. (Additionally, this law cannot be carried out in practice, for both practical and ethical reasons; see also parashat Emor). Since the Torah requires that penalties be universally applicable, the phrase cannot be

interpreted literally; it would be inapplicable to blind or eyeless offenders.

26. **Jump up ^** Tim Hegg: "Counting the Omer: An Inquiry into the Divergent Methods of the 1st Century Judaisms".
27. **Jump up ^** http://www.shemayisrael.com/parsha/bonchek/intro.htm
28. **Jump up ^** http://www.amazon.com/Haketav-Vehakabbalah-Demonstrating-Indivisibility-Commentaries/dp/9657108292
29. **Jump up ^** http://www.torah.org/advanced/netziv/
30. **Jump up ^** For more detail from a general perspective, see Rabbi Nathan Cardozo, *The Infinite Chain: Torah, Masorah, and Man* (ISBN 0-944070-15-9), and Rabbi Gil Student, *Proofs for the Oral Torah*. For a verse by verse analysis in light of the oral tradition, see the commentaries listed below.
31. **Jump up ^** Ken Koltun-Fromm, *Abraham Geiger's liberal Judaism*, Indiana University Press, 2006. p 53
32. **Jump up ^** Joseph A. Fitzmyer, *The Impact of the Dead Sea Scrolls*, Paulist Press, 2009. p 56
33. **Jump up ^** *Lowy, S. (1977). The Principles of Samaritan Bible Exegesis. Brill Archive. pp. 25–28. ISBN 9789004049253.*
34. **Jump up ^** *Danzger, M. Herbert (1989). Returning to Tradition: The Contemporary Revival of Orthodox Judaism. Yale University Press. p. 101. ISBN 978-0-300-10559-9.*
35. **Jump up ^** *Alan Silverstein (2001). Eli Lederhendler, ed. Who Owns Judaism?: Public Religion and Private Faith in America and Israel. 9780195148022. p. 54, fn. 56. ISBN 978-0-19-514802-2.*

Traditional Material

- "Maimonides introduction to the Mishnah Torah" (English translation)
- "Maimonides introduction to the Commentary on the Mishnah" (Hebrew Fulltext)

Bibliography

- *The Essential Talmud*, Adin Steinsaltz, Basic Books; 1984
- *Introduction to The Talmud and Midrash*, H.L. Strack and G. Stemberger, Fortress Press
- *The Infinite Chain: Torah, Masorah, and Man*, Nathan T. Lopes Cardozo, Targum Press Distributed by Philipp Feldheim; 1989

(Wikipedia contributors. "Oral Torah.")

APPENDIX V

TEMPLE, ADMINISTRATION AND SERVICE OF

The following is quoted from an article by the same name found in the Jewish Encyclopedia that will help explain the administration and service of The Temple from the Second Temple period:

REFERENCE:

Jacobs, Joseph, and Judah David Eisenstein. "Temple, Administration and Service Of." *Jewish Encyclopedia*.. 1901-1906. *JewishEncyclopedia.com. The unedited full-text of the 1906 Jewish Encyclopedia*. 2002-2011.Web. 08 June 2016. <http://www.jewishencyclopedia.com/articles/14303-temple-administration-and-service-of>

> The affairs of the Second Temple were managed by a board of fifteen appointed officers ("memunnim"). The Mishnah records the following names of officers of the Temple without stating their respective periods of activity; but it is presumed they were those appointed in the time of Agrippa: (1) Johanan b. Phinehas, in charge of the seals given in exchange for money to purchase sacrifices; (2) Ahijah, of libations; (3) Mattithiah b. Samuel, of allotments (*i.e.*, the selection of priests for the day); (4) Pethahiah, of the nests of fowls (for sacrifices); (5) Ben Ahijah, of the health department (treating especially a disease of the bowels caused by the bare feet touching the cold marble pavement); (6) Neḥunya, of the digging of wells (for the pilgrims on the highways leading to Jerusalem); (7) Gebini (Gabinimus), of announcements (the Temple crier); (8) Ben Geber, of the gates (opening and closing them); (9) Ben Babi, of the wicks for the candlestick ("menorah"); (10) Ben Arza, of the cymbals (leading the music of the Levites); (11) Hugras (Hugdas) b. Levi, of the musical instruments; (12) the Garmu family, of the preparation of the showbread; (13) the Abṭinas family, of the incense; (14) Eleazar, of the curtains; and (15) Phinehas, of the vestments (Sheḳ. v. 1; comp. Maimonides, "Yad," Kele ha-Miḳdash, vii. 1).
>
> Seven trustees ("amarkelim") and three cashiers ("gizbarim") had charge of the Temple treasury. In the courts were thirteen contribution-boxes in the shape of shofarim, with narrow necks and broad bases (Sheḳ. vi.). The half-shekel contribution for public sacrifices, etc., was demanded on the first of Adar and was payable by the twenty-fifth of the same month (*ib.* i. 1, 3). There was a special room, called "Lishkat Ḥashsha'im" (Secret Chamber), for anonymous donations, out of which fund the worthy poor were supported. Into the Vessel Chamber the people threw donations of silver and gold vessels. Every thirty days this chamber was opened by the

cashiers; who selected such vessels as could be utilized in the Temple, the rest being sold and the proceeds applied to a fund for repairing the Temple building ("bedeḳ, ha-bayit"; *ib.* v. 4).

The priestly officials were: the high priest, his deputy ("segan"), and his two attendants ("ḳatoliḳin" = "catholicus")...

A strict watch over the Temple was maintained, the guard being composed of three priests and twenty-one Levites. The priests were stationed one at the Chamber of the Flame ("Bet ha-Niẓoẓ"), one at the Chamber of the Hearth ("Bet ha-Moḳed"), and one at the Chamber (attic) of Abṭinas (see diagram, page 95). The Levites kept guard as follows: one at each of the five gates of the mount entrances; one at each of the four corners within the mount enclosure; one at each of the five important gates of the courts; one at each of the four corners within the court; one at the Chamber of Sacrifice; one at the Chamber of Curtains; and one behind the 'Kapporet' (Holy of Holies). The captain of the guard saw that every man was alert, chastising a priest if found asleep at his post, and sometimes even punishing him by burning his shirt upon him, as a warning to others (Mid. i. 1).

The priests were divided into twenty-four patrols ("mishmarot"), which were changed every week. The patrol was quartered partly in the Chamber of the Flame and principally in the Chamber of the Hearth, both of which were on the north side of the inner court ("'azarah"). The latter chamber was a capacious one, surmounted by a dome. Half of the chamber extended outside the court to the 'ḥel,' a kind of platform surrounding the courts, which was considered as secular, in contrast to the sacred premises within, where the priests were not allowed to sit down, much less to sleep. A fire was always kept burning in the outer extension, at which the priests might warm their hands and bare feet. Here also they might sit down and rest for a while. At night the elder priests slept here on divans placed on rows of stone steps one above another. The younger priests slept on cushions on the floor, putting their sacred garments under their heads and covering themselves with their secular clothing (Tamid. i. 1). The elder priests kept the keys of the Temple, putting them at night under a marble slab in the floor; to this slab a ring was attached for lifting it. A priest watched over or slept on the slab until the keys were demanded by the officer in the morning.

The king when visiting the Temple had no rights beyond those of the ordinary Israelite; only the kings of the house of David were privileged to sit down in the 'azarah (Soṭah 41b; Tamid 27a)....

The major Sanhedrin, composed of 71 members, sat in the Chamber of

Hewn Stone ("Lishkat ha-Gazit") on the extreme north of the priests' hall. Two tribunals of minor Sanhedrin, each composed of twenty-three members, sat one by the south gate of the mount and one in front of the hall on the north side. The sessions were held from the morning sacrifice till that of the afternoon. On Sabbaths and holy days, to facilitate increased business the major Sanhedrin sat outside on the ḥel (Sanh. 88b), and the minor Sanhedrin assembled in the bet hamidrash situated on the mount (Tosef., Ḥag. ii.)...

Entrance within the enclosure of the mount was permitted to any one who was decently attired and who carried no burden. Israelites when ritually unclean and Gentiles were not allowed to pass beyond the 'soreg,' a fence which surrounded the courts at a distance of ten cubits. The outer court, called 'Ezrat Nashim' (Women's Hall), was for the use of ordinary Israelites. The priests' hall was reserved for the priests and Levites; occasionally, however, men and women presenting sin-offerings, sacrifices on which they were required to place the hands ("semikah"), made use of it. At the festivals, to accommodate the large crowds, all Israelites were permitted to enter the priests' hall, on which occasion the curtain of the vestibule was raised to show the people the interior of the 'Hekal' (see Pilgrimage). The people, though tightly packed, were able to find sufficient space in which to prostrate themselves, this being one of the miracles associated with the Temple. The people crowded to within eleven cubits behind the Holy of Holies (Yoma 21a).

Another phenomenon was the water-supply. A spring rising below the Holy of Holies from an opening as narrow as the antennæ of a locust increased when it reached the entrance to the Hekal to the size of a warp-thread; at the entrance to the vestibule it assumed the size of a woof-thread; and at the house of David it became an overflowing brook (Yoma 77b, 78a). This spring is referred to in the passage 'And behold, waters issued out from under the threshold of the house . . . at the south side of the altar' (Ezek. xlvii. 1, 2); it was the mysterious spring that filled the bath of Ishmael the high priest, situated by the attic of Abṭinas on the south of the court, at the water-gate. There was another bath, in a passage under the Chamber of the Hearth, for the use of any ordinary priest who might become ritually unclean. This was reached by a winding staircase. The priest, having bathed, dried himself by the fire; he then dressed and returned to his comrades above, with whom he waited until the gates were opened, when he left the 'azarah, being unfit for service till sunset of the same day...

The order of the priests' daily service in the Temple was as follows: One of the priests arose early and bathed before the arrival of the officer, who usually came about cockcrow. The officer knocked at the door of the

Chamber of the Hearth, and the priests opened it. He called for the priest who had bathed, and ordered him to decide by lot which of the priests should serve that day. The officer then took the keys and entered through the wicket ("pishpush") of the door to the 'azarah, followed by the priests who formed the patrol, each holding two torches. The patrol was divided into two sections; one going through the colonnade on the east, and one on the west, the sections meeting on the south side at the chamber where they prepared the 'ḥabittin' (the baked cake for the meal-offering). The priests now asked one another 'Is all well?' and received the answer 'All is well.' The officer assigned by lot the making of the ḥabittin. Similarly he selected a priest to clean the altar of ashes, his comrades uttering the warning: 'Be careful not to touch the sacred vessels before thou sanctifiest [by washing] thy hands and feet at the laver; and see that the coal-shovel ["maḥtah"] is in ts place [near the "kebesh," the inclined plank or bridge leading to the altar].' Proceeding without any light save that of the pyre ("ma'arakah") on the altar, he disappeared below, and was next heard operating the machinery for raising the laver from the well. This consisted of a wooden wheel and shaft and a chain, a device designed by the high priest Ben Ḳaṭṭin. The noise caused by this operation fixed the time for washing hands and feet. The priest took the silver 'maḥtah' and ascended the altar; pushing the large coals aside, he took a shovelful of ashes and charred wood, and, descending, turned northward and deposited the ashes in a heap on the floor three handbreadths from the 'kebesh,' where also the ashes from the golden altar and the candlestick were placed. The authorities disagree as to the disposition of the ashes: some say they fell through a grate in the floor; others, that they were removed later. Observing his act, the priest's comrades hurried to wash their hands and feet at the laver. They then took large shovels ("magrefot") and made a heap ("tappuaḥ") of the ashes of the altar in the center, other priests meanwhile using flesh-hooks to place aside the portions of the sacrifices that had not been consumed during the night. When the heap of ashes was sufficiently large it was removed outside the city. The priests now brought pieces of all kinds of wood except olive and vine, and built a new pyre, on which they replaced the unconsumed portions of the sacrifices. For a second pyre, intended for the burning of incense, they selected the best fig-wood. Having lit the two pyres, they descended from the altars.

The officer then ordered the priests to decide by lot who should slaughter the sacrificial victim, who should sprinkle the blood, who should clean the ashes from the golden altar and from the golden candlestick, and who should attend to the sacrifices in detail. This being done, the officer commanded: 'Go ye and see if it is time to commence the sacrificial service!' Mounting to an eminence of the Temple, they looked toward the east, till at length one shouted, 'Barḳai!' (the morning light has appeared). Mattithiah b. Samuel said they asked him, 'Has the light in the east reached Hebron?' and he answered, 'Yes.' The mention of Hebron was made to honor the memory of the patriarchs buried there. The officer then said: 'Go and fetch a lamb from the Chamber of the Lambs' (situated at the northeast corner of the 'azarah). The priests entered also the Vessel Chamber and took therefrom ninety-three vessels of silver and gold. The lamb was now examined by the light of torches to see whether it was free from blemishes; and water from a golden cup was given it to drink. The priest selected by lot then dragged the animal to the abattoir, north of the altar. Meanwhile other priests advanced with the 'ṭeni,' a gold dish in the shape of a basket of a 'tarḳab' measure; the 'kuz,' a gold pitcher; and two keys wherewith to open the Hekal, one from the outside and one from within through the wicket or lattice of a cell on the north side of the vestibule. The bolt was thrown back and the doors unlocked, causing a noise which was heard a long distance and which was the signal for the shoḥeṭ to slaughter the perpetual morning sacrifice ("tamid shel shaḥarit.") at the abattoir, while the priest in the Hekal carefully gathered up all the ashes of the golden altar into the ṭeni, put this on the floor, and went out. The priest with the kuz cleared the candlestick of ashes, leaving the two lights nearest to the east to burn till the evening. If he found them extinguished he renewed and relighted them, after which he trimmed the other lamps. In front of the candlestick were three marble steps, on the top one of which the priest stood to trim and light the lamps. When he had finished he put the kuz on the second step and went out. On the first step the tongs and snuff-dishes were placed (Maimonides, "Yad," Bet ha-Beḥirah, iii. 11). The ṭeni was removed by the priest chosen to remove the ashes of the altar after the incense had been offered; the kuz, by the priest who in the afternoon attended to the two lights of the candlestick that had been burning all day...

The slaughter of the lamb was effected as follows: The front legs were bound to the hind legs, the head pointing south with its face toward the west. The shoḥeṭ stood facing the west. The morning tamid was slaughtered at the northwest corner, that of the afternoon at the northeast corner, of the altar at the second ring. There were twenty-four rings, in four rows, fixed to the floor on hinges; in these the heads of the animals were held in position. The priest who received the blood in a basin stood facing the south. He sprinkled the blood on both sides of the northeast and south west corners of the altar. The removal of the hide and the dissection of the carcass were shared by the priests, and were followed by the meal-offering (Lev. vi. 13). This accomplished, the priests went to the Chamber of Hewn Stone. There the officer directed them to recite one benediction ("Ahabah Rabbah") and to read the Ten Commandments and the 'Shema',' after which they blessed the people. On Sabbaths they blessed also with 'love, brotherhood, peace, and friendship' the patrol that was about to go off duty...

Finally, the priests drew lots for the incense service, and the various assignments were made, only those who had not been previously selected being admitted to the ballot. The priests that were not to share in the service of the day now removed their priestly garments and then, having delivered them to an attendant who placed them in the proper lockers, dressed themselves in their secular clothes and retired from the 'azarah till their next turn...

During the sacrifice the Levites were at their stations on the steps leading to the priests' hall, and in front of the dukan; but they did not commence their music until the libation at the conclusion of the service. The musical instrument called the 'magrefah,' somewhat similar to the organ, stood between the altar and the vestibule. Its tones, which could be heard a long distance, were the signal for the priests to prostrate themselves: this took place after the incense-offering...

Special honor was paid to the high priest. He was attended by three priests: one on his right, one on his left, and one holding up the breastplate adorned with precious stones. The high priest entered the Hekal alone, and after the curtain was lowered, he prostrated himself and retired. The officer who waited in the vestibule, on hearing the sound of the bells on the hem of the high priest's garment, raised the curtain. After the high priest had left, the officer who acted as sagan entered the Hekal and prostrated himself; and on his retirement the other priests entered and followed his example. In case the high priest desired to offer the incense he was assisted by the officer and two attendants.

At the conclusion the priests bearing the five empty vessels—the basket, pitcher, ladle, spoon, and cover—used in the service of the altar, and those carrying the candlestick and incense, stood in line on the staircase of the vestibule, and, raising their hands as high as their shoulders, recited the priestly benediction.

The high priest then offered the libation of wine ("nesakim"). The officer stood in the corner with kerchief (flag) in hand, and two priests; with silver trumpets by the table, the cymbals meanwhile playing between them. The trumpeters sounded 'teḳi'ah, teru'ah, teḳi'ah'; the high priest commenced the ceremony of the libation; the officer unfurled the kerchief; the cymbals clashed; and the Levites sang hymns accompanied by music. During the pauses the trumpet sounded 'teḳi'ah,' and the people in the 'azarah prostrated themselves; at every pause a teḳi'ah and a prostration. The order of the daily Psalms from Sunday to Saturday was as follows: Ps. xxiv., xlviii., lxxxii., xciv., lxxxi., xciii., xciv. (Jacobs, Joseph, and Judah David Eisenstein, "Temple, Administration and Service Of")

RECOMMENDED READING AND RESEARCH

Although I do not agree on every point with the following books, DVDs, websites, authors, or other resources listed, I have learned much since 2003 from these, particularly concerning the Written Torah. I would recommend that you pray for the Holy Spirit to reveal the truth to you as you read, watch or listen to them:

The King James Bible – Each word in the King James Bible is linked to the Strong's Concordance for further study in the Hebrew and Greek language definitions.

Arthur Bailey – Leads congregation of House of Israel in Charlotte, NC. As of 11/09/2016, their Sabbath Service is available to view live at www.arthurbaileyministries.com at 11:00 a.m. EST on the Sabbath. Ministry focuses on keeping The Written Torah from a Holy Spirit led perspective.

The Chronological Gospels: The Life and Seventy Week Ministry of the Messiah – John Michael Rood, 2013. Matthew, Mark, Luke, John, Acts, and The Revelation put in chronological order (according to the author). Reference Bible and research tool with many facts/notes/images not easily found elsewhere. Inquiries should be addressed to: Aviv Moon Publishing, P. O. Box 1559, Fort Mill, SC 29716 or www.TheChronologicalGospels.com.

Too Long in the Sun by Richard Rives (Book and Dvd available). Sun worship revealed to have crept into Christianity.

Michael Rood – Hosts "Shabbat Night Live" at his website at 8:00 p.m. EST www.aroodawakening.com. Also Aviv.tv. Pioneer in Hebraic Roots Movement. Sabbath fellowships worldwide can be located at his Aviv Fellowships Finder.

Fossilized Customs – Lew White. Also see www.torahzone.net. Paganism in Christianity revealed and how it came in. ISBN: 0-9584353-6-7

Chaim Goldman – www.RepairingtheBreach.org. Messianic Jew who understands the need for reformation in both the Christian Church and Judaism.

Batya Wooten – Founder, along with her husband, Angus Wooten, of Alliance of Redeemed Israel. www.redeemedisrael.com. Pioneer in Messianic Jewish teaching.

Brad Scott – www.wildbranch.org. Hebraic Roots Teacher.

Bill Cloud – www.BillCloud.org. Shoreshim Ministries. Hebraic RootsTeacher.

Dr. Kenny Russell – founder Hebrew Roots Center Galilee. www.BulldozerFaith.com. Sabbath Broadcast from Israel. Full Gospel ministry (Yeshua, Written Torah, and Power of the Holy Spirit).

Constantine's Sword: The Church and the Jews: A History by James Carroll, Houghton Mifflin Company, c. 2001

Jacob (Ya'acov) Damkani – www.TrumpetofSalvation.org – Messianic Jewish Israeli since the 1970's. His autobiography, Why Me?, very insightful and available on his website. Ministry focuses on bringing the truth of the Jewish Yeshua to his people, the Jews in Israel. Movie of his life has just been released in 2016, "The Messenger."

His Hallowed Name Revealed Again by Keith Johnson. The Name of the Father revealed as YeHoVaH!

23 Minutes In Hell: One Man's Story About What He Saw, Heard, and Felt in that Place of Torment Paperback – January 30, 2006 by Bill Wiese (Author) - also available on You Tube as a video.

GNU Free Documentation License

Version 1.3, 3 November 2008

Copyright © 2000, 2001, 2002, 2007, 2008 Free Software Foundation, Inc. <http://fsf.org/>

Everyone is permitted to copy and distribute verbatim copies of this license document, but changing it is not allowed.

0. PREAMBLE

The purpose of this License is to make a manual, textbook, or other functional and useful document "free" in the sense of freedom: to assure everyone the effective freedom to copy and redistribute it, with or without modifying it, either commercially or noncommercially. Secondarily, this License preserves for the author and publisher a way to get credit for their work, while not being considered responsible for modifications made by others.

This License is a kind of "copyleft", which means that derivative works of the document must themselves be free in the same sense. It complements the GNU General Public License, which is a copyleft license designed for free software.

We have designed this License in order to use it for manuals for free software, because free software needs free documentation: a free program should come with manuals providing the same freedoms that the software does. But this License is not limited to software manuals; it can be used for any textual work, regardless of subject matter or whether it is published as a printed book. We recommend this License principally for works whose purpose is instruction or reference.

1. APPLICABILITY AND DEFINITIONS

This License applies to any manual or other work, in any medium, that contains a notice placed by the copyright holder saying it can be distributed under the terms of this License. Such a notice grants a world-wide, royalty-free license, unlimited in duration, to use that work under the conditions stated herein. The "Document", below, refers to any such manual or work. Any member of the public is a licensee, and is addressed as "you". You accept the license if you copy, modify or distribute the work in a way requiring permission under copyright law.

A "Modified Version" of the Document means any work containing the Document or a portion of it, either copied verbatim, or with modifications and/or translated into another language.

A "Secondary Section" is a named appendix or a front-matter section of the Document that deals exclusively with the relationship of the publishers or authors of the Document to the Document's overall subject (or to related matters) and contains nothing that could fall directly within that overall subject. (Thus, if the Document is in part a textbook of mathematics, a Secondary Section may not explain any mathematics.) The relationship could be a matter of historical connection with the subject or with related matters, or of legal, commercial, philosophical, ethical or political position regarding them.

The "Invariant Sections" are certain Secondary Sections whose titles are designated, as being those of Invariant Sections, in the notice that says that the Document is released under this License. If a section does not fit the above definition of Secondary then it is not allowed to be designated as Invariant. The Document may contain zero Invariant Sections. If the Document does not identify any Invariant Sections then there are none.

The "Cover Texts" are certain short passages of text that are listed, as Front-Cover Texts or Back-Cover Texts, in the notice that says that the Document is released under this License. A Front-Cover Text may be at most 5 words, and a Back-Cover Text may be at most 25 words.

A "Transparent" copy of the Document means a machine-readable copy, represented in a format whose specification is available to the general public, that is suitable for revising the document straightforwardly with generic text editors or (for images composed of pixels) generic paint programs or (for drawings) some widely available drawing editor, and that is suitable for input to text formatters or for automatic translation to a variety of formats suitable for input to text formatters. A copy made in an otherwise Transparent file format whose markup, or absence of markup, has been arranged to thwart or discourage subsequent modification by readers is not Transparent. An image format is not Transparent if used for any substantial amount of text. A copy that is not "Transparent" is called "Opaque".

Examples of suitable formats for Transparent copies include plain ASCII without markup, Texinfo input format, LaTeX input format, SGML or XML using a publicly available DTD, and standard-conforming simple HTML, PostScript or PDF designed for human modification. Examples of transparent image formats include PNG, XCF and JPG. Opaque formats include proprietary formats that can be read and edited only by proprietary word processors, SGML or XML for which the DTD and/or processing tools are not generally available, and the machine-generated HTML, PostScript or PDF produced by some word processors for output purposes only.

The "Title Page" means, for a printed book, the title page itself, plus such following pages as are needed to hold, legibly, the material this License requires to appear in the title page. For works in formats which do not have any title page as such, "Title Page" means the text near the most prominent appearance of the work's title, preceding the beginning of the body of the text.

The "publisher" means any person or entity that distributes copies of the Document to the public.

A section "Entitled XYZ" means a named subunit of the Document whose title either is precisely XYZ or contains XYZ in parentheses following text that translates XYZ in another language. (Here XYZ stands for a specific section name mentioned below, such as "Acknowledgements", "Dedications", "Endorsements", or "History".) To "Preserve the Title" of such a section when you modify the Document means that it remains a section "Entitled XYZ" according to this definition.

The Document may include Warranty Disclaimers next to the notice which states that this License applies to the Document. These Warranty Disclaimers are considered to be included by reference in this License, but only as regards disclaiming warranties: any other implication that these Warranty Disclaimers may have is void and has no effect on the meaning of this License.

2. VERBATIM COPYING

You may copy and distribute the Document in any medium, either commercially or noncommercially, provided that this License, the copyright notices, and the license notice saying this License applies to the Document are reproduced in all copies, and that you add no other conditions whatsoever to those of this License. You may not use technical measures to obstruct or control the reading or further copying of the copies you make or distribute. However, you may accept compensation in exchange for copies. If you distribute a large enough number of copies you must also follow the conditions in section 3.

You may also lend copies, under the same conditions stated above, and you may publicly display copies.

3. COPYING IN QUANTITY

If you publish printed copies (or copies in media that commonly have printed covers) of the Document, numbering more than 100, and the Document's license notice requires Cover Texts, you must enclose the copies in covers that carry, clearly and legibly, all these Cover Texts: Front-Cover Texts on the front cover, and Back-Cover Texts on the back cover. Both covers must also clearly and legibly identify you as the publisher of these copies. The front cover must present the full title with all words of the title equally prominent and visible. You may add other material on the covers in addition. Copying with changes limited to the covers, as long as they preserve the title of the Document and satisfy these conditions, can be treated as verbatim copying in other respects.

If the required texts for either cover are too voluminous to fit legibly, you should put the first ones listed (as many as fit reasonably) on the actual cover, and continue the rest onto adjacent pages.

If you publish or distribute Opaque copies of the Document numbering more than 100, you must either include a machine-readable Transparent copy along with each Opaque copy, or state in or with each Opaque copy a computer-network location from which the general network-using public has access to download using public-standard network protocols a complete Transparent copy of the Document, free of added material. If you use the latter option, you must take reasonably prudent steps, when you begin distribution of Opaque copies in quantity, to ensure that this Transparent copy will remain thus accessible at the stated location until at least one year after the last time you distribute an Opaque copy (directly or through your agents or retailers) of that edition to the public.

It is requested, but not required, that you contact the authors of the Document well before redistributing any large number of copies, to give them a chance to provide you with an updated version of the Document.

4. MODIFICATIONS

You may copy and distribute a Modified Version of the Document under the conditions of sections 2 and 3 above, provided that you release the Modified Version under precisely this License, with the Modified Version filling the role of the Document, thus licensing distribution and modification of the Modified Version to whoever possesses a copy of it. In addition, you must do these things in the Modified Version:

- A. Use in the Title Page (and on the covers, if any) a title distinct from that of the Document, and from those of previous versions (which should, if there were any, be listed in the History section of the Document). You may use the same title as a previous version if the original publisher of that version gives permission.
- B. List on the Title Page, as authors, one or more persons or entities responsible for authorship of the modifications in the Modified Version, together with at least five of the principal authors of the Document (all of its principal authors, if it has fewer than five), unless they release you from this requirement.
- C. State on the Title page the name of the publisher of the Modified Version, as the publisher.
- D. Preserve all the copyright notices of the Document.
- E. Add an appropriate copyright notice for your modifications adjacent to the other copyright notices.
- F. Include, immediately after the copyright notices, a license notice giving the public permission to use the Modified Version under the terms of this License, in the form shown in the Addendum below.
- G. Preserve in that license notice the full lists of Invariant Sections and required Cover Texts given in the Document's license notice.
- H. Include an unaltered copy of this License.
- I. Preserve the section Entitled "History", Preserve its Title, and add to it an item stating at least the title, year, new authors, and publisher of the Modified Version as given on the Title Page. If there is no section Entitled "History" in the Document, create one stating the title, year, authors, and publisher of the Document as given on its Title Page, then add an item describing the Modified Version as stated in the previous sentence.
- J. Preserve the network location, if any, given in the Document for public access to a Transparent copy of the Document, and likewise the network locations given in the Document for previous versions it was based on. These may be placed in the "History" section. You may omit a network location for a work that was published at least four years before the Document itself, or if the original publisher of the version it refers to gives permission.
- K. For any section Entitled "Acknowledgements" or "Dedications", Preserve the Title of the section, and preserve in the section all the

substance and tone of each of the contributor acknowledgements and/or dedications given therein.

- L. Preserve all the Invariant Sections of the Document, unaltered in their text and in their titles. Section numbers or the equivalent are not considered part of the section titles.
- M. Delete any section Entitled "Endorsements". Such a section may not be included in the Modified Version.
- N. Do not retitle any existing section to be Entitled "Endorsements" or to conflict in title with any Invariant Section.
- O. Preserve any Warranty Disclaimers.

If the Modified Version includes new front-matter sections or appendices that qualify as Secondary Sections and contain no material copied from the Document, you may at your option designate some or all of these sections as invariant. To do this, add their titles to the list of Invariant Sections in the Modified Version's license notice. These titles must be distinct from any other section titles.

You may add a section Entitled "Endorsements", provided it contains nothing but endorsements of your Modified Version by various parties—for example, statements of peer review or that the text has been approved by an organization as the authoritative definition of a standard.

You may add a passage of up to five words as a Front-Cover Text, and a passage of up to 25 words as a Back-Cover Text, to the end of the list of Cover Texts in the Modified Version. Only one passage of Front-Cover Text and one of Back-Cover Text may be added by (or through arrangements made by) any one entity. If the Document already includes a cover text for the same cover, previously added by you or by arrangement made by the same entity you are acting on behalf of, you may not add another; but you may replace the old one, on explicit permission from the previous publisher that added the old one.

The author(s) and publisher(s) of the Document do not by this License give permission to use their names for publicity for or to assert or imply endorsement of any Modified Version.

5. COMBINING DOCUMENTS

You may combine the Document with other documents released under this License, under the terms defined in section 4 above for modified versions, provided that you include in the combination all of the Invariant Sections of all of the original documents, unmodified, and list them all as Invariant

Sections of your combined work in its license notice, and that you preserve all their Warranty Disclaimers.

The combined work need only contain one copy of this License, and multiple identical Invariant Sections may be replaced with a single copy. If there are multiple Invariant Sections with the same name but different contents, make the title of each such section unique by adding at the end of it, in parentheses, the name of the original author or publisher of that section if known, or else a unique number. Make the same adjustment to the section titles in the list of Invariant Sections in the license notice of the combined work.

In the combination, you must combine any sections Entitled "History" in the various original documents, forming one section Entitled "History"; likewise combine any sections Entitled "Acknowledgements", and any sections Entitled "Dedications". You must delete all sections Entitled "Endorsements".

6. COLLECTIONS OF DOCUMENTS

You may make a collection consisting of the Document and other documents released under this License, and replace the individual copies of this License in the various documents with a single copy that is included in the collection, provided that you follow the rules of this License for verbatim copying of each of the documents in all other respects.

You may extract a single document from such a collection, and distribute it individually under this License, provided you insert a copy of this License into the extracted document, and follow this License in all other respects regarding verbatim copying of that document.

7. AGGREGATION WITH INDEPENDENT WORKS

A compilation of the Document or its derivatives with other separate and independent documents or works, in or on a volume of a storage or distribution medium, is called an "aggregate" if the copyright resulting from the compilation is not used to limit the legal rights of the compilation's users beyond what the individual works permit. When the Document is included in an aggregate, this License does not apply to the other works in the aggregate which are not themselves derivative works of the Document.

If the Cover Text requirement of section 3 is applicable to these copies of the Document, then if the Document is less than one half of the entire aggregate, the Document's Cover Texts may be placed on covers that bracket the Document within the aggregate, or the electronic equivalent of covers if the Document is in electronic form. Otherwise they must appear on printed covers that bracket the whole aggregate.

8. TRANSLATION

Translation is considered a kind of modification, so you may distribute translations of the Document under the terms of section 4. Replacing Invariant Sections with translations requires special permission from their copyright holders, but you may include translations of some or all Invariant Sections in addition to the original versions of these Invariant Sections. You may include a translation of this License, and all the license notices in the Document, and any Warranty Disclaimers, provided that you also include the original English version of this License and the original versions of those notices and disclaimers. In case of a disagreement between the translation and the original version of this License or a notice or disclaimer, the original version will prevail.

If a section in the Document is Entitled "Acknowledgements", "Dedications", or "History", the requirement (section 4) to Preserve its Title (section 1) will typically require changing the actual title.

9. TERMINATION

You may not copy, modify, sublicense, or distribute the Document except as expressly provided under this License. Any attempt otherwise to copy, modify, sublicense, or distribute it is void, and will automatically terminate your rights under this License.

However, if you cease all violation of this License, then your license from a particular copyright holder is reinstated (a) provisionally, unless and until the copyright holder explicitly and finally terminates your license, and (b) permanently, if the copyright holder fails to notify you of the violation by some reasonable means prior to 60 days after the cessation.

Moreover, your license from a particular copyright holder is reinstated permanently if the copyright holder notifies you of the violation by some reasonable means, this is the first time you have received notice of violation of this License (for any work) from that copyright holder, and you cure the violation prior to 30 days after your receipt of the notice.

Termination of your rights under this section does not terminate the licenses of parties who have received copies or rights from you under this License. If your rights have been terminated and not permanently reinstated, receipt of a copy of some or all of the same material does not give you any rights to use it.

10. FUTURE REVISIONS OF THIS LICENSE

The Free Software Foundation may publish new, revised versions of the GNU Free Documentation License from time to time. Such new versions will be similar in spirit to the present version, but may differ in detail to address new problems or concerns. See http://www.gnu.org/copyleft/.

Each version of the License is given a distinguishing version number. If the Document specifies that a particular numbered version of this License "or any later version" applies to it, you have the option of following the terms and conditions either of that specified version or of any later version that has been published (not as a draft) by the Free Software Foundation. If the Document does not specify a version number of this License, you may choose any version ever published (not as a draft) by the Free Software Foundation. If the Document specifies that a proxy can decide which future versions of this License can be used, that proxy's public statement of acceptance of a version permanently authorizes you to choose that version for the Document.

11. RELICENSING

"Massive Multiauthor Collaboration Site" (or "MMC Site") means any World Wide Web server that publishes copyrightable works and also provides prominent facilities for anybody to edit those works. A public wiki that anybody can edit is an example of such a server. A "Massive Multiauthor Collaboration" (or "MMC") contained in the site means any set of copyrightable works thus published on the MMC site.

"CC-BY-SA" means the Creative Commons Attribution-Share Alike 3.0 license published by Creative Commons Corporation, a not-for-profit corporation with a principal place of business in San Francisco, California, as well as future copyleft versions of that license published by that same organization.

"Incorporate" means to publish or republish a Document, in whole or in part, as part of another Document.

An MMC is "eligible for relicensing" if it is licensed under this License, and if all works that were first published under this License somewhere other than this MMC, and subsequently incorporated in whole or in part into the MMC, (1) had no cover texts or invariant sections, and (2) were thus incorporated prior to November 1, 2008.

The operator of an MMC Site may republish an MMC contained in the site under CC-BY-SA on the same site at any time before August 1, 2009, provided the MMC is eligible for relicensing.

BIBLIOGRAPHY

"Carlstadt: Elevating Jesus Over Paul." *Jesus' Words Only*. N.p., n.d. Web. 24 Feb. 2015. <http://jesuswordsonly.com/books/193-carlstadt-research.html>

Carroll, James. *Constantine's Sword: The Church and the Jews: A History*. New York: Houghton Mifflin Company, 2001. Print.

"Constantine the Great (C.ad 285--337)." *The Hutchinson Unabridged Encyclopedia with Atlas and Weather Guide*, edited by Helicon, 2016. *Credo Reference*. Web. Accessed 08 Nov 2016. http://search.credoreference.com/content/entry/heliconhe/constantine_the_great_c_ad_285_337/0

Eusebius. *Eusebius' Ecclesiastical History*. Peabody: Hendrickson Publishers, 1998. Print.

Jacobs, Joseph, and Judah David Eisenstein. "Temple, Administration and Service Of." *Jewish Encyclopedia*.. 1901-1906. *JewishEncyclopedia.com. The unedited full-text of the 1906 Jewish Encyclopedia*. 2002-2011.Web. 08 June 2016. <http://www.jewishencyclopedia.com/articles/14303-temple-administration-and-service-of>

Johnson, Keith E. *His Hallowed Name Revealed Again*. 2nd ed. Minneapolis: Biblical Foundations Academy, 2011. Print.

JPS Hebrew-English TANAKH: The Traditional Hebrew Text and The New JPS Translation. 2nd ed. Philadelphia: The Jewish Publication Society, 1999. Print.

KING JAMES VERSION OF THE HOLY BIBLE [KJV]. N.p.:n.p., Authorized1611. *Blue Letter Bible*. Web.(<https://www.blueletterbible.org//kjv>)

Kohler, Kaufmann. "Sadducees." *JewishEncyclopedia*. 1901-1906. *JewishEncyclopedia.com. The unedited full-text of the 1906 Jewish Encyclopedia*. 2002-2011. Web. 6 Nov. 2016. <http://www.jewishencyclopedia.com/articles/12989-sadducees>

Rood, Michael John. *The Chronological Gospels: The Life and Seventy Week Ministry of the Messiah*. South Carolina: Aviv Moon Publishing, 2013. Print.

Schieffler, Michael. "Sunday is NOT the Sabbath!" *BIBLE LIGHT HOMEPAGE*. Web. 2015. <http://www.biblelight.net/notsun.htm>

"Separatist". *Encyclopedia Britannica. Encyclopedia Britannica Online.* Encyclopedia Brittanica, Inc. , 2016. Web. 04 Dec. 2016 <https://www.brittanica.com/topic/Separatists>.

'"Statues of Saints" God Ordained or Idolatry?' *Let Us Reason Ministries.* 2009. Web. 1 Jan. 2016. <http://www.letusreason.org/rc2.htm>

Stefano Assemani. *Acta Sanctorium Martyrum Orientalium at Occidentalium, Vol. 1,* Rome. 1748. Print.

Strong, James, S.T.D., LL.D. *Strong's Exhaustive Concordance of the Bible: Showing Every Word of the Text of the Common English Version of the Canonical Books, and Every Occurrence of each Word in Regular Order; Together with Dictionaries of the Hebrew and Greek Words of the Original, with References to the English Words.* Peabody : Hendrickson Publishers. n.d. Strong's Hebrew Lexicon (KJV). *Blue Letter Bible.* Web.

Townsend, Rev. George, D. D. *Ecclesiastical and Civil History Philosophically Considered with Reference to the Future Re-union of Christians, the First Three Books, Comprising the Period from the Ascension of Our Lord to the Death of Wycliffe, Vol. II.* London: Francis & John Rivington, 1847. Print.

White, Lew. *Fossilized Customs: The Pagan Sources of Popular Customs.* Special Edition. Louisville: Strawberry Islands Publishers, 2002. Print.

Wikipedia contributors. "Assumption of Mary." *Wikipedia, The Free Encyclopedia.* Wikipedia, The Free Encyclopedia, 21 Dec. 2015. Web. 1 Jan. 2016.

Wikipedia contributors. "Constantine the Great." *Wikipedia, The Free Encyclopedia.* Wikipedia, The Free Encyclopedia, 18 Aug. 2014. Web. 21 Aug. 2014.

Wikipedia contributors. "Council of Jerusalem." *Wikipedia, The Free Encyclopedia.* Wikipedia, The Free Encyclopedia,17 Dec. 2015. Web. 25 Dec. 2015.

Wikipedia contributors. "Immaculate Conception." *Wikipedia, The Free Encyclopedia.* Wikipedia, The Free Encyclopedia, 27 Dec. 2015. Web. 1 Jan. 2016.

Wikipedia contributors. "James (brother of Jesus)." *Wikipedia, The Free Encyclopedia.* Wikipedia, The Free Encyclopedia, 25 Apr. 2016. Web. 28 Apr. 2016.

Wikipedia contributors. "Oral Torah." *Wikipedia, The Free Encyclopedia.* Wikipedia, The Free Encyclopedia, 11 Jul. 2016. Web. 18 Sep. 2016.

Wikipedia contributors. "Pope." *Wikipedia, The Free Encyclopedia*. Wikipedia, The Free Encyclopedia, 14 Dec. 2015. Web. 1 Jan. 2016.

Wikipedia contributors. "Tetragrammaton." *Wikipedia, The Free Encyclopedia.* Wikipedia, The Free Encyclopedia, 26 Aug. 2016. Web. 28 Aug. 2016.

ABOUT THE AUTHOR

Joy Collins Lyle is a believer in Yeshua from a child and, after realizing in her thirties that much of her life she had actually been living in rebellion to her Father's will, she asked for forgiveness in Yeshua's Name, and became the grateful daughter that was on fire for her Lord! She has been filled with the Holy Spirit since 1991, and has endeavored to be Written Torah Observant since 2003, after learning of its great importance. She loves Israel, has visited once, and has recently taken a course in the Biblical Hebrew language. She has three grown children and three wonderful grandchildren! Joy earned a Bachelor of Business Administration Degree in Accounting from Georgia Southern College early in life, and completed elementary education coursework as well from Clemson University. She has had many vocations, including accountant, advertising salesperson, model, professional singer, home-school teacher of her children, and most recently, real estate sales broker associate. At this point in her life, serving her Creator and Father, and her Savior, Yeshua ha Mashiach, by preaching the true, full, balanced gospel of the Kingdom of God is her mission, **TO HELP ALL PEOPLE TRULY AVOID THE LAKE OF FIRE AND LIVE IN THE PRESENCE OF YEHOVAH ELOHIM FOREVER!!!**

www.ingramcontent.com/pod-product-compliance
Lightning Source LLC
Chambersburg PA
CBHW081454040426
42446CB00016B/3242

9780979934438